The Christopher Small Reader

ALSO BY CHRISTOPHER SMALL

Music, Society, Education

Music of the Common Tongue:
Survival and Celebration
in African American Music

Musicking: The Meanings
of Performing and Listening

Edited by Robert Walser

THE CHRISTOPHER SMALL READER

Wesleyan University Press   Middletown, Connecticut

Wesleyan University Press
Middletown CT 06459
www.wesleyan.edu/wespress

Manufactured in the United States of America
Designed by Mindy Basinger Hill
Typeset in Minion Pro

Library of Congress Cataloging-in-Publication Data

Names: Small, Christopher, 1927–2011. | Walser, Robert, editor.
Title: The Christopher Small reader /
Christopher Small; edited by Robert Walser.
Description: Middletown, Connecticut : Wesleyan University Press, [2016] |
Series: Music/culture | Includes bibliographical references and index.
Identifiers: LCCN 2015048308 (print) | LCCN 2015051357 (ebook) |
ISBN 9780819576392 (cloth : alk. paper) |
ISBN 9780819576408 (pbk. : alk.paper) | ISBN 9780819576415 (ebook)
Subjects: LCSH: Music—Philosophy and aesthetics. | Music—Social aspects. |
Musicology. | Small, Christopher, 1927–2011.
Classification: LCC ML423.S58 A25 2016 (print) |
LCC ML423.S58 (ebook) | DDC 780—dc23
LC record available at http://lccn.loc.gov/2015048308

5 4 3 2 1

CONTENTS

INTRODUCTION

Robert Walser

I am 75 years old and I have learnt that we are on the earth
to enjoy it together. Music serves to explore our identity,
helps us to know who we are, and to celebrate it.

Christopher Small[1]

Christopher Small was born in New Zealand in 1927 and died in Spain in 2011 at the age of eighty-four, having spent much of his life teaching in London. I believe he was the most profound musical thinker of the twentieth century. I say that because the breadth and depth of his work, in which he drew upon his training as both a scientist and an artist, his accomplishments as a classical musician and as a devoted student of African American music, and his practical experiences as a composer, a pianist, an accompanist, and a teacher, enabled him to become the consummate insider/outsider who could empathetically challenge our assumptions about the nature of music and help us account for the pleasures that it gives us.

Mikhail Bakhtin wrote powerfully about the importance of outsiders for helping insiders understand the significance of things they had taken for granted. Chris, as a New Zealander, as a gay man, as someone without a doctoral degree who had strong opinions about higher education, and as an enthusiastic amateur musician, had forged an identity that didn't quite fit into the contexts he inhabited during most of his life. And that helped enable him to become an original thinker. Yet it is also true that the insider brings to bear crucial intimate knowledge. The writers who are normally ranked highest in explaining the significance of the classical music tradition have been mostly quite parochial, and they usually did not even imagine that they should try to place that sort of music making in a larger context of human activity. More anthropologically oriented scholars have typically not had the familiarity with the classical tradition that would enable them to discuss its details and analyze its fundamental assumptions. And almost no one outside the official boundaries of music education has cared to question what we do and why we do it when we teach young people about music. Chris saw all of these things as part of the same web of human musicking, the understanding and elucidation of which was his lifelong passion.

Small was both personally modest and as intellectually ambitious as anyone ever has been. He was a bit self-conscious about his unimposing academic pedigree at the same time that he was keenly aware of the potentially revolutionary implications of his thinking. He was flattered that people sought him out and invited him to lecture, especially after his retirement and the gradual circulation of his books. But at the same time he never expressed any doubts about the rightness, the dignity and humaneness, of the stance he took in his writings.

As Thomas S. Kuhn argued half a century ago, paradigms don't shift when new answers are proposed; they shift when new questions are posed. After reading Christopher Small, to study the works of prominent philosophers of music is to realize that they are proceeding entirely from premises that Small spent his life calling into question. Roger Scruton's endorsement of the old saw that aesthetic experience involves the appreciation of something "for its own sake" presupposes that music has a "sake," which it patently does not, being as it is, as Chris always insisted, not a thing at all but an activity that people do. Or when Peter Kivy worries about what it means for music to express emotions, he skates over the fact that music doesn't express emotion at all—*people* express and experience emotions through their involvements with one another in various ways, including through the medium of musical sound. As Chris argued in response to something he had read about the effects of postmodern thought, "'Postmodern thought' can't do anything. Only people can do anything! By continuing this kind of . . . metaphor he's going back into the same . . . morass of Platonist assumptions."[2] Those who wrangle about exactly how musical works are to be defined are not thinking about the fact that musical scores are only useful as parts of specific musicking situations, in which their meanings change according to the contexts in which they are utilized. The old "hypodermic" model of musical meaning, in which artists use music to inject audiences with feelings or meanings, clashes with Chris's readings of musicking situations, in which people take part in social rituals. And it doesn't live up to his steadfast belief that any theorizing about how music works is worthless unless it sheds some light on how *all* music, of all times and places, becomes a valuable thing for people to do.

In an unpublished file called "Miscellaneous Observations," Chris wrote, "I am sometimes criticized for not having done research. But whatthehell is the use of doing all this research, a little bit of knowledge here, a little bit there, if someone doesn't come along and (at least make an attempt to) tell us what it all means. That's my job."[3] It depends on what you think research is, I guess. Chris's unpublished papers include thirty-six notebooks, begun in 1969 and continuing through the last dated item, in 2003, and the last dated comments in Chris's hand, from 2007. In those notebooks, he recorded quotations from and observations about works that comprise an astonishing array of intellectual sources.[4] Is reading such authors and grappling with the implications of their thinking not to count as research?

Small's three books in Wesleyan University Press's Music Culture series, *Music, Society, Education*, *Music of the Common Tongue*, and *Musicking*, comprise an extraordinary legacy and resource. This fourth volume brings previously published work, some of it available in disparate locations, together with key excerpts from the three books he published and other writings that remained unpublished at his passing. It both makes available ideas that were not included in the earlier books and presents an overview of his thought over the course of his life. I hope it rewards those who already know his work and hooks those who don't, so that they are drawn to read the other books.

I have included here two excerpts from each of Chris's published books, the introductory chapter and one other, as a way of tracing concisely in this volume the progress of his thought. In the first book, the contrasts between science and art particularly occupied him—art being understood as the classical tradition and its modernist extension, in which Small was trained as a composer—as ways of understanding the world and living well in it. Science, on the other hand—he was a zoology major in college—he understood as a means of mastering the world. By the time the second volume was being written, he had partnered with Neville Braithwaite (see the afterword to this collection), and his focus was on understanding the impact of African American music, which, he had realized, nearly all twentieth-century people had experienced as the only twentieth-century music that really mattered. And in the third book he returned mostly to the classical tradition—or rather its persistence in ritualized form in our time as the only music that could in educated circles be casually referred to as simply "music."

From *Music, Society, Education* I chose the chapter on the American experimental tradition, which I have always particularly admired because Chris didn't necessarily like much of this music, yet he made the best possible case for it. That's how I teach my students how to teach, and I learned it from him. The other piece from *Music of the Common Tongue*, in contrast, is a thoughtful meditation on the practice and history of jazz. The second chapter of *Musicking* I chose is called "A Solitary Flute Player," and about that I have a confession. Chris begins this piece by relating that certain friends, whom he left anonymous, had tried to discourage him from including it in the book on the grounds that the flute player could all too easily be read as a stereotypical representation of the non-Western Other. Well, those friends were I, I'm afraid, and I was wrong. Chris insisted on including that flute player because that solitary musician exemplified and illuminated some crucial points about musicking—and also because Chris admired and respected the never-heard musicking that he was writing about. So I include it here as a kind of repentance.

But it's here also because the flute player returns as a topic of discussion in Robert Christgau's extraordinary interview with Chris, so I've placed that chapter immediately before the latter. I call it "extraordinary" because I regard it as simply the finest interview about music I've ever read. Bob came to visit Chris in Spain after having studied all three books and thought deeply about their implications. His questioning proceeded from an understanding of Chris's work and an appreciation of its potential implications for all types of musicking that was second to no one's. Bob gently pushed Chris beyond what he had written and shows us some hints of where he might have gone in the future.

"Whose Music Do We Teach, Anyway?" is an unpublished address that was given at the Music Educators' National Conference in Washington, D.C., in 1990. Deliberately provocative, it summarizes his developing thoughts about "musicking," a concept he had introduced in *Music of the Common Tongue*, which appeared in print in 1987. Many of these ideas would later be expanded upon in his book *Musicking*.

"Why Doesn't the Whole World Love Chamber Music?" was commissioned for delivery in 2001 at an annual conference of Chamber Music America. It was later printed in the journal *American Music*, of which I was then editor. It builds upon his book *Musicking*, which had been published three years earlier, but it targets an audience that is obviously very devoted to classical music and challenges them to rethink that investment within larger historical, social, and ethical contexts.

As Chris cheekily pointed out in an interview published the following year in *La Vanguardia*, when those contexts change, so change the meanings of the musical sounds that occur.[5] He starts the interview by asking the interviewer a question: "Do you know the Fifth?"

> *Of Beethoven? Yes of course: Pom Pom Pom Pooooom . . .*
>
> CS: OK, when Beethoven performed it for the first time, these "poms" were like the new dominant class of Europe slapping its chest to proclaim its dominance since the French Revolution. If you listen carefully, you will hear in those notes how the aggressive new bourgeoisie was flexing its muscles for the conquest of the world.
>
> *But! The Fifth! Its message is universal and eternal. . . .*
>
> CS: On the contrary: it's different every time. Then it was the song of a class. It was written as a fist in the face of the old order. Things were about to change: pom pom pom pom!
>
> *And today how does it sound?*
>
> CS: Today it tells us that nothing is going to change. It tells those who are in charge: relax, everything's going to be the same, the same order: pom pom pom poooooom!
>
> *How?*
>
> CS: Because it tranquillizes, comforts and gives them security. They think of the Fifth as going on sounding the same in these times of vertiginous change. . . . Do you see? The composition doesn't exist without the act of performance.

This exchange raises a crucial point that has sometimes been missed even by some of Small's biggest fans: he never claimed that musicking was always a good thing. Expert musicking can sometimes yield results that we might consider oppressive or destructive, and amateurish musicking—as long as, Chris always said, everyone was doing the best they could with what they had—can sometimes be a transcendent experience.

After Chris's first two books were republished and the third was published by Wesleyan University Press in 1997–1999, he received even more invitations to speak abroad, not all of which he could accommodate, unfortunately, due to advancing age. "Creative Reunderstandings" was delivered at a conference at the University of Oslo in 2005. It is of all his writings the most explicitly political, although the moral implications of his work had always been clear enough. Chris was not very optimistic during his last decade about the state of the world, but much of the musicking he encountered continued to delight and encourage him.

"Exploring, Affirming, Celebrating—and Teaching" summarizes in three words the functions of musicking as Chris understood them. It was written for a Spanish journal of music education in 2003 and continues his tendency to become ever more provocative during the dozen or so years of writings and lectures that followed *Musicking*. He makes explicit here a suspicion that had grown over the course of his life, that it might be better overall not to teach music in schools at all—at a time when he was becoming more and more an intellectual hero to many music educators. This line of thought is extended in his 2009 "Afterword" for a book of essays on music education edited by Ruth Wright. "Six Aphorisms and Five Commentaries" is included here not because it breaks any new ground but because it schematizes briefly and thus handily the main tenets of Chris's musical thought.

This collection is roughly chronological, but shorter unpublished pieces have been interleaved with the longer ones. Interspersed among the more extended pieces you will find some brief occasional writings, postdating most or all of the books, such as "Deep and Crisp and Even," a graceful yet somewhat curmudgeonly meditation on Christmas carols that had originally been intended for *Musicking*. There is also "The Sardana and Its Meanings," Chris's warm analysis of the Catalonian circle dance that is a ubiquitous source of pride and community in the region where he resided for the latter part of his life. And we have "Rock Concert," a brief evaluation of a Barcelona concert by an unnamed American star. I regret that I didn't know he had written this and so never asked him who that star was. (My best guess would be Tina Turner, who performed for seventy-five thousand people at Barcelona's Olympic Stadium on October 5, 1990.)

The *Reader* begins with Chris's "Autobiography," written in 2004 and with an addition from 2008, and ends with a lovely lyrical piece called "Pelicans," which is not about music at all but rather about nature, which is where he started as an undergraduate student so many years earlier, and about aesthetics and human relationships, which is really what concerned him most. Susan McClary closes the book with reminiscences of Neville Braithwaite, Chris's partner for several decades; they were finally able to marry near the end of his life. I think Neville was the person who most kept alive Chris's faith in the power of music and dance to help us understand and live well in the world, keeping at bay the cynicism to which we are all too susceptible, and thus enabling Christopher Small to teach us so much.

NOTES

1. Christopher Small, interview in *La Vanguardia*, September 21, 2002, La Contra (back page). This appeared in Chris's files in English. I don't know if the original publication has been translated, and if so by whom.

2. Christopher Small, notebook 36, p. 68, Robert Walser private collection. Chris was a dear friend. Over the years that we knew one another, Susan McClary and I spent a dozen months visiting him and Neville in Sitges, the Catalan town to which they had retired.

3. Christopher Small, "Miscellaneous Observations," March 10, 1996, Robert Walser private collection.

4. The following are only some of the authors whose books he excerpted: John Berger, C. G. Jung, Herbert Marcuse, Gregory Bateson, Colin McPhee, R. G. Collingwood, William P. Malm, Thomas Mann, Francis Bebey, John Storm Roberts, J. H. K. Nketia, Max Weber, Bruno Nettl, Raymond Williams, Thomas Kuhn, Daniel Bell, Timothy Leary, Herbert Read, Marshall McLuhan, Edgard Varése, Desmond Morris, Norman Mailer, Cornelius Cardew, Pierre Boulez, R. D. Lang, Carlos Castenada, Mircea Eliade, George Steiner, Charles Ives, Henri Pousseur, David Toop, Ivan Illich, Henry David Thoreau, Clifford Geertz, Colin Turnbull, Arnold van Gennep, Paul Feyerabend, Eugene Genovese, E. P. Thompson, Harry Partch, Jacques Attali, John Blacking, Lewis Mumford, Bill C. Malone, Lawrence Levine, Henry Pleasants, Alan P. Merriam, Mantle Hood, Ernest Cassirer, Simon Frith, Stuart Hall, Theodor W. Adorno, Paul Oliver, Charlie Gillett, Paul E. Willis, Albert Murray, Charles Keil, David P. McAllester, Richard Hoggart, John F. Szwed, Eileen Southern, Peter Guralnick, William Ferris Jr., Friedrich Blume, André Hodier, Val Wilmer, LeRoi Jones, Howard Zinn, Aldous Huxley, Robert Farris Thompson, Alan Lomax, Richard Waterman, Nancy Cunard, Charles Hamm, Paul Henry Lang, Andrew Tracy, William Weber, Ben Sidran, Jacques Chailley, Henry Raynor, Claude Lévi-Strauss, Janet Wolff, Roland Barthes, Pierre Bourdieu, Carl Dalhaus, Joseph Kerman, Gunther Schuller, Jeff Todd Titon, Robert Palmer, Greil Marcus, David Toop, Dave Laing, Christopher Ballentyne, Suzanne K. Langer, John A. Sloboda, Leonard B. Meyer, Noam Chomsky, Lucy Green, John Chernoff, Henry Kingsbury, Joseph Horowitz, Richard Middleton, George Lipsitz, Daniel K. L. Chua, Martha Feldman, George Lakoff, Mark Johnson, Lawrence Kramer, Paul Gilroy, Thrasybulos Georgiades, Eric R. Wolf, Mark Slobin, Gerald Edelman, Carlo Ginsberg, M. M. Bakhtin, Neal Zaslaw, Richard Taruskin, Tricia Rose, María Rosa Menocal, Richard L. Crocker, John Potter, Michel Foucault, Mark Johnson, Bruno Latour, Dave Hickey, and Marshall Berman.

5. Small, interview in *La Vanguardia*.

Autobiography

(2004; REV. 2008)

When I left school at eighteen, with a three-year university scholarship under my belt, I thought I was clear about what I was going to do with my life. I was going to be a doctor—not any old common-or-garden GP or even surgeon but a public health doctor. My father's cousin's husband was public health officer in Dunedin, and I had accompanied him on his rounds in that quaint Victorian city and seen some of its messy underside. I was going to get my medical degree and then study for the Diploma of Public Heath, which included topics like geology, hydrology, plumbing, economics, and even, if I remember correctly, a little seismology—all to me topics of much more interest than the messy structure of people's insides.

At that time, music was little more than an intensely practiced avocation. It was in the family, though there was very little stimulation from the dull town in which we lived. My early memories include my mother singing me to sleep with lovely Edwardian music-hall songs, and we had a gramophone—phonograph to you—a big windup acoustic HMV console model ornamented with machine-carved curlicues, and an assortment of records, 78 rpms of course, which I had the run of from an early age. When I was ill, which was often when I was a child, I used to have the big HMV beside my bed, which would be strewn with records. I can still hear one, called *Herd Girl's Dream*, played by a trio of flute, violin, and harp, which at six or seven I thought the most beautiful music in all the world. I remember every note of it, though the record disappeared, as they do, more than fifty years ago.

We had other records too, album sets proudly proclaiming the "new electrical process": Beethoven's Fifth Symphony and Emperor Concerto; the New World

Symphony, which at age twelve or so I prided myself on being able to whistle my way through from start to finish; *The Gondoliers* of Gilbert and Sullivan, which my sister and I used to sing over the washing up; Schubert's B-flat Trio; excerpts from act 3 of *Tristan und Isolde*; and the suite from *Swan Lake* (when I hear any of those longer works today I still have a kinesthetic memory in the seat of my pants of where I had to get up to turn the record over). I liked also to play some of the jazz records that my elder brother brought home from university in the late thirties in the teeth of our parents' disapproval: some Duke Ellington, whose sound fascinated me with its fine-drawn, plangent quality, along with Nat Gonella and his Georgians and Harry Roy and his Tiger Ragamuffins (you won't have heard of them, but they were good musicians who were trying to establish jazz in Britain in the 1930s in the face of the indifference or hostility of the middle-class-dominated BBC and entertainment industry). Our parents wouldn't let him desecrate the big HMV in the dining room with such terrible noises so he had to listen to them in his own room on a tinny little portable. When he was in the mood he would sometimes let me come in with him and listen in, as we used to say in those days. Later, after seeing the George Gershwin biopic with Alan Alda's father as the composer, our parents relented somewhat and the records were allowed to be brought downstairs.

There was also Paul Whiteman making a lady out of jazz, "vocal gems" from operettas, and a lot of dance records, foxtrots and quicksteps, hits of the day now forgotten with titles like "Goodnight Sweetheart" and "In a Little Gypsy Tearoom"—the word had much more innocent connotations in those days. Or maybe it didn't—who knows?

And we had the six-foot contralto Clara Butt belting out "Land of Hope and Glory," Gounod's "Serenade," black spirituals, Layton and Johnson's "It Was a Lover and His Lass," a few comic monologues, and one record from a four-record set—all I knew of the piece for years—of the second movement and the start of the third of Schumann's Piano Concerto. I played and loved them all indiscriminately, blissfully unaware at that age that there was one thing called "classical music" and another called "popular music" and that one was better than the other.

Then there was the piano, which I started learning at the age of seven. It seems that my teacher, to whom I'm eternally grateful, didn't approve of those grade examinations of the Royal Schools of Music to which my contemporaries were put, painfully learning three set pieces a year, but instead presented me with easy pieces of Grieg, Tchaikovsky, and Palmgren along with easy arrangements of popular songs (those from *Snow White and the Seven Dwarves* were contemporary favorites), and later Granados, Debussy, and Bartok—all moderns in those days. I remember also in my early teens triumphantly bringing him an ancient volume of Mozart sonatas that an old lady had given me, as if I'd rediscovered them all by myself—which in a way I had—and this while my contemporaries were learning their boring exam pieces and practicing scales (never in my whole life have I practiced scales) and were being taught *The Robin's Return* and *Blumenlied* (though I later found *Blumenlied* for myself and played it con amore).

My mother didn't play an instrument, although she was proud of the fact that her father, who was a printer by trade, had conducted a choral society in Wellington. I still have the baton that his choir presented to him in 1896. It's made of polished oak and bound in silver engraved with his name and the date and weighs about half a pound. They must have been giants in those days. My father played the piano quite well and had a nice baritone voice. He loved to sing to his own accompaniment—sea songs, old popular songs, Tom Moore, and Burns; his party piece was the Cobbler's Song from the cod-Chinese musical *Chu Chin Chow*, which he and my mother had seen in London in 1919 when he was there as an army dentist. He also liked to do *The Holy City*, although he never could quite manage the repeated triplet chords in the accompaniment. Years later, when I went to live in Catalonia, I made an arrangement of it for a friend of mine who has a magnificent tenor voice to do with the local choir. It may be an old warhorse in Anglo-Saxon countries, but it was a breathtaking novelty in Spain and for a while they couldn't get enough of it.

As my sister and I began to get a bit good on the piano (she is still, in her eighties, a fine pianist with a string of pupils in the lovely little New Zealand country town where she has lived and brought up a family for more than fifty years), he stopped, and I never heard him sing or play in later years. I wonder if my priggish adolescent attitudes might have had something to do with it; I remember being ashamed when he played and sang in front of my intellectual school friends, and I daresay I showed it. He did, however, snap back at me once (I loved him, as did everyone, but he did have his fits of irritation) when I ridiculed a ukulele-playing British film comedian called George Formby: "I bet he practices his uke at least as hard as you practice your bloody piano." Touché; my skills at the piano came all too easily, and at that teenaged time I was fonder of showing off to visitors (showers of wrong notes, but ah, the *expression!*) than I was of practicing.

My brother's violin teacher played lunchtimes in a trio in the elegant wood-paneled restaurant of the town's posh department store. They were scarcely audible at times over the conversations and the noise of serving and eating, but they were a treat for me (three musicians at a time were still the most that I had ever heard!), and today the sound of that despised genre, café music, all too rarely heard these days, retains a special magic, especially when heard through the noise of cutlery and plates. Years later, on my first visit to Venice, the café bands in Saint Mark's Square brought it all back to me in a wave of intense, nostalgic joy. On occasional evenings the British Music Society would bring musicians from Wellington, and my parents and I would make our way through the darkened haberdashery department of that same department store, at four stories the tallest building in town, and up to the restaurant where the concerts were held. I haven't the faintest recollection of what was played or sung on those occasions, but I remember the delicious feeling of being initiated at that early age into an adult society that was in some way defined by attendance at those concerts. It was around that time too that I learned the skills of sitting still and concealing boredom, during long evenings at the home of a record-collecting lecturer in the local agricultural college, while he played his records: the complete *Saint Matthew Passion*, it might be, or what seemed like a couple of hundred Scarlatti sonatas played by Wanda Landowska one after the other on the harpsichord, a sound I have never managed to like—all at that time as incomprehensible as music from Mars. Those record evenings resonate down the years so that, even today, to hear the *Matthew Passion* gives me a distinct feeling of being on the outside looking—or listening—in.

There was not much live popular music. There was an exuberant boy in high school whom we intellectuals affected to despise but whom I secretly envied for his ability to play pop tunes by ear; "Darktown Strutters Ball" was his signature tune. He later had a very good dance band. But it never occurred to me to try it for myself.

Playing by ear was a skill I acquired only years later in my first teaching job in a large country secondary school with no money to buy sheet music. Every Friday morning I had to take the whole school—750 pupils—for singing, with a huge brute of a piano missing one caster so it looked like the *Titanic* going down. Each pupil had a copy of the school songbook with words only of a hundred or so hearty, patriotic, and folksy songs, leaving me to make up the accompaniments. I remember the thrill when in the third line of "Santa Lucia" I discovered the V of II–II progression.

The only other live popular music I heard came from a dreary little trio of bored local musicians—piano, sax, and drums—that droned its way, Victor

Sylvester style, through foxtrots, quicksteps, and waltzes at teenage dances organized by the upper-class mothers of the town. I attended these affairs under bitter protest seething with a rebellion that hadn't yet acquired the nerve to surface.

I vividly remember hearing a symphony orchestra live for the first time. I was twenty, and it was the newly formed New Zealand National Orchestra in the fine old Wellington Town Hall, built barely sixty years after the first British settlers had landed on the foreshore. It didn't sound at all like the records I'd been listening to. Those records gave an impression of a sonic space that was completely saturated by the sounds, but this sound was thinner, finer, and there was space around it. It didn't completely fill the hall but left the music room to breathe. I was, and remain, enchanted by it. Later I discovered that the London Royal Festival Hall, despite all attempts to "fix" the acoustics, had something like the same sound (interestingly, it was not liked by either performers or audiences).

My medical ambitions had to be postponed, as the year in which I passed the entrance exam for what was then the only medical school in New Zealand was the year in which the soldiers came back from the Second World War, many of them already holding medical entrance certificates and wanting to get back to study. Rightly, they were given preference over youngsters like me, so there was no room in the medical school for me and a number of my contemporaries. They told us that science graduates would get preference for admission, so a dozen or so of us gritted our teeth and set out on science degrees.

To my astonishment I found the whole course fascinating: zoology, botany, organic and inorganic chemistry, and geology (geomorphology opened my eyes to the New Zealand landscape, while paleontology and stratigraphy vanquished convincingly and forever any literal interpretation of the Old Testament and with that most of its authority). Zoology in those days was mostly comparative anatomy, and I did my dissections of those unfortunate creatures with a zest and a perpetual astonishment at the unity in variety that they displayed. What I didn't understand then was that I was learning about relationships—relationships between the parts of an individual creature, relationships between those relationships in another creature, and relationships between relationships between relationships between groups and groups and so on until the whole living world could be seen to be related. Can you imagine how I felt when, in May 1975, according to the date I wrote on the flyleaf, I read Gregory Bateson's *Steps to an Ecology of Mind*, picked up casually in a bookshop in London?

I remember our prof of zoology giving us a few lectures on a new science, called ecology (none of us had heard the word before), while our geology prof, one of the last of the old-style heroic Victorian naturalists, talked to us about Alfred Wegener's theory of continental drift ("Most geologists think it's rubbish, but some of you might find something in it"). I used to spend weekends at the marine biological station down by the harbor, up to my thighs in gooey mud, counting ascidians and other creatures of the tidal zone, and other weekends up the rivers of North Otago looking for, and finding, abundant creatures of the Cretaceous, and even a perfect vertebra of a moa, the two-meter-high flightless bird that was hunted to extinction by the Maori in the eighteenth century. I polished it and used it for years as a paperweight.

In the meantime my interest in music was broadening and deepening. I took piano lessons from a German Jewish refugee musician and read everything I could find about it and listened to whatever I could hear. I even composed a few little pieces including an attempt at a piano sonata, not really knowing what I was doing as I had never studied what was called "theory." Finally, with my BS degree behind me, I confronted my parents with what I now really wanted to do, which was to practice music. They grilled me carefully and finally agreed to support me through a music degree. In March 1949 I began my studies in the newly established Department of Music at Victoria University of Wellington, with one classroom over the chemistry labs, so that there was always the faint smell of hydrogen sulfide. It doubled as concert room with the addition of a standard lamp. It had a piano and a record player, a senior lecturer and a lecturer, and that was it. The lecturer was Douglas Lilburn, New Zealand's first professionally trained composer—he had studied at the Royal College of Music and with Vaughan Williams—and although the bachelor of music syllabus didn't require one to play a note on an instrument, we were taught very thoroughly the rudiments of composition. In order to graduate we were required to compose a large-scale piece for chorus and orchestra. Mine was a setting of W. H. Auden's *Look, Stranger*, composed in ignorance that it had formed part of Benjamin Britten's cycle *On This Island* (I still like mine better). The choir of Wellington Teachers' College did a roughish but enthusiastic performance of it with two pianos, and it turned out pretty well I think. I studied piano with a wonderful teacher who had been a pupil of Bartok in Budapest and had done a PhD in Vienna (thank you again, Adolf Hitler), and I became a competent pianist with an LRSM (Licentiate of the Royal Schools of Music) behind me.

We were thoroughly grounded in the history of Western music, harmony, canon, fugue, orchestration, and so on. When I look at some of the posh American universities with their millions of dollars of buildings and equipment, I don't feel at all envious. I was taught pretty well. My one regret is that when in my second year I was offered a post as a kind of répétiteur with the Wellington Amateur Operatic Society (despite the name they did mostly musicals, pre-*Oklahoma!*), I asked Douglas if I should take the job. His reply was terse: "If I were you I'd keep my ears clean." So I turned the job down and have regretted it ever since as an opportunity lost to learn essential skills on the job.

I started at Wellington Teachers' College in 1952 but left after one year, with the blessing of the principal, to work with a small group that was trying to get an educational animated film studio started in a small town north of Wellington. It was a bad time; to keep the place alive I taught all day in the local secondary school and worked on filmmaking all night—that is, when we were not taking part in endless rows provoked by the pugnacious little Scot who had started the thing and finally destroyed it with his quarrelsomeness and touchiness. It was at the end of 1958 that I finally got up the courage to get the hell out and went back to teaching. I had written a handful of scores for short films and had learned a lot, so that when I got a letter from a dance teacher in Wellington inviting me to compose a score for the first ballet to be entirely created by New Zealanders, I jumped at it. It was in two acts, three quarters of an hour long, the biggest thing I had ever attempted. It was performed in Wellington in February 1960 with a mainly amateur cast and was reckoned a success, though today I find its treatment of Maori culture cringe making—it was based on a sentimentalized version of a Maori legend and featured Maori maidens in brown body stockings dancing on points. I don't think anyone would dare produce it today, although it was revived and toured in 1970 by the newly formed Royal New Zealand Ballet.

I've never had such a high in all my life as on the night of the orchestral rehearsal, hearing my music played by twenty-five good musicians from the New Zealand National Orchestra (NZNO). A friend of mine described the music as Sibelius and water, which I took as a compliment. I was happy not to conduct. That was done by the leader of the NZNO, a fine musician who had played pre-World War II in the London Philharmonic Orchestra under Thomas Beecham and had managed to keep alive for many years a good semipro string orchestra, taking it to audiences of farmers and coal miners in the backblocks, and playing them Bach and Britten, Warlock and Tchaikovsky, as well as pieces by NZ composers who were starting to emerge. National radio later broadcast a suite from my ballet, in an arrangement I had made for full orchestra.

I applied for, and won, a New Zealand government scholarship that would give me two years' study abroad at five hundred pounds a year, not much even in those days, but with a little copying for the BBC (sweated labor at a shilling and ninepence a page—seven and a half pence in today's money), I managed to survive.

In those days for us colonials, "abroad" meant England, and I arrived in London in April 1961 with not much idea what I was going to do with my two years of freedom and no one to advise me. I went to the Royal College of Music, where they told me politely that they didn't want me. I now know that I'd have done better career wise to enroll at, maybe, Cambridge or York University, where I could have done a doctorate full time in the two years, but I didn't know that then, and so I wrote to Michael Tippett asking for lessons (I thought I might as well start at the top). He politely refused but told me that in his opinion the best teacher in England was Priaulx Rainier, so I wrote to her, made an appointment, and went to see her. She was in her sixties then, a composer of gritty and dissonant though not serial music. She looked through my precious ballet score and one or two other things, finally putting them aside and saying, "Now let's see what you can really do."

I was working entirely on my own, living in a bedsitter, with no opportunities for performance, not even a piano, and no acquaintance among musicians in London. It was really more or less hopeless, but I persevered and composed a number of instrumental pieces and songs under Priaulx's supervision and a large orchestral piece, rather in the manner of Schoenberg's *Five Orchestral Pieces* Opus 16. In August 1962 she sent me to the summer school of music at Dartington in Devon. There I found myself in a new world, the young lions of the avant-garde, whose talk was all about aleatoricism and total serialism, whose heroes were Boulez and Stockhausen, Berio and Cage, none of whom I had then heard of. I enrolled in the composition class, with Luigi Nono as tutor. The young lions (I was thirty-five at that time) excluded me, were deaf to my pleas to tell me what it was they were talking about, made it clear they thought Priaulx Rainier was something out of the ark, and generally treated me and my idols with contempt. Sibelius? What's that? One bright spot was that I got an eminent clarinetist to look at some duos for clarinets I had written for Priaulx. He liked them and got two of his pupils to play them at an informal afternoon concert. Another was meeting Bernard Rands, fresh from study in Florence with Luciano Berio, and currently a lecturer in the University of North Wales in Bangor. He spent a whole afternoon with me with pencil and manuscript paper explaining the principles of serial composition and other concepts. I shall always be grateful to him for that. We become good friends, and in subsequent years I spent a lot of time at his home in Bangor, and later at York, and through him met Berio and Cathy Berberian and a number of other luminaries of the time. It was also Bernard who introduced me to the idea of music as gesture, though I really didn't understand it at the time, and in any case he was thinking more in terms of a musical work than of performance. Berio's series of pieces for solo instrument, called *Sequenzas*, I found interesting, especially the one for trombone, which I heard at the Queen Elizabeth Hall played by the marvelous jazz trombonist Paul Rutherford. It was wildly applauded and praised by the critics, until Rutherford admitted that he'd played the first measures of the score and improvised the rest. The avant-gardists never forgave him, but Berio didn't seem to mind too much.

But for all Bernard's help I never got on with serial composition, Schoenbergian, Webernian, or Boulezian. I just couldn't make myself believe that what I had written sounded like music. I went to every avant-garde concert I could find in London and enjoyed many of them, while others I couldn't make head or tail of. I kept writing pieces in the hope that someday they might get performed, but I found myself drifting back into my old tonal habits. When the scholarship ran out I found myself faced with the task of finding a way of making a living. I drifted for a couple of years, doing supply teaching and working for a couple of years for a cheapjack publisher that made pirated versions of Soviet publications on science and technology. They paid quite good money, but I realized one day that this wasn't what I wanted or ought to be doing with my life, and applied for a teaching post. I had to go right back to a rookie's job, but that was good for me, and in April 1967 I found myself appointed to a wonderful secondary modern girls' school in north London.

The first thing I saw when I walked in the place was a play rehearsal going on in the school hall. What were they rehearsing? My god, the *Antigone* of Sophocles, with a tall, hugely intelligent black girl as the blind seer Tiresias. These were supposed to be the dumb kids! I got stuck in, went to any number of teachers' courses, and started developing some ideas on how to get the kids composing. All my ideas were of course based on the avant-garde, but I did have some successes, including a twenty-minute Christmas cantata based on New Testament texts, with each class in the school's first year contributing a section. They did it at the school's pre-Christmas concert, and it went over like a bomb. The idea that I worked on had come to me fully formed: that all children have the potential to be composers as well as performers. Another idea that came to me very quickly when I attempted to teach recorder to the kids is that recorders are not instruments that children ought to be required to play. They are very difficult, and especially difficult to keep in tune, which makes them very unrewarding for young children. The fact that an instrument is technologically simple doesn't mean that it's easy to play. Quite the opposite in fact—the complexities of modern wind instruments come from the need to make them easier, not harder, to play. (I have long suspected that the ubiquity of recorders in schools originated in a very skillful commercial ploy by the Dolmetsch family, playing on the snobbery of the "early music" movement). The other thing about them is the (to me at least) horrible sound they make. After a few months of persevering I bought a set of despised penny whistles and handed them out to one class—instant improvement! They were easier to keep in tune, provided a much pleasanter sound, and gained much more enthusiastic participation from the class.

I didn't get far with these developments, as I was appointed in 1968 to a teachers' college in Birmingham, a small (about two hundred students) women's physical education college. I had hoped to do a lot of music for dance, but to my surprise I received no encouragement from the dance staff. I had so little to do in fact that I offered myself to a local primary school and spent Friday afternoons teaching there. That was a lot of fun, but my superiors didn't think I ought to be working outside the college and it ended after a term. I also worked weekends with the Schools Outreach section of the Belgrade Theater in nearby Coventry and spent an exhilarating fourteen hours one Saturday with the actors creating and recording music for a play they were touring in schools. It later won a prize. Then there was an adults' Saturday-afternoon music workshop in the Birmingham and Midland Institute that I ran for a couple of years. I also started getting invitations to talk about and demonstrate my ideas on pupils' composition around the English Midlands and beyond.

All these engagements helped me in two ways. First was that I got to do work that I never managed to do in London, and the second was that it all helped me little by little to evolve my ideas, which include (1) music is basically performance and (2) all normally endowed human beings are capable of taking an active part in a musical performance. The idea of "musicking" itself came later, around the time when I was writing *Music of the Common Tongue* in the mideighties.

A landmark in my musical experience was going to the last of the great Isle of Wight rock festivals in July 1970. I could find no one of my age to go with me, so I bought a backpack and a sleeping bag and off I went on my own. I was taken up by a group of young U.S. Air Force conscripts and their wives/girlfriends, who found the old man (I was forty-two) amusing and were nice to me and kept me happily stoned the entire weekend. The experience of sitting out in the (mostly) beautiful weather in the midst of this vast crowd and being immersed in music for nearly twenty-four hours a day for three days was for me staggering—The Who, Joni Mitchell, Joan Baez, Chicago, Donovan, Miles Davis, and Jimi Hendrix. Oh yes, and Tiny Tim . . . I remember my American friends' disgust at the tasteless behavior of a group near us, who were drinking alcohol—not just that but *cider* for god's sake! I arrived back in Birmingham exhausted, saturated with music and marijuana and generally mindblown, and took about a week to come back to earth. What the experience did to my senses and my feeling for the order of things is something I am still coming to terms with.

I returned to London in 1981, having been appointed senior lecturer in music at Ealing Technical College, later Ealing College of Higher Education, later Ealing Polytechnic, and currently Thames Valley University. Still the same grotty dump that we loved back in '71, the only difference is that the standard of teaching and general adventurousness have gone down in proportion as the status of the place has gone up. For me it was, at least initially, a great experience. The head of the Music Division was a straight-up-and-down Royal College of Music musician, a fine organist and choral conductor of the most traditional kind. But he used to say to me, "I don't know what the hell you're doing, Chris, but if you think it's music, go ahead and do it." We got on well for the fifteen years I spent there until I retired in 1986.

In the early seventies we constructed a new BA in humanities degree under the aegis of the Council for National Academic Awards, and I was entrusted with the design of the first-year music course. I insisted that it be accessible to anyone interested, regardless of his or her level of musical expertise or previous musical experience. I included a three-hour practical composition workshop each week, which proved popular and useful.

We attracted some very offbeat students, one of whom introduced me to one of the finest musicians and teachers I have ever met: the jazz drummer John Stevens. His drumming was beautiful, and I could listen to him alone for hours—always different, always wonderfully fluid, and yet you never had the slightest doubt where the beat was (unless he wanted you to be unsure, of course). He had a group called the Spontaneous Music Ensemble, which included everyone from the best British jazzmen to tyros like me. I remember we did a BBC gig with two pianists in the group. When the other pianist arrived, it was the great Stan Tracey, doyen of British jazz pianists! I went through John's "Search and Reflect" process with him, a very liberating experience, and we spent many hours talking and listening to music. He loved Anton Webern's works and could explicate them better than any PhD. Like so many of the best British jazzmen (Americans seem to know little and care less about the very beautiful and lively British jazz scene of that time, which was enlivened by a number of superb, exiled, black South African musicians—your loss), John had come through the Royal Air Force Band at Uxbridge, not far from Ealing. He also helped me in my first tremulous attempts to play jazz, and though I never got good at it I did gain more understanding of the complexity of the art. One of my students, a good R&B saxophonist, who wanted to use the performance option in the degree to improve his jazz skills, asked me to act as pianist for his lessons. That was a steep learning curve if ever I got onto one.

In 1980, when I was on a year's secondment to Dartington College of Arts in Devon, I got John down to give a workshop to the students. The workshop, predictably I'm afraid, attracted more students of drama than of music. John, clearly nervous of being in such posh surroundings, had put on his best Italian suit, very sharp, with white shirt and narrow black tie. He was an enormous success. One fledgling theater director said to me afterward, "Here comes this dude looking like everyone's idea of a used-car salesman and just manages to blow everyone's mind."

John died of a heart attack in 2000, aged only fifty-three.

Also around that time I got involved in a sound poetry and music group around the sound poet Bob Cobbing. There was a young woman singer who wove marvelous lines of sound around Bob's voice; a flutist, David Toop, who played some beautiful, big Andean flutes he had made; a percussionist, Paul Burwell, who had the biggest collection of hubcaps I have ever seen; a trombonist, and me at the piano. I loved it. We even did a BBC Radio 3 gig.

I had been working for some years on a translation of Henri Pousseur's *Fragments théoriques sur la musique expérimentale*, a massive task, and had been trying to get a publisher to look at it. It was only when I offered it to Calder and Boyars, who had been the British publishers of a number of interesting music books, including the Cage books and Ives's *Essays before a Sonata*, that I received any response, in the form of an invitation to talk with the great man, John Calder, himself. He looked at my manuscript, and we talked for a while about music (he is a great opera buff), and then he offered me a contract to write a book for him, just like that. That was the origin of *Music, Society, Education*, which I wrote more or less off the top of my head from my lectures and classes. I expected it just to sink from sight like dozens of other academic music books (every academic thinks he has a book in him), and no one was more surprised than I was when it started to get good and even rave reviews—and some bitchy ones. I had been in doubt as I wrote it whether I was just mouthing platitudes (after all, it all seemed to me so obvious) or making wild, unsupported, and maybe unsupportable, assertions. I certainly had no idea that I was writing an "important" book. I remember meeting the U.S. cultural attaché at a conference a few months after it was published, and when he asked me over lunch if I was "the" Christopher Small I had no idea how to answer.

I shall always be grateful to John Calder for giving me the chance to write and be published, but he did rip me off rotten, and still owes me a lot of money that I shall never see. I finally told him in a letter that I was grateful to him but that I had run out of gratitude. But I was frightened to take the rights back from him, although he was flagrantly in breach of our contract, thinking that I would never get another publisher and that a dud publisher was better than no publisher.

The breakthrough came when Rob Walser, whom I had met at the 1988 meeting of the Society for Ethnomusicology at MIT, contacted me in Sitges and asked if he and his wife Susan McClary could stay with us for a couple of nights. Sitting out on the terrace of our apartment one evening, I told them about my woes with Calder, and they said that, as two-thirds of the music editorial committee of Wesleyan University Press, they could guarantee that if I could get the rights off Calder they would reprint my (then) two books. It took a while, but we managed it. Later Wesleyan published the third book, *Musicking*, so all three are now under the same imprint.

The other big influence on my feelings and ideas about music was knowing Neville Braithwaite, my friend and companion of thirty years. When I dedicated *Music of the Common Tongue* to him "for showing me what it was all about," I meant it—not only for himself but also for so many West Indian friends (he is Jamaican by birth) whom I met through him and through his profession of youth worker, and from his wonderful welcoming family, scattered around the world, who view life from a viewpoint intriguingly different from my own, and who have enriched my life and especially my understanding of the act of musicking. Alas, he died of a brain tumor in October 2006, and I shall miss him forever.

People like to label me a musicologist, but I feel that the label puts me in a nice, safe pigeonhole and makes me innocuous. If I have always tried, not always successfully, to refuse it, it is not out of modesty, real or assumed, although it is true that I have no formal musicological training. Rather, it is because my ideas, such as they are, have grown more out of my musical experiences than out of any theory, which for me has always come after the musical fact. I consider myself, therefore, simply as a musician who thinks about his art.

SITGES, JULY 2004

I am also starting to realize that I have been lassoed into the music education corral, where I don't feel I really belong either. True, I have been a teacher of music most of my professional life and have theorized some about my job, but being a teacher of music is not necessarily the same thing as being a music educator, although it is to be hoped that the latter category is always to be subsumed into the former. I have always tried to put my performing money where my theorizing mouth is.

I have a sneaky feeling that both these "disciplines" are some kind of—no, not scams, which implies a degree of deliberate deception that I don't intend—but that neither is really necessary for the universal practice of musicking. Perhaps I oversimplify (a sin of which I have been accused), but I cannot help feeling that these great intellectual (and career) structures have been erected around what are really two very simple propositions—that all normally endowed human beings are born with the capacity to music and that everyone wants to have the power to music just as they want to have the power to speak.

POSTSCRIPT, 2008

Introduction to *Music, Society, Education*

(1977)

It is generally acknowledged that the musical tradition of post-Renaissance Europe and her offshoots is one of the most brilliant and astonishing cultural phenomena of human history. In its range and power it is perhaps to be matched by only one other intellectual achievement—the science of post-Renaissance Europe. It is understandable, therefore, if those of us who are its heirs (which includes not only the Americas and many late and present colonies of Europe but also by now a large portion of the non-western world as well) are inclined to find in the European musical tradition the norm and ideal for all musical experience, just as they find in the attitudes of western science the paradigm for the acquisition of all knowledge, and to view all other musical cultures as at best exotic and odd. It is in fact precisely this inbuilt certainty of the superiority of European culture to all others that has given Europeans, and latterly their American heirs, the confidence to undertake the cultural colonization of the world and the imposition of European values and habits of thought on the whole human race.

We should not, however, allow the brilliance of the western musical tradition to blind us to its limitations and even areas of downright impoverishment. We may be reluctant to think of our musical life, with its great symphony orchestras, its Bach, its Beethoven, its mighty concert halls and opera houses, as in any way impoverished, and yet we must admit that we have nothing to compare with the rhythmic sophistication of Indian, or what we are inclined to dismiss as "primitive" African music, that our ears are deaf to the subtleties of pitch inflection of Indian raga or Byzantine church music, that the cultivation of bel canto as the ideal of the singing voice has shut us off from all but a very small part of the human voice's sound possibilities or expressive potential, such as are part of the everyday resources of a Balkan folk singer or an Eskimo, and that the smooth mellifluous sound of the romantic symphony orchestra drowns out the fascinating buzzes and distortions cultivated alike by African and medieval European musicians.

It is only comparatively recently that Europeans have developed sufficient interest in these and other musical cultures to hear in them anything more than quaintness or cacophony; we were in the position of the fish in Albert Einstein's metaphor, not aware of the water because it knows nothing of any other medium. Today, partly through our increasing knowledge of other musical cultures, we have the opportunity to become aware of our own tradition as a medium surrounding and supporting us and shaping our perceptions and attitudes as the needs of hydrodynamics shape the fish's body; this book is in part an attempt to examine the western musical tradition through this experience as well as in itself, to see it through the mirror of these other musics as it were from the outside, and in so doing to learn something of the inner unspoken nature of western culture as a whole. We shall try to look beneath the surface of the music, beneath the "message," if any, which the composer consciously intended (and even the fact that a message is intended may be in itself significant), to its basic technical means, its assumptions, which we usually accept unawares, on such matters as the nature of sound, the manner of listening, the passing of time, as well as its social situation and relations, to see what lies hidden there.

For it is in the arts of our, or indeed of any, culture, that we see not only a metaphor for, but also a way of transcending, its otherwise unspoken and unexamined assumptions. Art can reveal to us new modes of perception and feeling, which jolt us out of our habitual ways; it can make us aware of possibilities of alternative societies whose existence is not yet. Many writers and critics have undertaken, in the visual and plastic arts and in literature, to make plain the social implications of their chosen arts; it is to me perpetually surprising that so few writers have made any comparable attempt in music, whose criticism and appreciation exists for the most part in a social vacuum. Perhaps it is the lack of explicit subject matter in music that frightens people off. I make the attempt here with much trepidation, but feel it imperative, not merely for the sake of constructing yet another aesthetic of music (though even to do this in a way that takes note of the musical experience of other cultures would be a worthwhile project) but because of what I believe to be the importance and urgency from the social and especially the educational point of view of what I have learnt from my explorations. In following these explorations in this book the reader will notice that I occasionally return to the same point more than once; I must ask the reader to regard these repetitions not as signs of simple garrulousness but rather as nodal points in that network structure which my argument resembles more than it resembles a straight logic-line. The explorer (to introduce a metaphor which will become familiar) in a strange territory may cross and re-cross the same point many times, but will come towards it from a different direction each time as he traverses the terrain, and, if he is lucky, will each time obtain a new point of view. And if I appear to leave the subject and introduce irrelevancies I must ask the reader to trust me eventually to make relationships plain.

I shall begin my investigation with an exposition of what I see as the principal characteristics of western classical music, and of the conventions, both social and technical, of that music. I shall try to show how both western classical music and western science speak of very deep-rooted states of mind in Europeans, states of mind which have brought us to our present uncomfortable, if not downright dangerous condition in our relations with one another and with nature. I shall suggest that education, or rather schooling, as at present conceived in our society has worked to perpetuate those states of mind by which we see nature as a mere object for use, products as all-important regardless of the process by which they are obtained, and knowledge as an abstraction, existing "out there," independent of the experience of the knower, the three notions being linked by an intricate web of cause and effect. In holding up some other musical cultures to the reader's attention I shall try to show that different aesthetics of music are possible that can stand as metaphors for quite different world views, for different systems of relationships within society and nature from our own. I shall describe the various attempts, in the music of our century, to frame a critique of our present society and its world view, while a brief survey of music in the United States will show that that country possesses a culture which is not only more remote from Europe than we imagine but has also long contained within it the vision of a potential society which is perhaps stronger and more radical than anything in European culture. And finally, I shall attempt to show how the new vision of art revealed can serve as a model for a new vision of education, and possibly of society.

I have based my investigations upon two postulates: first, that art is more than the production of beautiful, or even expressive, objects (including sound-objects such as symphonies and concertos) for others to contemplate and admire, but is essentially a *process*, by which we explore our inner and outer environments and learn to live in them. The artist, whether he is Beethoven struggling to bring a symphony into being, Michelangelo wresting his forms from the marble, the devoted gardener laying out his garden or the child making his highly formalized portraits of the important people and things in his life, is exploring his environment, and his responses to it, no less than is a scientist in his laboratory; he is ordering his perceptions and making a model of reality, both present and potential. If he is a sufficiently gifted artist his art will help others do the same. Art is thus, notwithstanding its devaluation in post-Renaissance society, as vital an activity as science, and in fact reaches into areas of activity that science cannot touch. The second postulate is that the nature of these means of exploration, of science and of art, their techniques and attitudes, is a sure pointer to the nature and the preoccupations of the society that gave them birth. We shall find that our culture is presently undergoing a transformation as profound as that which took place in the fifteenth and sixteenth centuries which we call the Renaissance, and that this transformation, like the Renaissance, is taking place not just on the level of conscious opinions and concepts but, more importantly, on that of perception and the often unconscious habits of thought on which we base our everyday speech and action. And since it is perception and the subconscious that are the concern of art, it is the methods of art rather than of science which can provide a model and a guide for the new conceptual universe towards which we are moving.

It is a grave but common error to think of the aims of art and of science as identical, or complementary, or even much in tune with each other. Art and science, it is true, are both means of exploration, but the intention, the method and the kind of reality they explore are very different. This is not simply the Cartesian split between matter and mind (we must indeed start from the assumption that they are identical); it is rather that the aim of art is to enable us to live in the world, while that of science is to enable us to master it. It is for this reason that I insist on the supreme importance of the art-process and the relative unimportance of the art-object; the essential tool of art is the unrepeatable experience. With science it is the finished product that counts, the theory, the hypothesis, the objectified knowledge; we obtain it by whatever means we can, and the tool is the repeatable experiment. Art is knowledge as experience, the structuring and ordering of feeling and perception, while science is abstract knowledge divorced as completely as possible from experience, a body of facts and concepts existing outside of and independently of the knower. Both are valid human activities, but since the Renaissance we have allowed the attitudes and values of science to predominate over those of art, to the detriment of the quality of our experience.

Our schools, for example, concern themselves almost exclusively with abstract knowledge, which pupils are expected to absorb immediately and regurgitate on demand. The pupils may or may not wish, or be able, to absorb the knowledge, but the one lesson that all do learn is that they can be consumers, not producers, of knowledge, and that the only knowledge that has validity is that which comes to them through the school system. They are taught much about the world, but their experience of it, apart from the hermetic world of classroom and playground, is seriously impaired. And so, too, of our culture as a whole. We know more about the world, and experience it less, than perhaps any previous generation in history; so, too, musicology has made available to us more knowledge about music than ever before, and yet our experience of it is greatly diluted by being mediated through the knowledge of experts. We become afraid of the encounter with new musical experience, where knowledge and expertise are no guide and only the subjective experience honestly felt can serve, and retreat into the safe past, where we know what to expect and connoisseurship is paramount.

This book will suggest that artistic activity, properly understood, can provide not only a way out of this impasse in musical appreciation, in itself an unimportant matter, but also an approach to the restructuring of education and even perhaps of our society. Simply because the artist sets his own goals and works with his whole self—reason, intuition, the most ruthless self-criticism and realistic assessment of a situation, freely, without external compulsion and with love—art is a model for what work could be were it freely and lovingly undertaken rather than, as it is for most today, forced, monotonous and boring. The spectacular changes which western art has undergone in our century are metaphors for changes that are still only latent in our culture. They show, however, that there are in fact forces within the matrix of society that are favorable to these changes, which could bring about our liberation from the scientific and technocratic domination of our lives, from the pointless and repetitious labor that passes for work for most people, and, for our children, from the scars inflicted by our present schools, well-intentioned though they may be, on all those, successful and unsuccessful alike, who pass through them.

A Different Drummer—American Music

From *Music, Society, Education*

(1977)

It is a characteristic of tonal-harmonic music that it requires a high degree of subordination of the individual elements of the music to the total effect. Not only is the progress of each individual voice required to conform to the progression of chords, but also each individual note or chord is meaningless in itself, gaining significance only within the context of the total design, much as the authoritarian or totalitarian state requires the subordination of the interests of its individual citizens to its purposes. It is therefore interesting to see in the music of those British colonies, which become the United States of America, a disintegration of tonal functional harmony taking place long before such a process became detectable in Europe, and it is not too fanciful to view this as one expression of the ideal of individual liberty on which the United States was founded, an ideal that, however meagerly realized or even betrayed during the course of its history, has never quite disappeared.

The colonists who arrived in New England in the early seventeenth century had left behind the last days of a golden age of English musical culture. Many were, in the words of the first Governor of the New England colonies, "very expert in music," and although the Pilgrims and Puritans favored sacred over secular music, they had no objection to secular instrumental music, and even dance, as long as decorum was preserved. However, the Mayflower and her successors had little room for any but the most essential cargo, and only the smallest and hardiest musical instruments could be accommodated—certainly nothing so bulky and liable to damage as a virginal or organ. So far as is known, the early colonists could and did enjoy only music that was simple and functional, that is, social music and worship music. As far as the former is concerned, we do know that there were instruments around, though what they played is unclear—possibly from English collections like those of Thomas Ravenscroft, and later John Playford. Secular song was not unknown, not only in the Anglo-Celtic ballads, which belonged to the ancient oral rather than to the literate tradition, and which in America proved extremely durable, but also songs from the various collections that had crossed the Atlantic with them. Worship music, on the other hand, meant almost exclusively the singing of the psalms in metrical translation, a practice that was not unknown in England even in the Established Church. This may seem a limited repertoire, but there are after all a hundred and fifty psalms, many of which are very long, and their emotional range is very wide. The version favored by the early colonists was that of Henry Ainsworth, who used a variety of poetic meters and provided no less than thirty-nine different tunes, which were printed at the back of the book in the form of single lines of melody. Dissatisfaction was, however, early expressed by the Puritan divines, who alleged that faithfulness to the literal word of God was too often sacrificed to literary grace, and in 1640 a new metrical translation was made by a committee and published—the first book to be printed in the New England colony.

The translations were made into only six metrical schemes, mostly in four-line stanzas, so that the same tune could be used for several psalms, and the number of tunes that needed to be learnt was kept to a minimum. The new psalm book was adopted, after much disputation, throughout the New England colonies by the end of the seventeenth century; under the name of *Bay Psalm Book* it ran through innumerable editions over the next century. It was not until the ninth edition, of 1698, that tunes were provided—a mere thirteen—to which the psalms could be sung.

Irving Lowens makes a valuable comment on the American culture of this period:

> The story of the arts in seventeenth century New England is the tale of a people trying to plant in the New World the very vines whose fruit they had enjoyed in the Old, while, at the same time, it is the chronicle of the subconscious development of a totally different civilization. The seventeenth-century history of the *Bay Psalm Book* is a case in point, for although the psalm-tunes may superficially appear nothing more than a parochial utilization of certain music sung in the mother country, a mysterious qualitative change took place when

> they were sung on different soil. Here, they proved to be the seed from which a new, uniquely American music was later to flower.[1]

The first flowers did not appear until late in the eighteenth century, but even within the psalm-singing tradition some very interesting departures from European practice were very soon to appear. There was an inevitable decline in musical literacy after the first generation of the Pilgrims, brought about by the wilderness conditions in which they found themselves; psalm-singing was transformed from a written to a mainly oral tradition, and despite the efforts of the divines and the 'educated' musicians to instill what they called "regular singing" (singing, that is, at that neat brisk jogtrot which every church organist still today likes to hear from his congregation), the folk persisted in planting their own fingerprint on the singing of the psalms. It is fascinating to see, at the very beginning of America's cultural history, the kind of clash between native and imported European tradition that was to recur again and again.

Because it was a folk and an oral tradition and frowned upon by educated people, we have only unsympathetic accounts of what was happening; the people, as usual, had no spokesman. Here is the Reverend Cotton Mather, writing in 1721: "It has been found . . . in some of our congregations that in length of time their singing has degenerated into an *odd noise*, that has more of what we want a name for, than any Regular Singing in it."[2] And, in the same year, one Thomas Walter: "I have observed in many places, one man is upon this note, while another is on the note before him, which produces something as hideous and disorderly as is beyond expression bad."[3]

We can infer from these and other contemporary accounts that what was happening was that the people, singing unaccompanied as was usual, had evolved their own style, slowing up the putative beat almost to immobility (though probably each carrying within himself his own beat), gradually sinking in pitch and then perhaps jumping up an octave or a fifth to regain his own natural compass. Then, within each enormously prolonged note (as written), each would proceed to ornament each note with "turnings and flourishings," grace notes and arabesques, with arbitrary alterations of melody and time. It must have been an astonishing noise; one would wish to have had a tape recorder in Plymouth, Massachusetts, in the 1690s. And, at least in the country areas, there seemed little that the cultivated musicians could do to prevent it; the people sang in their own way as long as the singing remained unaccompanied and there were not enough trained musicians around to confine their musical devotions to the written note.

Christopher Small at a restaurant in Sitges, Spain, 2008.
Photograph by Robert Walser.

This continual clash between those who want to regulate and those who do not want to be regulated recurs time and again throughout America's history. Thoreau, for example, writing a hundred and thirty years after Cotton Mather, set the matter eloquently: "Why should we be in such desperate haste to succeed, and in such desperate enterprises? If a man does not keep pace with his companions, perhaps it is because he hears a different drummer. Let him step to the music which he hears, however measured and far away. It is not important that he should mature as soon as an apple-tree or an oak. If the condition of things which we were made for is not yet, what were any reality which we can substitute?"[4]

The validity of this way of singing, reviled and ridiculed as it was by the cultivated musicians of two centuries, was affirmed by the town bandmaster of Danbury, Connecticut, George Ives, and his son Charles. The persistence of the tradition of spontaneous hymn-singing can be appreciated when we realize that what Charles writes of below must have been taking place in the 1880s: "I remember when I was a boy—at the outdoor Camp Meeting services in Redding, all the farmers, their families and field hands for miles around used to come through the trees—when things like *Beulah Land, Woodworth, Nearer My God to Thee, The Shining Shore, Nettleton, In the Sweet Bye and Bye* and the like were sung by thousands of 'let out' souls. The music notes and words on paper were about as much like what they 'were' (at those moments) as the monogram on a man's necktie may be like his face. Father, who led the singing, sometimes with his cornet or his voice, sometimes with both voice and arms, sometimes in the quieter hymns with a French horn or violin, would always encourage the people to sing in their own way. Most of them knew the words and music (theirs) by heart, and sang it that way. If they threw the poet and the composer around a bit, so much the better for the poetry and the music. There was power and exultation in these great conclaves of sound from humanity."[5]

The proponents of "regular singing" were not slow to take action against what they regarded as the corruption of hymn singing. Innumerable books were published with the intention of schooling singers, and, more important, the institution of singing schools grew up. These were generally run by itinerant musicians, often doubling as peddlers of quack medicines or the like, who would settle in a village or town for a few weeks, announce their intention of instructing those who wished it in regular singing, and conduct classes for all comers in the evenings. This institution prospered for reasons that probably had as much to do with social as with purely musical factors, and became an important part of the life of the New England colonies, right down the eastern seaboard. It was these travelling singing masters who built up a musical community that gave rise in the late eighteenth century to the first group of native American composers.

The group who became known as the First New England School were humble men, who called themselves "tunesmiths" rather than composers, since they regarded themselves as artisans whose function, like that of the blacksmith or wheelwright, was to serve the community. As H. Wiley Hitchcock says:

> This was a music completely in tune with the society for which it was written. These journeymen composers had a secure and respected function in Colonial and Federal-era life in general; viewed historically from a point two hundred years later, theirs was a sort of golden age of musical participation in which teachers, composers, singers and populace in general worked together fruitfully. If ever there was a truly popular music, the music of the New Englanders was popular; it arose from the deep, old traditions of early America; it was accessible to all and enjoyed by all; it was a plain-spoken music for plain people, and assessed on its own terms it was a stylistically homogeneous music of great integrity.[6]

These were down-to-earth men, then, and they had down-to-earth names; among them were Justin Morgan, Supply Belcher, Timothy Swan, and, the best-known and most articulate member of the group, William Billings of Boston. Born in 1746, he was a tanner by trade; quite self-taught in music (though doubtless tutored in a singing school), he abandoned his trade and hung a shingle outside his house which read, simply, "Billings—Songs." He was apparently a remarkable man; a contemporary description says he was "a singular man of moderate size, short of one leg, with one eye, without any address, with an uncommon negligence of person. Still he spake and thought as one above the common abilities."[7] He published a number of collections of songs, hymn tunes, and anthems, usually prefacing them with pungently expressed opinions, which give the flavor not only of the man but of the confident young society in which he lived in an intimate relationship that must be the envy of many a contemporary composer. For example:

> Perhaps it may be expected that I should say something concerning rules for composition; to those I answer that Nature is the best dictator, for not all the hard, dry, studied rules that ever was prescribed, will not enable any person to form an air . . . It must be Nature, Nature who must lay the foundation, Nature must inspire the thought . . . For my own part, as I don't think myself confined to any rules of composition, laid down by any that went before me, neither should I think (were I to pretend to lay down rules) that any one who came after me were in any ways obligated to adhere to them, any further than they should think proper; so in fact I think it best for every composer to be his own carver.[8]

Brave words! But Billings has more for us:

> Perhaps some may think I mean and intend to throw Art entirely out of the question. I answer, by no means, for the more art is displayed, the more Nature is decorated. And in some sorts of composition there is dry study required, and art very requisite. For instance, in a fuge, where the parts come in after each other with the same notes, but even here, art is subservient to genius, for fancy goes first and strikes out the work roughly, and art comes after and polishes it over.[9]

Billings was fourteen years younger than Haydn, ten years older than Mozart, but his music inhabits another world than that of European classicism. In some ways it seems to hark back to an earlier European style; it is modal rather than tonal, with a folkish flavor, deriving perhaps from the Anglo-Celtic folk tradition. It is to all intents and purposes non-harmonic; certainly tonal functional harmony plays no part in its repertory of expressive means. Any conflict between the needs of chord progression and the shape of an individual melodic line is invariably resolved in favor of the latter, even if this produces a harmonic clash, so that astounding dissonances unknown in contemporary European music are used freely and often without any feeling of need for resolution. Open and parallel fifths, both proscribed by European rules, are heard here so frequently that it is clear that the sound was positively enjoyed by these composers and their congregations. To harmonically attuned ears the music may sound tonally monotonous, the more so as modulation, apart from the occasional perfunctory movement to the dominant, is virtually non-existent, but to feel this is to miss the point of the music, which is concerned with other matters, and pursues its concerns in a remarkably stylish and consistent way. The music is mainly for unaccompanied chorus—at least, no accompaniment is provided, although wind and even string instruments might join in doubling the vocal parts should they happen to be available. Keyboard instruments were rare and played no part in the world of these composers—which may have been a contributing factor to the absence of harmonic device in their works, obliging them to think in terms of lines rather than of chords (the role of the keyboard, with its power of bringing complex textures under the control of a single individual, in the development of tonal harmony has already been remarked on).

A typical New England anthem consists of a number of short sections cunningly put together, with chordal sections alternating with sections in simple imitative counterpoint ("fuging") and remarkable manipulation of textural effect in which the whole group may be set against one, two or three voices, as well as contrasts of tempo, dynamics and vocal timbre, all used as structural rather than as decorative elements. That the first western non-harmonic music since the Renaissance should have been composed in a society founded on the ideal of individual liberty (Billings was an active supporter of the Colonial cause and wrote not only its principal rallying-song, *Chester*, but also an eloquent *Lament Over Boston* on the occasion of the burning of the city by the British) by a musician who believed that "every composer should be his own carver" and that "nature must inspire the thought" should come as no surprise to the reader who has thus far followed the argument of this book.

Billings, like his colleagues, was very concerned for the manner of performance; many of his ideas would have shocked his European contemporaries, and even today show a very cavalier attitude to the demands of traditional tonal-harmonic music, especially the importance it assigns to the real bass. He liked, for example, to have male and female voices on each part, producing an octave, and occasionally a double-octave, doubling—a kind of organ sonority in six or eight parts. His ear was very idiosyncratic, but it is clear that he knew the kind of sound he wanted:

> Suppose a company of forty people; twenty of them should sing the bass, and the other twenty should be divided according to the discretion of the company into the upper parts. Six or seven voices should sing the ground bass, which sung together with the upper parts, is most majestic, and so exceeding grand as to cause the floor to tremble, as I myself have often experienced . . . Much caution should also be used in singing a solo (*sic*); in my opinion 2 or 3 at most are enough to sing it well. It should be sung soft as an echo, in order to keep the hearers in agreeable suspense till all the parts join together in a full chorus, as sweet and strong as possible.[10]

It was also apparently not unusual for these composers to place the various parts at some distance from one another, making use of the spatial separation between them—attesting further to a concern for the individual part, which was virtually unknown in the European music of the time.

Here, then, was the stuff of a new, democratic tradition in music, strong, confident, firmly rooted in the life of the people, and accessible to them, which could match the aspirations of Jeffersonian democracy. Yet it vanished without trace for almost two hundred years, swamped by the movement towards gentility and European-style "correctness" which took place under the leadership of musicians such as Lowell Mason in the early years of the nineteenth century. To Mason, who, appropriately enough, was also the first to bring to music the methods of that typically American institution, Big Business (which was just getting under way in the early nineteenth century), music was principally a commodity. He published an enormous quantity of music, hymns, church music generally, children's instructional manuals and songbooks, secular songs, some of them his own compositions (*From Greenland's Icy Mountain* is his) but mostly taken from the work of lesser European composers and the lesser works of greater, often rearranged to take out their most striking features, leaving a bland and bloodless mixture, not unlike the products of present-day American television, and for much the same reasons. Mason grasped the fact that if music was to be treated as a commodity then clearly it had to appeal to the widest number of people and antagonize the fewest. Good quality, yes—but not so original as to disturb or frighten off a potential customer. (This blandness is still to be found today in many American collections of music for high school orchestras, bands and the like.) In any case the raw but richly alive works of the New England tunesmiths clearly would not do.

It is not too fanciful to see in this betrayal of the ideals of the early composers a parallel of the betrayal of the idea of the rights of man that began to take place in the early nineteenth century as industrialism got under way. America in the nineteenth century produced writers of real greatness who preserved an aggressive stance of independence—Melville, Twain, Whitman, Emerson, for example, and above all Thoreau, while American art music produced only Louis Moreau Gottschalk and Stephen Collins Foster, both interesting figures but scarcely of comparable stature. Could not this be because music, for the very reason that it is less precise in its outward meanings, less conscious of exactly what it is saying, gives even deeper expression than literature to the subconscious motivations of a culture? In any case, the history of nineteenth-century American art music is a dismal affair; one after another, young composers crossed the Atlantic, to Dresden, to Leipzig, Vienna or Weimar, rarely to Paris, coming back with music that was no more than a pale imitation of German romanticism. As David Wooldridge in his recent biography of Charles Ives remarks, the vision of the New England tunesmiths "went forfeit to the competent . . . Only music malingered dismally, generation over generation of American composers making the pilgrimage to Europe like dowagers to a spa, to fetch back the continuing seed of a foreign culture for the continuing delight of old ladies."[11]

It was not, however, the Europeanized American composers who dominated the art-music scene; indeed, they were hard put to it to get a hearing at all. It was European, and especially German, music, its apparatus and standard repertoire—a state of affairs that largely continues even today with the large and socially accepted concert organizations. And precisely because this music had, and has, no organic relationship with indigenous American culture it proved sterile, without roots; it is perhaps for this reason that, while in Europe those who find in themselves no point of contact with classical music (in the popular sense of the word) are content to ignore it and go their own way, in America it seems to arouse positive hostility. A standard plot for the Hollywood musicals of my youth concerned the confrontation between "longhair" musicians and the "regular kids," as portrayed by the young Mickey Rooney, Judy Garland, Bonita Granville and Jane Withers, who wanted to "Hey kids, let's put on a show!" There is malice, too, in the Marx Brothers' hilarious destruction of a performance of *Il Trovatore* in *A Night at the Opera*, and in the cutting loose of the floating platform in *At the Circus* allowing the symphony orchestra under the baton of the outrageously caricatured Italian conductor to float out to sea still energetically playing Wagner—an architypal image if ever there was one. But we must be clear; it was not music that the average American disliked, then as now. His culture was full of it, from minstrel shows to southern hymnody, jazz, cowboy songs, vaudeville, "burleycue" and military marches—all vigorous growths, all indigenously and characteristically American and all popular in the widest sense. It was specifically European art music that was and is rejected by the vast majority.

The triumph of the European tonal-harmonic tradition in the nineteenth century among Americans who considered themselves to be cultured went parallel to that of the post-Renaissance scientific world view, and its cognates the Protestant ethic, capitalism and industrialism. Only for those who lived outside the mainstream of American life did the older traditions survive. We have seen how the tradition of communal hymn singing in the old style persisted in rural areas into the late years of the nineteenth century; even today in the backwoods areas of Kentucky and the Carolinas one comes across thriving groups who sing the old hymns in the old way, using shape-note notation and "fasola" syllables which date back to the days of the eighteenth-century song schools. The survival of modal Anglo-Celtic folksong among the remote rural populations of the Appalachian mountain region is well known; indeed, British folk-song collectors such as Cecil Sharp and Maud Karpeles found in the nineteen-twenties that these areas were an altogether richer source of British folk song than anywhere in England.

By far the largest group, which until recently has been excluded from the mainstream of American economic, political, and cultural life, is the Negro population. We have already observed that the collision between the African and the European, notably Anglo-Celtic, traditions, has proved one of the most fruitful in the entire history of music, and although this is not the place for an examination of that collision and its fruits, we may perhaps make some observations on the music and its relation to Negro society.

First, the blues. In its classic form this consists, verbally, of stanzas of two lines of rhyming verse, with the first line repeated, so that the second when it comes forms a kind of punchline. The words are characterized by an unsentimental melancholy tinged with an ironic humor, frequently connected with deprivation of love, such as:

I'm gonna buy me a bulldog, watch you while I sleep
(*I said*) *I'm gonna buy me a bulldog, watch you while I sleep,*
Just to keep those men from making their early mornin' creep'

Often the imagery is explicitly sexual:

My baby got a little engine, call it my Ford machine,
(*I say*) *My baby got a little engine, call it my Ford machine,*
If your generator ain't bad, baby, you must be buying bad gasoline.

and is surprisingly little concerned with topics concerning racial discrimination or economic deprivation.

Musically the classic blues consists of twelve bars of music on a very simple and conventional sequence of I-IV-I-V-(IV)-I chords, alternating two sung bars with two bars of instrumental improvisation. Although it would thus seem to be based firmly on European harmonic progressions, the music preserves, as do black singers towards white American society, a very ambiguous relationship towards tonal harmony. Leaving aside the fact that the progression is an unvarying one which can therefore play no part in the actual expressive means, since what is expected, harmonically speaking, always arrives, we find that the favored accompanying instrument, at least in country blues, is the guitar, an instrument that lends itself, especially when played with a sawn-off bottleneck, to bold pitch distortions, and is commonly used that way. We find, too, that the seventh degree of the major scale is frequently flattened, undermining the V-I progression, and that the third degree of the scale is commonly placed somewhere between the major and the minor third thus weakening if not destroying the distinction between major and minor scale so basic to the emotional expressiveness of tonal-harmonic music. The more sophisticated urban blues tends to use the piano, whose pitches are fixed on the tempered scale; the "neutral" third is simulated by playing major and minor third simultaneously (a feature that it shares with jazz) giving the characteristic sound to piano blues and its offshoots, barrelhouse and boogie-woogie, both of which use the blues harmonic framework. In any case, the tremendous proliferation of styles, of melodies and types of texture, which can be heard over that simple, conventional bass, shows that the interest of the music lies elsewhere than in harmony.

Many of the features are undoubtedly related to survivals of African music (the tenaciousness and persistence of African cultural elements in black people through generations of degradation and deliberate disruption is one of the cultural miracles of modern times) but that is not the present point; in the blues we see once again how the attitude to tonal harmony is a clear indicator of the ambiguity of its singers' position within and their attitude towards white society.

Blues was, and remains, an essentially oral tradition, with strong and close links with the society from which it arose. The blues singer, like his society, was, with a very few exceptions, and those only recently, poor. He was often itinerant, travelling large distances throughout the South, not infrequently blind, led, Tiresias-like, by a boy, and, like Tiresias, often treated by his people as a seer who "saw" more than the sighted. As in many oral traditions, the material comes largely from a common stock, not only of musical phrases but also of verbal expressions and images such as "I woke up this mornin' . . . ," or "Just a poor boy, long ways from home," or "Laughin' just to keep from cryin'." This common stock of phrases, which was often shared by poor white, no less than black, musicians, is a universal characteristic of oral poetry (one thinks of Homer's stock of phrases such as "the wine-dark sea" or "bright-eyed Athene") and is a great aid to communality of expression. Everyone can play; the modestly talented singer can fall back on the common stock and by selection and permutation can make something that expresses how he feels, while the greatly gifted artist can take the common stock, building on it and creating something new and uniquely expressive, giving voice to feelings that all his hearers can recognize in themselves, thus remaining always in touch with the community as a whole and comprehensible to them.

These blues singers were—and still largely are—the seers and prophets of the black community. There is much cross-fertilization between blues and gospel music; Charles Keil points out that many black blues singers go on to become preachers in later life: "The word 'ritual' seems more appropriate than 'performance' when the audience is committed rather than appreciative. And from this it follows that perhaps blues singing is more a belief role than a creative role—more priestly than artistic . . . Bluesmen and preachers both provide models and orientations; both give public expression to privately held emotions; both promote catharsis; both increase feelings of solidarity, boost morale and strengthen the consensus."[12]

Blues began, and has remained, very much a people's art. It preserves in its techniques similarly ambiguous attitudes to the European tonal-harmonic tradition to those of the community that gave it birth towards white American society. Jazz, on the other hand, is in its origins and its history much closer to white music and to white society. As Gunther Schuller points out,[13] the legend of the illiterate jazz musician in New Orleans in the early years of the century is not in general substantiated by the statements of musicians who were around at the time; many were highly trained in the western concert tradition with a wide knowledge of the various kinds of western concert music that New Orleans presented so richly. Many influences went into the shaping of jazz; Wilfrid Mellers, writing about Jelly Roll Morton's *Didn't He Ramble* sums them up thus:

> The military march becomes a rag, the hymn becomes a blues and a Latin-American dance-song brings in hints of French or Italian opera and maybe a whiff of Europeanized plantation music in the manner of Stephen Foster also. This melting-pot of a piece gives us an idea of the variety of music that shook New Orleans in the first decades of this century. Parade bands in the streets were so numerous that they were apt to bump into one another. Party bands in the streets and squares might be playing Negro rags or Latin-American tangos or French quadrilles or German waltzes.[14]

Jazz shows in its techniques that it is closer to white music. In fact the first jazz musicians to gain popular attention, especially those we know from the record companies, were white (King Oliver, Louis Armstrong, Bessie Smith, and their black contemporaries were initially relegated to the "race records" category). From its earliest days until, in the music of Ornette Coleman, John Coltrane, and Albert Ayler, it abandoned contact altogether with the idea of the fundamental bass, at about the same time as the post-Webernian revolution in European art music, it has maintained the harmonic progression to a greater or lesser degree as one of its expressive devices. Throughout its history it has maintained a flirtation with European art music (the word is apt; it is the sheer *playfulness* of jazz that is one of its most enduring features, giving it a personal quality and almost physical presence that the other lacks), and the closeness of its contact with white society at any time can be assessed from the importance of the harmonic element in the music. The swing era, for example, was characterized by complex harmony in elaborate arrangements played from written scores; it was at the time a largely white and perfectly "respectable" art in the eyes of the middle-American majority. The revolt against the over-smooth banalities of swing in the late forties, which became known as bebop, in its origins an entirely black movement, diminished the importance of harmony to a point where its role was associative rather than explicit (much of it was blues-derived), while rhythm regained the central position it had lost. Bop was also, quite explicitly, a music of black social revolt, so it is understandable not only that tonal harmony was the first casualty but also that at the time white people mainly detested it (today, of course, bop is history and thus safe to like).

It is a commonplace that much of the vitality of jazz comes from the tension between the African and the European elements that it incorporates. It is interesting, therefore, to see that the moment when it rejected tonality altogether in favor of a modal or even atonal heterophony in the music of Coleman, Coltrane, Ayler, and others was the point at which it stopped being a popular art and became virtually another branch of art music appealing to a public of *cognoscenti* rather than to a community. Blues, on the other hand, remains a communal art, and it was blues rather than jazz that became, along with country and western music, the main source of the other major non-harmonic (although still tonal) music of our time, rock'n'roll, and its successors in the sixties and seventies. These will be discussed more fully in the next chapter [*Music, Society, Education*].

I stated earlier that American culture is full of music, a line of thought that brings us directly to Charles Edward Ives, the one composer who brings together all the threads of specifically American music and links them with the European tradition. He had a wide knowledge of European music and a comfortable mastery of its techniques, yet his relationship to it was highly ambivalent and his commitment was first and foremost to America. I have already remarked on his experience of the outdoor camp meetings at which his father led the singing, and there is a memorable passage in his *Memos* telling how his father rebuked a smart young Boston musician for ridiculing the out-of-tune hymn singing of an old stonemason: "Watch him closely and reverently, look into his eyes and hear the music of the ages. Don't pay too much attention to the sounds—for if you do you may miss the music. You won't get a wild, heroic ride to heaven on pretty little sounds."[15]

The view of Ives as a cranky amateur who stumbled almost unawares on some of the most revolutionary musical discoveries of the century is now, one hopes, well and truly dead. He was a sophisticated, cultured musician with a powerful mind and an incredibly alert ear, and was very clear about what it was he was doing, as can be seen from his *Essays Before a Sonata*,[16] and the more recently published *Memos*. The reason why his music makes so little appeal to so many European academic composers and critics is that it celebrates, not some beautiful, orderly ideal world but the *real* world, contradictory, untidy, even chaotic as it is. He accepts and glories in the multiplicity of human experience, and the asymmetry and unexpectedness of the music is not the result of incompetence or naivety but arises naturally from his personality, from his belief in the freedom and autonomy of the individual, and above all in the unity that underlies all the variety of nature. There are those who, like David Wooldridge in his biography, and John Cage, blame Ives for abandoning the full-time profession of music and going into business. Cage writes: "I don't so much admire the way Ives treated his music socially (separating it from his insurance business); it made his life too safe economically and it is in living dangerously economically that one shows bravery socially."[17] Wooldridge and Cage reveal what is in fact an inappropriately romantic view of the position of a composer in society, which would no doubt have been quickly dismissed by William Billings and his colleagues. Ives's life in business is an expression of his faith in the unity of life; it was a gesture towards life and against fragmentation and the isolation of the artist. The rightness of his course is shown by the fact that his inspiration dried up as soon as he retired from business.

In considering both his beliefs and his techniques, the idea of Ives held by many Europeans, even among those who are sympathetic to his music, as a great original who sprang from nowhere, dissolves when we become aware of the nature of the American musical tradition, outside that of the Europeanized art music of the nineteenth century. At the same time, he had been thoroughly grounded in the European tradition both by his father (whose own musical training had included the working of Bach chorales and the transcription of opera scenes from Gluck and Mozart as well as of baroque masses, and whose small-town orchestra was capable of turning in excellent performances of Rossini, Mendelssohn, Verdi, Meyerbeer and even Mozart) and by the conventional but expert Horatio Parker at Yale. But his attitude towards the great masters of that tradition remained equivocal; on the one hand he could assert with confidence that "Bach, Beethoven, and Brahms are the strongest and greatest in all art, and nothing since is stronger than their strongest and greatest," while at other times he could voice interesting doubts, speaking of "a vague feeling that even the best music we know—Beethoven, Bach, and Brahms—was too cooped up—more so than nature intended it to be—not only in its chord systems and relations, lines, etc, but also in its time, or rather its rhythms and spaces—blows or not blows—all up and down even little compartments, over and over (prime numbers and their multiples) all so even and nice—producing some sense of weakness, even in the great." And again: "I remember feeling towards Beethoven that he's a great man—but Oh for just one big strong chord not tied to any key."[18]

His relationship with the indigenous music of the United States, on the other hand, was much more positive. His awareness of the continuity of the outdoor camp meetings with the psalm singing of the early colonists is as obvious as his love of the music. There is little in his compositions that actually suggests the quality of such meetings in a literal way, although the marvelous choral outburst at the end of the *Thanksgiving* movement of the *Holidays Symphony* comes near to it. But this wild, highly individualistic quality runs through all of his music. The *Second String Quartet* is in fact based on it; the four instruments are all characterized (the second violin is cast as Rollo, the type of prissy milksop musician whom Ives so despised), while the three movements are entitled: *Four Men Have a Discussion, Arguments and Fight*, and *They Climb a Mountain and Contemplate*. Other examples are to be found in the early scherzo, *Over the Pavements*, a representation of the different independent walking rhythms that could be heard in a busy street before the advent of the internal combustion engine.

In most of Ives's work, as in that of the New England tunesmiths, the needs of the individual voice or part take precedence over the neatness or consistency of the over-all effect (one is reminded of Whitman's bold "Do I contradict myself? Very well, I contradict myself!"). It is this fact that accounts for the notorious dissonance of his work, as well as for its rhythmic complexity. In allowing each voice to go its own way he was expressing his version of the ideal of individual freedom, but we should notice that while the relationships between the voices are complex in the extreme, often allowing no room for the stately, logical chord progressions of tonal functional harmony, they are not chaotic; Ives has them under control. There are accounts from those who knew him well of his ability to keep a number of rhythmic patterns going simultaneously, and he was well able to play his own music on the piano. His ideal of liberty remained firmly within the law, although the law was to be subtle and flexible to allow for the greatest degree of variety of individual interaction. He could be tolerant when it came to performances of his own music; provided that the music was attempted with sincerity and simplicity of purpose, he did not mind too much if it did not come out exactly as he wrote it—hence his famous comment on an early well-intentioned but botched performance of *Three Places in New England*—"Just like a town meeting—every man for himself. Wonderful how it came out!" One wonders, in fact, whether he would have liked some of today's recorded performances by the same kind of superstar conductor and instrumentalist as those who once pronounced the music unplayable, so smoothly and perfectly co-ordinated; in their very technical proficiency they are regressing towards the mean of European music, and the quality of adventure which he treasured is lacking from the experience.

In the multiplicity of his sources, from Beethoven to American folk tunes, gospel hymnody and ragtime, in the protean variety of his musical styles, from straightforward tonal harmony (regarded by him as only one of an infinite number of expressive means) to polytonality, polyrhythm and polymeter, proto-serial music, spatial music, Ives introduced something completely new into western music, which has become an increasingly important factor in it, especially to those Americans who succeeded him. In European music we obtain a hint of this all-embracing quality only in the work of Mahler, and in his famous remark, made to Sibelius, that "A symphony must be like the world; it must contain everything!" In the music of Ives, in fact, the work of art becomes not just an expression of nature or of an attitude to nature; it becomes a part of nature, flowing along in the flux of time as much as a rock or a tree. Like a natural object it contains not one but many meanings; the extraction of meaning requires more work on the part of the hearer, but the music allows the hearer to enter in and find his own meaning, rather than have it presented to him ready-made, depending on the aspects of it on which we concentrate our attention. This, for example, is what he says of the pieces which he calls *Tone Roads*:

> The *Tone Roads* are roads leading right and left—"F.E. Hartwell & Co., Gents' Furnishings"—just starting an afternoon's sport. If horses and wagons can go sometimes on different roads (hill road, muddy road, straight, hilly hard road) at the same time, and get to Main Street eventually—why can't different instruments on different staffs? The wagons and people and roads are all in the same township—same mud, breathing the same air, same temperature, going to the same place, speaking the same language (sometimes)—but not all going on the same road, all going their own way, each trip different to each driver, different people, different cuds, not all chewing in the key of C—that is, not all in the same key—or same number of steps per mile . . . Why can't each one, if he feels like trying to go, go along the staff-highways of music, each hearing the other's "trip" making its own sound-way, in the same township of fundamental sounds—yet different, when you think of where George is now, down in the swamp, while you are on Tallcot Mountain—then the sun sets and all are on Main Street.[19]

And elsewhere in the *Memos* he discusses the structure of a piece and comments, "This may not be a nice way to write music, but it's one way!—and who knows the only real nice way?"[20]

In his multiplicity Ives draws together many threads of American music and brings them to the surface from where they had lain, submerged and neglected, for more than a century. He celebrates the fact that what people play or sing is not necessarily the same as what they *think* they are playing and singing, and acknowledges their right to sing or play as they wish; indeed, given the right attitude in the listener, the result can be just as beautiful as more accurate or more formally disciplined music making.

Ives seems never to have seriously considered studying in Europe; those who did go to Europe either before or after him came back imbued with European attitudes, no matter how "American" they believed themselves to be. The music of Aaron Copland, Virgil Thomson, Roy Harris, even of Elliott Carter and Milton Babbitt, remains European-style concert music with an American accent, not unlike the nationalist concert music of such nineteenth-century composers as Smetana, Dvorak, Greig, whose national accents (this is not to deny their many virtues or even genius) remain mere dialects of the prevailing European polyglot. Of the generation following Ives, only Henry Cowell showed anything of Ives's bent for uninhibited experimentation with sound, free from harmonic preconceptions. Cowell's early pieces for piano, using tone-clusters (a term which was in fact invented by him) and plucked and rubbed strings may have been naïf (some were published while he was still in his teens) but their spirit was the same as had animated the eighteenth-century tunesmiths, and is directed towards liberating the inner nature of the sounds themselves. If his later work falls back into the European concert-music manner, albeit with an exotic seasoning, he had opened up some important new resources, and, as editor of the journal *New Music*, he became, in the words of John Cage, "the open sesame for new music in America . . . From him, as from an efficient telephone booth, you could always get not only the address and telephone number of anyone working in a lively way with music, but you could also get an unbiased introduction from him as to what anyone was doing. He was not attached (as Varèse also was not attached) to what seemed to many the important question: Whether to follow Schoenberg or Stravinsky."[21] The last is an important point; to be aware of the essential irrelevance of both Schoenberg and Stravinsky (obscured by the fact that both composers were resident in the United States, Schoenberg since 1934 and Stravinsky since the 1940s) to the growth of a genuinely American tradition was a state which Cage himself reached only in later life.

It is in fact in the music and the writings of Cage that the tendencies we have been observing over the three-hundred-and-fifty-year history of American music finally become explicit. His first confrontation with European concepts of harmony seems to have occurred when he was studying with Schoenberg, that most committedly European of all twentieth-century composers. He tells the story as if he were unaware of its significance, a fact that testifies to the depth, albeit perhaps unconscious, of his feeling. When he had been with Schoenberg for five years the master said that to write music one must have a feeling for harmony. "I told him," says Cage, "that I had no feeling for harmony. He then said that I would always encounter an obstacle, that it would be as though I came to a wall through which I could not pass. I said, 'In that case I will devote my life to beating my head against that wall.'"[22] Schoenberg, from his own point of view and that of the European tradition was of course right, but in fact Cage has felt no such necessity; going ahead as if western concepts of harmony and the associated ideas of linear time and climax had never existed, he has found in rhythm the organizing principle for which harmony served in traditional western music. "Sounds, including noises, it seemed to me, had four characteristics (pitch, loudness, timbre, and duration) while silence had only one (duration). I therefore devised a rhythmic structure based on the duration, not of notes, but of spaces in time . . . It is analogous to Indian *Tala* (rhythmic method) but it has the Western characteristic of a beginning and an ending."[23] The first sentence here seems to take Cage close to the position of Webern in the thirties; the last two emphasize how far from that position he actually was.

A piece by Cage, in fact, rarely develops, rarely works towards any kind of climax or apotheosis, but deals in what is known in Indian aesthetic theory as "permanent emotion" (one ancient work of theory lists these as Heroic, Erotic, Wondrous, Mirthful, Odious, Fearful, Angry and Sorrowful)—a single emotional state that persists through the piece. The music may thus be boring to some; once it has made its point, many feel, there seems little purpose in continuing it. Virgil Thomson, for example, says, "The Cage works have some intrinsic interest and much charm, but after a few minutes very little urgency. They do not seem to be designed for holding the attention and generally speaking they do not hold it."[24] This is the verdict of a western composer accustomed to the concept of music as drama, but it may also be a just criticism; it could be, as used to be said of Berlioz, that Cage just has not enough talent for his genius.

He has taken the denial of the European spirit even further than the simple rejection of harmony, and has attempted to eliminate as completely as possible the imposition of the composer's will upon the sounds, finding justification for this in his studies of Zen Buddhism. His renunciation of harmony "and its effect of fusing sounds in a fixed relationship," his desire to allow sounds simply to "be themselves," to refrain from imposing any outside order on them, is clearly anarchistic (we remind ourselves that the word "anarchism" is not a synonym for "chaos" but indicates rather a state in which men *need* no externally imposed laws), a metaphor for a potential society, which few Europeans have so far dared to imagine. His refusal to impose his will on the sounds has led him to his well-known use of chance operations, by the throwing of dice, the consultation of the Chinese *Book of Changes*, the *I-Ching*, or, more recently, the use of computers; he tries "to arrange my composing means so that I won't have any knowledge of what might happen. . . . I like to think that I'm outside the circle of a known universe and dealing with things I literally don't know anything about."[25] Boulez' criticism, made from his *echt*-European viewpoint, that such procedures merely cover "weaknesses in the compositional methods involved,"[26] is regarded by Cage as irrelevant, since if compositional methods are designed to assist the composer to submit the sound materials to his will, the absence of any desire to do so renders all such methods superfluous.

The use of chance operations has a further consequence: that one accepts the validity of whatever sound chance turns up, without making any kind of value judgment on it. "Value judgments are destructive to our proper business, which is curiosity and awareness. How are you going to use this situation if you are there? That is the question,"[27] he says, and quotes the Hindu aphorism, "Imitate the sands of the Ganges who are not pleased by perfume and who are not disgusted by filth." And again: "Why do you waste your time and mine by trying to get value judgments? Don't you know that when you get a value judgment that's all you have?"[28]

It is true that the European habit of placing value judgments on everything pervades our thinking to a degree that we hardly realize. Our minds are full of hierarchies; among composers, for example, we are accustomed to think of Bach and Beethoven, perhaps of Mozart (the hierarchy differs in detail between individuals but the main outlines are clear), with Brahms and Haydn perhaps a little below them, and so on down through Tchaikowsky, Schumann, Delibes, to Chaminade and Ketèlby to the lady next door who makes up little songs. This habit of thought is a cognate of the value placed on the art object rather than the creative process, since once a value is placed on the art object the natural question is, what value? Part of the reasoning behind Cage's frequent refusal to fix his works in final form, behind his use of chance and indeterminacy, is the desire to preserve as much of the art process as is possible for the performer and even the listener; "Art instead of being an object made by one person is a process set in motion by a group of people. Art's socialized. It isn't someone saying something but people doing things, giving everyone (including those involved) the opportunity to have experiences they would not otherwise have had."[29] So, at least in many later works, he provides the structure leaving the performer to fill in the actual material in his own way. So, too, the apparent chaos of vast multi-media works such as HPSCHD is intended to allow the listener to put his own meaning on the piece, rather than to present him with a ready-made meaning. He makes an interesting antitheses between "emerging" and "entering in"; "Everybody," he says, "hears the same thing if it emerges. Everybody hears what he alone hears if he enters in."[30] Again, to an interviewer who claimed to hear a sense of logic and cohesion in one of his indeterminate pieces, he replied, sharply, "This logic was not put there by me, but was the result of chance operations. The thought that it is logical grows up in you."[31]

With Cage, then, it would appear as if the emancipation from the drama, tension and domination of the will of European music is complete. And yet a doubt remains; the simple refusal to make any kind of value judgement, the unquestioning acceptance of any sound that happens along (which obliges us, it must be said, to accept at times some pretty excruciating sounds), is based on perhaps too facile an interpretation of Zen doctrines of art. Alan Watts points out, "Even in painting, the work of art is considered not as representing nature but as being itself a work of nature." So far so good, but he goes on, "This does not mean that the art forms of Zen are left to mere chance . . . The point is rather that for Zen there is no duality, no conflict between the natural element of chance and the human element of control. The constructive powers of the human mind are no more artificial than the formative action of plants or bees, so that from the standpoint of Zen it is no contradiction to say that artistic technique is discipline in spontaneity and spontaneity in discipline."[32] Not even his worst enemies would accuse Cage of lack of discipline; nevertheless, to deny the reality of value is simply to continue the discourse on value on the same level as it has been conducted since the time of Aristotle. What is needed is a new concept of value that transcends western hierarchical thinking, and this Cage, for all the magnitude of his achievement, for all the new freedom he has brought into ways of musical thinking, has not succeeded in establishing.

Since Cage, however, tonal harmony has no longer been a concern to those American musicians whose thinking does not follow that of Europe. American music no longer needs to protest its independence; that can now be taken for granted as American musicians compose their own models of the potential society that owe little to European precedents. I must emphasize again that this chapter makes no claim to being a comprehensive survey of American music, but simply attempts to offer an interpretation of certain aspects of that music in the light of the ideas presented in the earlier chapters, and in particular in the light of the ideal of individual liberty upon which the Republic was founded. With this in mind, let us consider only four of those musicians whose work is making the American scene today so much more lively than its European counterpart. The language may have changed, but the vision of the potential society remains as pervasive as ever.

The principal concern of these musicians seems to be the projection of sounds into time, the loving exploration of the inner nature of sounds, in a world where the structures that contain the sounds are relatively unimportant—a complete reversal, in fact, of the classical European aesthetic of music. The antithesis is summed up neatly in an exchange, reported by the pianist John Tilbury, which is supposed to have taken place between Morton Feldman and Stockhausen:

> KARLHEINZ STOCKHAUSEN: Morton, I know you have no system, but what's your secret?
>
> MORTON FELDMAN: Leave the sounds alone, Karlheinz, don't push them around.
>
> KARLHEINZ STOCKHAUSEN: Not even just a little bit?[33]

Feldman, who acknowledges Cage as having given him "early permissions to have confidence in my instincts," takes sounds, as it were, and holds them up for our pleasure and admiration. The sounds he presents to us are generally quiet and unobtrusive, changing gently, creating stillness and peacefulness. The temporal order of the sounds scarcely matters, so that conventional concepts of musical time have no meaning; one feels that if it were possible to project the entire piece simultaneously Feldman would do so.

La Monte Young is concerned also in the exploration of the inner nature of sounds. He recalls from childhood his fascination with the sound of the wind in telephone wires and says, "I noticed about 1956 that I seemed more interested in listening to chords than in listening to melodies. In other words, I was more interested in concurrency or simultaneity than in sequence."[34] The result of this concern was, for example, *Composition 1960 No 7*, which consists of the instruction "B and F sharp. To be held for a long time," and the very long composition *The Tortoise, His Dreams and Journeys*, in which "Young and three associates chant an open chord of intrinsically infinite duration, amplified to the point of aural pain. Public performances usually consist of two sessions, each nearly two hours in length, within a darkened room illuminated only by projections of pattern-art."[35] Young's music, then, has little to do with listening in the traditional western sense, and much with absorption in the timeless rituals of Buddhism and Lamaism. The extreme length of time each sound lasts is vital to the awareness of each nuance of its nature; just as the ethologist must sit and wait for a long time for the living community to reveal itself, so Young's music can be regarded as a kind of ethology of sound, as an observation of sounds when they are allowed to be themselves, not fashioned into shapes determined by human will.

Steve Reich, for long an associate and friend of Young, is also an observer of the behavior of sounds, but sounds not stationary but gradually changing from within, following their own natural evolution. His compositions are, as he himself says, literally processes, which happen extremely gradually, much as a plant unfolds. One often fails to perceive the process happening, but only becomes aware that a change has taken place. Reich compares such processes to "pulling back a swing, releasing it, and observing it gradually come to rest; turning over an hour glass and watching the sand slowly run through to the bottom; placing your feet in the sand by the ocean's edge and watching, feeling and listening to the waves gradually bury them."[36] Such processes, though fascinating to the mind that is prepared to sit and let them happen, are essentially undramatic; so is Reich's music, which might be dismissed as monotonous by minds attuned to the violent and dramatic contrasts of classical music. A piece tends to consist of an extremely small amount of material, both rhythmic and melodic, played by several performers (or, in the earlier pieces, on several tape recorders) who are slightly out of phase with one another, so that material is constantly being revealed in new, gradually changing relationships with itself; fascinating and beautiful new melodic and rhythmic patterns are constantly being created. The music is not difficult to play in terms of the actual notes, which tend to be simple repetitions of melodic patterns, but the task of playing the same pattern as one's neighbor at a slightly different but perfectly controlled speed requires intense discipline and months of rehearsal for each piece. Reich has collected around him a group of musicians who have developed the kind of social rather than individual virtuosity, which is perhaps the most important fruit of his period of study under a master drummer in Ghana. The nature of the processes at work is always perfectly clear to the listener; unlike tonal-harmonic or serial music it keeps no secrets. As Reich says, in the same article, "We all listen to the process together since it's quite audible, and one of the reasons why it's quite audible is because it's happening extremely gradually. The use of hidden structural devices has never appealed to me. Even when all the cards are on the table and everyone hears what is happening in a musical process there are still enough mysteries to satisfy all. These mysteries are the impersonal, unintended, psycho-acoustic byproducts of the intended process. These might include sub-melodies heard within repeated melodic patterns, stereophonic effects due to listener location, slight irregularities in performance, harmonics, difference tones, etc."[37]

Reich's largest and most ambitious work to date is *Drumming*, a work for tuned tomtoms, glockenspiels and marimbas, with singers, whistlers and piccolo to outline the melodic patterns that are implied as the highly disciplined performers move in and out of phase with one another; it was for me a musical experience of great beauty and joy when it was first performed in London in 1972. Reich's gift is the ability to set up situations in which, as the sounds unfold according to the rules of their own evolution, they make continuously beautiful and interesting patterns without the apparent intervention of the composer's will. There is an openness and a complex simplicity about this exploration of sounds that parallels the workings of nature herself.

The music of Terry Riley, a Californian and friend of both Young and Reich, takes place in a similar area of musical sound; it first struck a wide public at least, in this country with *In C*, where some fifty short melodic fragments, all diatonic on the scale of C, are played by as many instrumentalists as desired; each player plays each fragment as many times as he wishes before moving on to the next, the performance being held together rhythmically by a rapidly repeated high C on the piano. The result is an extremely pleasing music, not unlike Reich's in sound, but governed more by the whims of the performers than by the internal logic of the sounds; it is a less rigorous, more engaging, perhaps finally less satisfying music than Reich's. Later works have included tape loops and feedback systems, sometimes with delays built in; the sound is relaxed and slow-changing, and takes the listener again far into the awareness of the sounds themselves.

In these and other ways the ideas of Cage have been taken forward, ways which in the purely musical results are perhaps more sympathetic to the uncommitted ear than those of Cage himself. There has always been a strong didactic, even dogmatic, streak in Cage; one sometimes has the impression that certain pieces were composed more to prove a point than from any genuine aesthetic impulse in any traditionally comprehensible sense of the word, and having heard the piece, one frequently has no real desire to hear it again; the point has been made, the idea got across, and there seems no need to repeat the experience.

There is perhaps a parallel here with the modern movement in American painting, discussed wittily in a recent magazine article by Tom Wolfe, who sees it not as the consequence of an aesthetic impulse but as a response to a theory of art, usually propounded by a critic. He says, "Frankly, these days, without a theory to go with it I can't *see* a painting,"[38] and suggests, tongue only half in cheek, that when the final great retrospective exhibition of American art 1945–75 is presented at the Museum of Modern Art in the year 2000 the exhibits will consist of blow-ups of the writings of critics with, by way of illustration, tiny reproductions of the paintings themselves. Cage does not always avoid the trap of the piece written to illustrate a point about perception, sound, silence or society. If music is to be alive, however, Art, to parody Billings, must go first and strike out the work, then Theory comes after and polishes it over.

For this reason, it could be that despite the power of Cage's ideas to shock and disturb our preconceptions, a much more seminal figure will in time prove to be Harry Partch, who, born in 1901, was vouchsafed a mere four lines in a recently published history of music in the United States; his death at the end of 1974 passed almost unnoticed in the musical, not to say the general, press. If we compare Cage with the African and Balinese musicians discussed in chapter 2 [*Music, Society, Education*], it will be clear that he remains, for all his invaluable study of non-European ways, very much tied to western urban culture, and that his discourse is still carried on within the conditions of the western concert tradition. It is Partch, more than any other twentieth-century western musician, who represents a real challenge to that tradition, a challenge which stems not from the "Tomorrow's World" optimism of Cage, who is still, it seems, hung up on the engaging technological lunacy of Buckminster Fuller and the behaviorist nightmares of B. F. Skinner, but from the old, universal and forever new ways of ritual theatre. "The work that I have been doing these many years," says Partch, "parallels much in the attitudes and actions of primitive man. He found sound-magic in the common materials around him. He then proceeded to make the vehicle, the instrument, as visually beautiful as he could. Finally, he evolved the sound-magic and the visual beauty in his everyday words and experiences, his ritual and drama, in order to lend greater meaning to his life. This is my trinity: sound-magic, visual beauty, experience-ritual."[39]

Partch, in fact, may be the first musician of the west to have transcended the limitations of its concert tradition—or at least to have pointed a way in which this can be done. He is unique, not only in the thoroughness and explicitness of his rejection of European classical music, a rejection more complete than that of Cage or indeed of anyone since Billings and the New England tunesmiths, but also in the fact that he has succeeded in erecting a living alternative to it, growing not out of theory (though well supported by theory, coming *after* the creative fact) but out of "an acoustical ardor and a conceptual fervor"[40]—out of the fundamental creative impulse. In a single robustly-written chapter in his book *Genesis of a Music*, he surveys the whole of western music from Terpander in 700 BC to the present and finds it wanting in what he calls corporeality, that quality of being "vital to a time and a place, a here and now,"[41] of being "emotionally tactile." To him, the overwhelming majority of western musical compositions, including almost all of the post-Renaissance tradition (he has an interesting list of honorable exceptions, which includes the Florentine Camerata and Monteverdi, Berlioz, Mussorgski, the Mahler of *Das Lied von der Erde*, Debussy's *Pelléas et Mélisande*, the *Pierrot Lunaire* of Schoenberg—but nothing else by him—and Satie) is irretrievably lost in abstraction, in the denial of the physical being of man. In its place "We are reduced to specialisms—a theatre of dialogue, for example, and a concert of music without drama—basic mutilations of ancient concept. My music is visual—it is corporeal, aural *and* visual . . ."[42] The development of polyphony, of tonal harmony, and of the large abstract forms based on them, he sees as a distortion of the essential reality of music, which is the making of magic; and the principal bearer of that magic, as he sees it, is the human voice bringing the word.

So his music is composed around the human voice and the word—which of course means the theatre. His works are almost exclusively large music dramas, a theatre of mime, of farce and dance, of shouting and vocalizing, relating clearly to the great traditional dramas of Japan, of Ancient Greece, of Java and Bali—wherever in fact men have not forgotten how to act out ritually the myths that sustain their lives. Were this all, Partch would have little claim to uniqueness; many western musicians have looked in this direction for fresh inspiration. But he has gone further. Wishing to transcend the, to him, wholly artificial and unacceptable tempered scale, with its twelve equal out-of-tune intervals to the octave, he developed a different scale based on just intonation with natural acoustic intervals, comprising no less than forty-three tones to the octave, all of whose intervals are derived from the perfect fifth and perfect third, permitting not only an enriched concept of harmony owing little to European tonal-harmonic music but also a tremendously enriched source of melody which can approach the subtlety of speech inflection. As Peter Yates says:

> With a scale of intervals so finely divided, one is able to speak to exact pitches as easily as to sing. The artificiality of recitative is done away with . . . Instead there is by the use of the forty-three-tone scale a continuous field of melodic and harmonic relationship among the degree of spoken, intoned, chanted, sung, melismatic and shouted vocal utterance, a tonal spectrum filling the gap between the vocal coloration of opera and the spoken drama. Spoken drama can be taken over by the instruments and translated back into change and song.[43]

But how can spoken melody of forty-three tones to the octave—feasible for sensitive singers—be taken over by instruments, when all the instruments of the western tradition are built to a specification of only twelve? This was the problem Partch faced and solved with the simplicity of genius; he invented and built his own instruments. Over a period of more than forty years he designed and built nearly thirty new instruments, with an eye no less for visual than an ear for aural beauty, not to mention a considerable verbal flair in naming them. He has been responsible for inventing possibly more new instruments than Adolph Sax, yet he described himself modestly as "not an instrument builder but a philosophical music-man seduced into carpentry."[44] The instruments are mainly plucked and plectrum stringed instruments, often with the strings arranged three-dimensionally, as well as variations of the marimba and xylophone, with adaptations of more conventional instruments such as harmonium and viola (he was later to find wind players who could realize his scale on their instruments), and, apart from the beauty and expressiveness of their sounds, they represent as important a conceptual challenge as does the music itself. In the first place, they are hand-built by the composer to his own purposes, not mass-produced to a conventional specification; there is in existence only one set of instruments, and if one wants to hear Partch's music and see his dramas one has to go to them. Secondly, the instruments are as important a part of the musico-dramatic work as the actors; Partch specified that they be placed in full view of the spectators as part of the set, and that the musicians playing them take a full part in the dramatic action.

And, further, the construction of the instruments is regarded, not as a necessary task to be carried out before the real job of music making can be got on with, but as an essential part of the musical process, just as with any African musician; *his* music requires *his* instruments. While many of the instruments, built in that most beautiful of all materials, wood, are triumphs of the woodworker's skill, being beautiful and dramatic in appearance as well as sound, others equally are triumphs of bricolage, being made from old shell cases ("Better to have them here than shredding young boys' skins on the battlefield"[45]), light bulbs, Pyrex glass jars, hub caps and other cast-offs of technological society, materials available to anyone with the imagination to perceive their possibilities. Partch was not anti-technology; years of working with his own hands made him too wise to fall into that trap. His attitude towards the instruments of music resembles that of Robert Persig towards the art of motorcycle maintenance: He says,

> Musicians who are generally awkward with common tools, nevertheless expect faultless perfection from their instruments. These are mechanical contrivances, however, and it would be salutary if musicians developed the elementary skills needed to maintain them. In particular, the elementary skill of tuning is of supreme importance to musicianship, and a deeper understanding would certainly ensue if it were developed . . . The instruments do not maintain themselves, especially under the wear and tear and sometimes violent treatment (which I myself stipulate) of daily playing. And not a small part of the element of good condition is the visual; the instruments must be kept *looking well*, since they are almost always on stage as part of the set.[46]

In Partch's music, writings, and above all in his instruments, we see a vision of a communal musical art, and of a technology made human by the element of commitment, of care. Here the composer—or any other maker—is not merely the producer of a commodity for others to consume but the leader and pacemaker in the common activity. From the music of Partch, western music could learn to take a large step towards rejoining the musical community of the human race.

He was fond of quoting some lines written by a child:

> *Once upon a time There was a little boy And he went outside.*[47]

This childlike (not to be confused with childish) ability to "go outside" has been a recurring feature of American music, indeed of American culture, since the earliest days, and it remains no less a feature, despite recent disasters and betrayals, of the contemporary scene. This is not to deny that there flows, and has always flowed, a strong counter-current in the direction of Europe and of conformity to European rules, a music of academic formalism as strict as or stricter than anything practiced in Europe. That this is so should not be surprising; America has always been a country of extremes of conformism and non-conformism. Of the latter group no one, not even Cage, has shown such integrity, such humor, such staying power, and such sheer, beautiful musicality as has Partch, such ability to "go outside" (where, as far as the American and

European musical establishments are concerned he still largely remains), and, naturally and unselfconsciously, to propose new relationships in society as in music, to work untrammelled by "all the hard, dry, studied rules that ever was prescribed." If American music contains within it the possibility of becoming a force for the regeneration of western music in its society, a state which, however long heralded on both sides of the Atlantic, and however wished for, is still to come about, the music and the simple, complex, eloquent, and loving personality of Harry Partch will prove an important factor in bringing about such an event.

NOTES

1. Irving Lowens, *Music and Musicians in Early America* (New York: Norton, 1964), 37.

2. Quoted in Gilbert Chase, America's Music, 2nd edn. (New York: McGraw Hill, 1966), 23–24.

3. Ibid.

4. Henry David Thoreau, *Walden, or Life in the Woods* (1854) (Everyman Edition, n.d.), 287.

5. Charles E. Ives, *Memos*, ed. John Kirkpatrick (London: Calder & Boyars, 1973), 132.

6. H. Wiley Hitchcock, *Music in the United States: A Historical Introduction* 2nd ed. (New York: Prentice-Hall, 1974), 20.

7. Quoted in Gilbert Chase, op. cit., pp. 129–30.

8. Ibid.

9. Ibid.

10. Ibid.

11. David Wooldridge, *From the Steeples and Mountains: A Study of Charles Ives* (New York: Knopf, 1974), 6.

12. Charles Keil, *Urban Blues* (Chicago: University of Chicago Press, 1966), 64.

13. Gunther Schuller, *Early Jazz* (New York: Oxford University Press, 1968), 56ff.

14. Wilfrid Mellers, *Music in a New Found Land: Themes and Developments in the History of American Music* (London: Barrie & Rockliff, 1964), 283.

15. Charles E. Ives, op. cit., p. 132.

16. Charles E. Ives, *Essays Before a Sonata and Other Writings*, ed. Howard Boatwright (London: Calder & Boyars, 1969).

17. John Cage, "Two Statements on Ives," *A Year From Monday* (London: Calder and Boyars, 1968), 40.

18. Charles E. Ives, *Memos*, ed. John Kirkpatrick (London: Calder & Boyars, 973), 100, 135, 44.

19. Ibid., 63–64.

20. Ibid.

21. John Cage, *Silence* (Wesleyan University Press, 1961) (London: Calder and Boyars), 71.

22. John Cage, op. cit., p. 261.

23. John Cage, "On Earlier Pieces," *John Cage,* ed. Richard Kostelanetz, p.127 (London: Allen Lane The Penguin Press, 1971).

24. Virgil Thomson, *Twentieth-Century Composers 1: American Composers Since 1910* (London: Weidenfeld & Nicholson, 1970), 76.

25. Cage, John; op. cit., p. 146.

26. Pierre Boulez, "Alea," transl. David Noakes and Paul Jacobs, *Perspectives of New Music* 3, no. 1 (Fall-Winter 1964): 42–53.

27. Quoted in Richard Kostelanetz, op. cit., p. 196.

28. Ibid., 21.

29. John Cage, *A Year from Monday* (London: Calder & Boyars, 1968), 151.

30. Ibid., 39.

31. John Cage, Sleeve note to recording of *Fontana Mix*, Turnabout TV 34046S.

32. Alan Watts, *The Way of Zen* (Harmondsworth: Pelican Books, 1962), 193.

33. John Tilbury, Untitled article in *Ark*, no. 45 (Winter 1969): 43.

34. LaMonte Young, and Marion Zarzeela, eds., *Selected Writings* (Munich: Heiner Friedrich, 1969), n.p.

35. Richard Kostelanetz, in ibid., n.p.

36. Steve Reich, *Writings About Music* (London: Universal Edition, 1974), 9–10.

37. Ibid.

38. Tom Wolfe, "The Painted Word," *Harper's and Queen* (February 1976): 70–96.

39. Harry Partch, *Genesis of a Music*, 2nd ed. (New York: Da Capo Press, 1974), viii.

40. Quoted in Jonathan Cott, "Partch: The Forgotten Visionary," *Rolling Stone* (April 11, 1974): 20.

41. Ibid.

42. Harry Partch, Recorded comment on record accompanying *Delusion of the Fury*, Columbia MS 30576.

43. Peter Yates, *Twentieth Century Music* (London: Allen & Unwin, 1968), 297.

44. Quoted in Jonathan Cott, op. cit., p. 20.

45. Ibid.

46. Harry Partch, op. cit., p. 196.

47. Quoted in Harry Partch, op. cit., p. xiii.

Introduction to *Music of the Common Tongue*

(1987)

I have been prompted to write this book by two impulses, one public and general and the other personal and specific, which are inextricably intertwined with each other. The first is a conviction that the time has come, if it is not well overdue, for a recognition, a celebration even, of the central contribution which Africans and people of African descent scattered over the face of the earth have made to the very mainstream of human culture, that is, to the human race's awareness of itself and of the way in which we relate to the world in which we live. That the principal medium through which this contribution has been made is not words but music and dance is itself important and, indeed, part of the message, and there can be very few people living in industrial societies who do not owe something, whether they admit or even realize it or not, to the power of the African vision of the world. A scholar has called African music and dance "nonverbal formulations of philosophies of beauty and ethics";[1] the way in which, all unacknowledged, those philosophies have passed into the culture of Europeans and Euro-Americans is a story of endurance and ingenuity which forms much of the substance of this book, since the medium of their passing has been that music and dance of African descendents in the Americas, and elsewhere, to which we can only give the awkward name of "Afro-American."

The more personal reason I have for writing is in order to acknowledge, and even perhaps to return something of, what I owe to musicians of the Afro-American tradition, both black and white. As a musician and teacher of entirely European descent, trained in the most academic tradition of European music,

I have nonetheless believed ever since I started giving thought to such matters that the gift of music was for everyone, as natural and universal a part of human endowment as the gift of speech, and I have sought for ways to make this belief an actuality. In my early years as a school music teacher, in New Zealand, I believed—or rather, assumed—that it was possible for the European classical tradition to satisfy the musical needs of my pupils, and I tried, as I had been trained to do, to inculcate in them a love of the great European masters, and something of the foundations of their art. The fact that my successes were at best patchy challenged me to look further afield, and when during my studies in London I encountered the European and American avant-garde, and the claims of its practitioners that a radical rethinking of the whole musical process was taking place, I tried to bring my pupils and, later, my students to participation in, and understanding of, something whose real nature I now realize I myself understood only dimly. But at the time it seemed that here was a fresh start, which would allow all to take part without the prior need for formal training in all the skills of traditional classical composition and performance. A series of educational experiments took place at that time, in which I played a minor part, which was designed to bring school pupils into the culture of the avant-garde, not only as listeners but also as performers and even composers. I suppose, looking back, that any practical experience in music is worthwhile, but the fact remained that while my amiable pupils were willing to go along with my enthusiasm, they showed nothing of that real commitment which might impel them to make a lifelong practice of music. At any rate, I do not know of any of them who continued either to perform or to compose such music after leaving school.

That was in the 1960s, a time of general loosening of bonds and a tremendous outpouring of creative energy in popular music. It is fashionable to sneer today at the sixties, but at their best they were characterized by an awareness of the social and political power of music, even if most of us did not understand the nature of that power. It was at that time that I started to become aware, at first dimly but then with increasing clarity, of the existence of a music that had been all around me but which I had hardly noticed other than as light entertainment or as a rather intrusive noise from juke-boxes. One key moment was when, inquisitive about the nature of what was then the still quite new phenomenon of rock music, I attended the last great Isle of Wight festival in August 1970; another was meeting and talking with the drummer John Stevens in London and taking part in his spontaneous music workshops in Ealing College of Higher Education, where I was teaching in the early 1970s. From these and other beginnings, I started to explore more widely, if initially quite indiscriminately, across the whole spectrum, or at least as much of it as a middle-aged music lecturer could gain access to, of Afro-American music in both its contemporary and its past forms. As I explored further, and made my first hesitant attempts at playing jazz (the experience of finding myself, after thirty years or more as a pianist, once again a fumbling beginner was both chastening and enjoyable), I was struck increasingly with the profound differences, in both the musical and what I can only call the social assumptions of the music, from the tradition in which I had been brought up, as well as by the coherence and consistency of the culture. It seemed, and still seems, to me (it is in fact a major part of the argument of this book) that such seemingly disparate musics as, say, country-and-western, reggae, jazz, punk rock, Broadway popular songs and calypso were all in fact aspects of one brilliant tradition, which resulted from the collision in the Americas, during and after the times of slavery, between two great musical cultures (perhaps one should say, groups of cultures): that of Europe and that of Africa, a tradition which partakes of the nature of both but is not the same as either. I found increasingly that the music of this tradition fulfilled in me not only an emotional but also an intellectual and a social need, which European classical music, however much I loved and admired much of it, did not, and if I was honest, never had fulfilled. I decided to try and investigate what it was in the music that could produce so many kinds of satisfaction and joy, while at the same time disturbing, if not disrupting, the comfortable ways in which I had been accustomed to listening to, performing and thinking about music. The desire to do so was strengthened by encountering the warmth, sophistication and humor of those Afro-Caribbean friends whom I had at that time begun to meet, and by the way they seemed to view the world from an angle that was intriguingly different from my own. This book, then, is a thank-offering to the untold numbers of musicians who created the music and an exploration of my own feelings about it. If I say that whatever understanding I now possess of my experience began with that feeling of "rightness" in the music which was only later confirmed by thinking about it, it may perhaps suggest something of that unity between mind and nature which is one of its lessons.

My training and background in classical music have obliged me in writing this book to attempt a task which most of those who write on Afro-American music do not as a rule attempt: to consider the position of the music in modern western society, especially vis-à-vis the socially dominant European and Euro-American classical tradition. The one major attempt that I know of to fill this curious gap, and to confront the nature of the European classical tradition as it exists today from inside the tradition itself, is a trio of books by Henry Pleasants.[2] But Pleasants was more interested in the classical tradition than in the Afro-American, and in any case his books were published nearly thirty years ago, and thus antedate most of what has been called the Rock Revolution of the 1960s, which changed the popular-music scene radically. Nevertheless, I do acknowledge here my debt to those brave books, even if I am not setting out to emulate them.

What I am setting out to do is simple, even though I find the magnitude of the reversal from the musical values in which I was brought up unnerving; it is to show that, by any reasonable reckoning of the function of music in human life, the Afro-American tradition is the major music of the west in the twentieth century, of far greater human significance than those remnants of the great European classical tradition that are to be heard today in the concert halls and opera houses of the industrial world, east and west.

To this purpose I need to carry on two discussions simultaneously: first, an examination of the various aspects of the Afro-American tradition in both its contemporary and its historical forms, in an attempt to show them all as aspects of the one great and coherent culture, and, second, a study of what seem to me some important aspects of the art of music in general, in an attempt to understand something of what it is that gives Afro-American music its power in the lives of so many people across the whole world in our century. As music does not take place in a social vacuum, but springs from the ways in which people regard themselves and their relationships with their fellows, I cannot carry out such an investigation without looking also at the social components of music, and especially at the encounter between people of African and of European origins as it has taken place over the centuries; I can only ask black readers of this book to pardon my impertinence in my attempts, obviously made from outside, to understand what seem to me important aspects of their culture.

It is not easy to write about the Afro-American tradition as a whole, perhaps because, as a music that does not in the main rely on written or printed notes, it not only is decentralized but also does not reveal itself in that linear manner which is characteristic of the notation-dependent tradition of European classical music. Blues, jazz, rock, and so on, are not separate musical categories, however much the analytical temper of Europeans would have it so, but are constantly shifting and interacting facets of the great tradition, meeting and flowing into one another, grouping and regrouping with dizzying rapidity, and without regard for the labors of specialists or archivists. In writing this book I have been obliged by the nature of the printed word to follow some of the streams as if they were separate, and I can only ask the patience of the reader as I attempt to make the connections plain. For me, it is this persistently anarchistic resistance to classification of both the musicians and their music that is one of the enduring delights of Afro-American music; I have therefore no wish to tidy it up, but rather hope that I can convey something of this anarchistic delight, which is, I am sure, part of the profoundly pluralistic inheritance that black people carry around with them still, not as a set of beliefs but as a style of thinking, feeling, perceiving—and of playing, listening and dancing.

It may then be thought that I am trying to write two books at once, but my purpose will only have been achieved if I can show that they are in fact one. To this end, I have interspersed chapters from one "book" with those of the other, so that discussion of one or another aspect of the Afro-American tradition alternates with more general discussion of music as a human social activity. It is through this discussion, notable for its absence in most accounts of classical music, that I shall try to show the primacy of Afro-American music in the west today, and to establish that this is so on several levels, not just in the simple appeal of the music to vast numbers of people (though this is not without importance, however much the clerics of the classical tradition may protest) but also in its openness to development, its universal accessibility and the ability of its musicians to evade capture by the "official" values of the industrial state, which has proved the ruination of the classical tradition in the present century.

I am aware that my free use of the words "classical" and even "Afro-American" for the two traditions causes problems. It should be clear, of course, that I am not using the former term to signify that period in European music, between about 1770 and 1830, which music specialists know by that name; rather, I am using it in the vulgar sense, to mean the music of the European concert, church and opera tradition since about 1600 (since it is essentially a dramatic tradition, the date of the first real opera, performed in that year, sets its beginning neatly) as performed today by symphony orchestras, concert soloists and chamber ensembles as well as by opera companies, and including the music of the post–world war two avant-garde and its offshoots and successors. I shall use it in this way in the knowledge that not only would it have meant little to the masters of the tradition in the past but also that it is used today mostly by those who are not in sympathy with the music; those who do subscribe to its values feel no need for the qualifying adjective, since to them it is, *tout court*, music, and it is other styles of music making that need qualification: "popular," "folk," "ethnic," "contemporary" (an odd one, that) and so on. We know what to expect when we open the pages of *The Musical Times*, *Music and Musicians* or *Musical America*, or any number of *Histories of Music*. Similarly with classes in Music Appreciation, while Music Departments in schools, colleges and universities, not to mention conservatoires of music, mostly direct their attention entirely towards the one tradition. I am only too aware, however, that the boundaries of what is meant by "classical music" are maddeningly difficult to define, the more so as I believe the meaning of the music—or, rather, the meaning of performing it—has changed considerably over the past sixty years or so.

It would probably not be necessary to define it at all were it not for the disastrous pulling-away of the classical tradition from the vernacular over the last hundred years. I shall have more to say about that later, but note here that the disaster (and it *has* been disastrous, for both traditions) can be laid more at the doors of classical musicians and of critics, scholars, teachers and those who are responsible for the financial support of classical music than at those of the musicians of the Afro-American tradition who, as we shall see, have always possessed an easy mastery of classical styles; if they have played in the style we know now as Afro-American, it has never been because they could not play in the European manner but because they have preferred to play in that way.

I shall have to leave to a later work a discussion of the very interesting question of the boundaries of classical music, and ask the reader to accept my rough-and-ready definition as sufficient for the present book. At the same time we might keep in mind that what is and what is not regarded as classical is often as much a matter of performance style as of the actual musical content, and also that classical music can be distinguished from vernacular in that it gives more attention to the musical work in itself than to its social meaning.

For music that does not come under the rubric "classical," I prefer the term "vernacular" to either "popular" or "folk," both of which have become loaded with secondary meanings and are involved in their own demarcation disputes. The basic meaning of the word, of course, has to do with speech, and its use in respect of music does remind us that the ability to take part in a musical performance is as natural and universal a part of the human endowment as is the ability to take part in a conversation. It can subsume both "folk" and "popular" (although I shall use both these words on occasion when their meaning is clear) to mean music of the common tongue that is made for *use*, with little pretension to Art and its high social status, but by no means unselfconscious pipings either; like virtually all music everywhere and at all stages of human history, it is made by musicians who, even if they do not verbalize it, are well aware of what they are doing and who work hard to do it. An outside observer of music as a whole in western society would conclude that classical and vernacular music represent different and even opposed values, but this has not always been so; indeed, it would seem as if during the greatest period of European music its practitioners did not think of themselves as in any way separate from the vernacular of their day but both drew on it (after all, the Viennese classical style even at its most elevated has its roots firmly in Austrian folk music) and actively contributed to it. They strove to reach the widest possible audience (Mozart was delighted to find that everyone in Prague was whistling the airs from *Figaro*) and if they made music sometimes for the broader and sometimes for a more exclusive audience they did not feel impelled to make any break in their style; Beethoven remains as recognizably Beethoven in his ballroom dances as in his last string quartets.

I was reminded of this not long ago when I heard a fine British jazz quartet on three successive evenings, on the first evening playing to an audience of connoisseurs in a concert hall, on the second blowing up a storm and setting all the teenyboppers, much to *their* surprise, dancing at a local hop, and on the third playing discreetly for the entertainment of the patrons in a pub, all without any dislocation of style or the slightest hint of condescension or of playing anything but their best. It is possible that Afro-American music has developed its own kind of classical music that, unlike today's European or Euro-American classical music, remains in close touch with its vernacular, both feeding on it and feeding back to it. To my knowledge, the last European master of the classical tradition who was able to inhabit that kind of unified musical universe without strain was Erik Satie, who died in 1925; appropriately, he was one of the few major musicians of the tradition who really did die in poverty—and voluntary poverty at that.

One might say, perhaps tautologically, that vernacular music, "the music of the common tongue," is, like vernacular speech, the normal experience of the human race. Classical musics are comparatively rare; they seem to need for their existence not only a leisured class able to command a quantity of surplus resources but also a situation where that class is to some degree isolated from the majority of the people and possesses the social power to represent its own tastes as superior. Thus classical musics developed not only in Europe but also in India and China, though not, despite the equal richness and sophistication of the culture and the music, in the African kingdoms or in Bali, in both of which the royal courts and their music were accessible to all. If jazz is today acquiring some of the characteristics of a classical music we might be able to discover comparable social factors at work—but that must wait for a later chapter.

There is another pair of terms that I am going to have to use extensively in this book: "black" and "white" as applied to people. The absurdity of these terms when used in this way can be seen from the start by anyone who cares to look, in that those who are labeled "white" may be anything from greyish pink to mid brown in skin tone, while those labeled "black" may be anything from pale brown to rich dark brown; not only is literal blackness of skin color rare but also many of those who are labeled "black" may be lighter in complexion than many who are labeled "white." The two terms, when used to mark off two genetically separate human groups, make no sense at all; what they amount to in terms of human relationships is a highly asymmetrical form of classification which assigns all those who bear the slightest visible sign of African descent to the category "black," and thus automatically to inferior status, even though, to the unprejudiced eye, they may appear more European (or, to put it pseudo-scientifically, Caucasoid) than African (or Negroid). In societies that are dominated by European values, European appearance is the norm and taken for granted, becoming in this way invisible, while African is the aberration, and thus highly visible, even, as in the Americas, after nearly five hundred years of daily interaction. The asymmetry requires that only those with no visible sign of the "aberration" can qualify as "white." This paradox of racism compounds its absurdity through the fact that while to be "black" carries considerable social disadvantage throughout Europe and America, to be "white" does not carry, as any number of unemployed white people can testify, any balancing advantage, other perhaps than the dubious advantage of being able to look down on a fellow human being. In the long run the only people who derive any real benefit from the whole sorry business are those who have an interest in dividing and ruling.

If "white" means having exclusively European ancestry while "black" means possessing any mix of European, African and, indeed, any number of other ethnic backgrounds from one hundred per cent of the latter to ninety-nine per cent of the former, then "black" has any real significance only as a cultural term. It is worn thus, as a badge of pride, by those who have historically been obliged to accept a definition of themselves by reference to European norms—that is, they have been defined as contravening in their very existence the society's norms of Caucasian racial purity. Black culture, and especially black music and dance, has over the past five hundred years or so been a tool by means of which people so defined have struggled, and continue to struggle, to assert their own definition of themselves. If this has necessarily entailed compromises and accommodations with the prevailing definition (and, as we shall see, Afro-American music and dance are shot through with, and indeed have their origin in, such accommodations) and an at least outward acceptance of them, nonetheless the self-definition of those who are classed as "black" has for the most part been affirmative rather than negative, proud rather than humble, self-assertive rather than self-effacing. And thus, while to label such great American musicians as Charles Mingus, Duke Ellington and Jelly Roll Morton as "black" may be a genetic absurdity, given their very visible genetic makeup, it does, given the ethno-cultural situation, make a certain kind of sense, since they, and countless others, found their cultural roots among those who had been similarly defined. It makes it possible to find a livable sense in a situation that is essentially nonsensical.

One need not assume from this that "black" culture is monolithic—far from it. One of the distinguishing features of the culture of the people of the African diaspora has always been an openness and an adaptability which, as I hope to show in due course, is a part of the African cultural inheritance. This is why the variety of Afro-American music is so astonishingly wide, representing as it does any number of different accommodations to the dominant white culture, as well as to other cultures. It is, if anything, white culture that through its exclusionist tendency can be said to be impoverished. We can see this in the music of the classical tradition in our own time; by comparison with the musical whirlwind which is Afro-American music the so-called "new music" which is associated with the names of Schoenberg and Stravinsky and later of Messiaen, Boulez, Stockhausen and Cage is a mere breeze, imprisoned in its luxurious concert halls and quite possibly heralding the end of the tradition in a state of isolation, solipsism and spiritual anorexia. There seems to be a kind of rule in these affairs, that whenever a policy of exclusion is practiced, it is the excluders who are the ultimate losers.

If it were a matter of the mere cultural survival of black people, that would be a remarkable enough achievement, given what they have endured for five hundred years. But there is more. Despite their exclusion, black people in the Americas and elsewhere have been during the present century at the heart of an outburst of creative energy surely unparalleled in the known history of the human race. Its vigor has taken it beyond the shores of the Americas and caused it to become acclimatized throughout most of the world, usually over the dead bodies of the guardians of the official musical culture, but its power to seize the imagination and the sensibilities of so many different kinds of people, most of whom have no direct contact with the black experience, is a phenomenon which still lacks a satisfactory "official" explanation—understandably so, for the only explanation that makes sense would not be good news to those guardians. So it tends either to be taken for granted, like a force of nature, or to be attributed to the pressures of cynical media manipulators. Neither explanation is anything like adequate—even though it is obviously true that commercial forces have played a considerable (though perhaps less than is generally assumed) part in its development and dispersion. Rather, it is a ceaseless and spontaneous activity of countless human beings, all of them living within, responding to and trying to make sense of, certain social, political and economic situations. But the question of why this music has not remained simply the property of an underdog group in the Americas (after all, there are many such underdog musics the world over, but most of them stay firmly within the societies from which they came), but has instead moved out to transform the musical sensibilities of a large part of the human race, is an important one, to which I propose addressing myself in this book.

How, then, do we define Afro-American music? At first sight, the question seems easy enough; we know about jazz, yes, and blues, we are possibly aware of the debt owed to the blues by all those varieties of music that are collectively called rock or pop and which are the most audible kinds of Afro-American music to be heard today. There is also disco perhaps, and there are styles that seem to have remained mostly the province of black artists, such as gospel and reggae and soul, although there are white artists who have made soul, if not gospel, their own. There is also calypso and the steel band, among its more exotic manifestations, and rapping, scratching and hip hop. We should also include styles which, although shot through and through with black idioms, are almost exclusively the domain of white musicians, such as country-and-western in all its considerable variety, and Cajun music from Louisiana—in fact not much vernacular music of our time has escaped its powerful presence. And we have not yet mentioned the beguines, the merengues, the sambas and rumbas, the mento and salsa, the reggae and soca, that come from South and Central America and the Caribbean, or the riotous proliferation of styles that has taken place in the various parts of Africa to which the music has returned. We could continue enumerating for a long time, through the ramifications of rock, for example, and it might be possible to compile a catalog that had some claim to completeness. Possible but pointless, for by the time it was completed it would be obsolete; the art is in such a state of headlong development and change that cataloging it is rather like painting the Forth Railway Bridge—the job gets finished just in time to start it all over again.

But the key to all this magnificent confusion lies in any case not in a catalog at all, however complete, since catalogs enumerate objects and music is not an object, or even a collection of objects, but an activity. Afro-American music making (I should prefer, for reasons which will become clear in chapter 2 [*Music of the Common Tongue*], to use the word "musicking," the present participle of the regrettably non-existent verb "to music") has resulted, seemingly, in the production of innumerable music-objects—and we have the records and the tapes and the sheet music that we can hold in our hands—but as we examine these objects we find that they are not as stable as we thought, but are mere stages in a process of creative evolution, caught for a moment on disc, tape or paper.

The other trouble with the simple enumeration of various styles of Afro-American music is that many of them are merely the creation of those commercial and marketing interests which have intersected at so many points with the musical process, and were often invented either to give the appearance of something new to a way of musicking that has had a long subterranean history or to evade reference to that racism which has also intersected in a significant way with the music. Categories in any case are *never* watertight, but flow ceaselessly into one another; certainly the musicians who play it, the listeners who listen to it and the dancers who dance to it rarely allow themselves to be neatly pigeonholed but move freely across categories according to their own inclination at the time—as well as according to who is paying. Categories are only convenient abstractions, and useful in discussion, if we understand that there is, for example, no such thing as jazz, but only musicians who play in a certain manner and listeners who like to listen to them doing so (for that matter, there is no such thing as music, only musicking). The musician who plays in the manner we call jazz is himself also a listener, and does not confine his listening to other musicians who play in the same or similar ways to himself (he may feel a greater sympathy, of course, with such musicians) but will feel free to listen to, and to use, any kind of musicking from any performer who he feels will help to make his own performance more interesting, more satisfying. That such listening is not random in its focus but depends on a measure of social and cultural empathy is a matter which I shall discuss in due time.

What we call Afro-American music, then, is not a collection of sound-objects, or a repertory of pieces, or even a group of musical styles narrowly considered, but an approach to the act of music making, a way of playing and of responding to music, which derives from those two great ways of making music which came together in the Americas. It is this way, or rather, it is these ways, since there is no one way, which I mean to celebrate in this book. I make no claim for it as a comprehensive survey of either the history or the present of Afro-American music; that would require whole libraries. Rather, I hope to present what seem to me important aspects of both that history and that present in order to suggest an approach, a conceptual and historical framework, in which listeners, and indeed performers, may place the experience of the music, to find out a little of what it can have to say to us on the important concerns of human life, and how it can help us in constructing an identity that is appropriate to ourselves and our time. At the same time I hope that this book may suggest something of the richness and complexity of both the culture and the history, which have been so fraudulently denied by the majority culture, of black people in the Americas.

In order to keep my study to manageable proportions I have had to confine it to those aspects of the music that originated in the United States, with brief glances only toward Latin America, the Caribbean and Africa. But while this restriction does represent a loss of scope, it does not really affect my argument, which is that Afro-American music is a unified culture through which are explored and celebrated aspects of human experience and identity that are not dealt with in either the European or indeed the African tradition.

Let us now, without more ado, look at what it was that the people from each of the two continents brought with them to America in the way of human social and musical values.

NOTES

1. Robert Farris Thompson, "An Aesthetic of the Cool: West African Dance," *African Forum*, 2, no. 2 (Fall 1966): 85.

2. Henry Pleasants, *The Agony of Modern Music* (New York: Simon and Schuster, 1955); *Death of a Music*? (London: Victor Gollancz, 1961); *Serious Music—And All That Jazz* (London: Victor Gollancz, 1969).

Styles of Encounter III—Jazz

From *Music of the Common Tongue*

(1987)

Of all the styles of Afro-American music, in so far as they can be separated out from one another, that which is known as jazz is the one with which white intellectuals and classical musicians today feel most at ease. They manage to assimilate the values and the aesthetic of jazz to those with which they were brought up, and they feel able to accord to its artists a status and a respectability denied to other Afro-American musicians, and not far beneath that accorded to classical artists. This almost classical status is illustrated neatly by the fact that the British Broadcasting Corporation devotes about four hours of a total weekly airtime of some 120 hours on its classical-music channel to jazz. Among intellectuals and classical musicians the names, and the work, of Brubeck, Basie and Beiderbecke are almost as familiar as those of Boulez, Beckett and Bergman, and there exists a literary tradition of jazz scholarship, criticism and exegesis, not shared by any other Afro-American style, going back fully fifty years to the pioneering writings of André Hodier and Hugues Panassié. All this suggests that jazz has affinities with classical music that other Afro-American styles do not have.

Of all Afro-American musicians jazzmen, and jazzwomen, have always been the most eclectic; everything they hear, from blues to symphonic music to Anglo-Celtic folksong, from gospel to opera arias to the post-war avant garde, is grist to their mill. It may even be possible to propose a definition of jazz as that aspect of Afro-American musicking that has closest links with classical music. It is not a satisfactory definition, but it does have the merit of drawing attention to the fact that a major source of creative energy for the artist in jazz has come from the tensions between European, or Euro-American, and Afro-American values.

These tensions can be perceived in a number of ways. We can see them as between, on the one hand, the literate culture of western industrial society, with all its tendency towards centralization and standardization, and on the other the orality and decentralization of black American culture. In musical terms this can be heard as, on the one hand, composition through notation, the separation of composer from performer and the authority of the written text, and, on the other, improvisation, non-literate composition and the autonomy of the performer. As we have seen, the composition-improvisation antithesis has important implications for the kinds of relationship that are brought into being by a musical performance—how close to or distant from one another the participants are, how active or passive the listeners, and so on. We have seen, too, how the classical tradition has abandoned improvisation, and it is interesting to see how whenever that tradition has become dominant in jazz the space for improvisation has become curtailed; one could use the extent to which the musicians are obliged to rely on notation as a yardstick for determining which of the two cultures is dominant at any point in the history of jazz performance.

It is important to bear in mind that these two tendencies, or orientations, are not mutually exclusive, but exist side by side in most western people, white and black. We have seen that even the most literate of western people still acquire some of their most important cultural attitudes and assumptions through the oral-aural mode, from parents, elders and peers, even if in our society the superiority of the literate mode is assumed without discussion. Conversely, it should not need to be pointed out that black Americans are just as much at home in the literate mode as are their white compatriots—but they continue to place a higher value on orality, and tend to be more proficient and imaginative with the spoken word, than whites. The fact that a literate society is a centralized and hierarchical one, which Africans and Afro-Americans have traditionally resisted, is also important.

If the fundamental concern of all music is human relationships, the problem in group music making of all kinds, from symphony orchestras to Balinese *gamelans* to heavy-metal bands, is the establishment of workable relationships between the participants, which will allow room for the individual player to make full use of his or her musical skills and imagination to explore, affirm and celebrate an identity, while preserving that over-all order which is essential if the musicking is to generate any meaning either for performers themselves or for whoever is listening. Those relationships incarnate ideal human relationships as imagined by the participants, and both the technical problems encountered and the techniques used to solve them are metaphors for the problems, and the methods, of maintaining an acceptable social order. In a symphony orchestra those problems have been solved, once and for all, by the evolution of a hierarchical structure and centralized authority vested partly in a composer and partly in a conductor, each of whose authority in his own area is absolute—an uneasy combination at best, at least when the composer is around to make his views known. Those who have worked in or with professional symphony orchestras know that while an orchestra's power structure may, in theory, be precisely defined and static, the actual day-to-day relationships are as edgy as those in any other industrial organization, with the players constantly challenging the conductor's authority and subjecting each new piece to the most merciless scrutiny. But, grumble and smoulder as they may, they make no serious attempt to depose either authority from his (it is rarely *her*) position, not surprisingly since without a conductor and a score they would be at a complete loss for anything to play or for how to play it. In a symphony orchestra, then, as in other kinds of classical performance today, the question of order has been settled in the way most contemporary governments would like to be able to settle it. The performances that are made possible by this centralized and authoritarian order can be of an indubitable splendour and brilliance, but they are bought at the price of the players' autonomy and of creative satisfactions that ought to be commensurate with the skills and the musicality that are demanded of them. The players are rewarded for this sacrifice in other ways, with a social status and a degree of financial security that is denied to their colleagues in vernacular musicking.

That there is necessarily an antithesis between individual freedom and social order is a notion that Europeans, and those who have absorbed European and Euro-American culture, have interiorized so completely that they scarcely even notice that they are thinking in that way, still less consider the possibility of alternatives. The notion is implicit in the activities of all contemporary governments, who take it for granted that considerable sacrifices of individual freedom are necessary to preserve a social order in which it is possible to live free from the fear of rape, pillage and robbery—and of conquest by the forces of other, like-minded governments. It is implicit in the writings of some of the greatest of European thinkers; the whole line of thought that is descended from Thomas Hobbes's *Leviathan* is based on it, while even Freud, in his last writings, mused despairingly on the repression that seems to be necessary if civilization is to exist at all. It is noticeable also in the whole organizational structure and the teachings of the Christian church, even if it is less in evidence in the recorded words of its founder. But in traditional African culture such an antinomy is by no means self-evident. As the Ewe proverb has it, "Man is man because of other men"; individual and society live, not in antagonism but in mutual dependency, the individual coming to fullest development only within the social framework, and the society flourishing only on the basis of fully realized individuals whose individuality is necessary for social health. The elaborate rituals of traditional African societies, the musicking, the dancing, the masking, the cult ceremonies, are all designed ultimately to mediate social and individual necessity, to bring them into harmony rather than merely to effect compromises between antagonists. We have seen how the Africans brought their social attitudes with them on the Middle Passage and how those attitudes became a powerful factor for survival in the terrible conditions of slavery and its aftermath, and I have suggested that Afro-American musical performances in this century, especially in blues and gospel, have been rituals that have continued to affirm and to celebrate the mutual support of individual and community.

To play jazz, for a black musician, is to go beyond such rituals into a more complex and even dangerous task; it is to move out from one's base in the community (that is, from blues and gospel music) and to engage oneself with the values and the assumptions of white society, going to meet them and to play with them, and trying on roles in symbolic fashion in relation to that culture and society through its musicking, discovering what is of use for oneself and for the community. Black jazz musicians are thus no less the ritual representatives of the community than are bluesmen and gospel singers, and their task is in many ways even more important. Conversely, when white musicians play jazz, they are in almost a complementary situation in exploring the values of the black culture. How deeply they are able to do this will depend on the extent to which they are able to submit to the social and musical values they find there; it is in a sense even more difficult for them than for their black confrères, since as members of the socially dominant culture they have more to unlearn, and more intellectual baggage to dispose of, before they can enter fully into the engagement.

But both are also engaging with that most pressing of twentieth-century problems: that of the relationship between freedom and social order, and they are empowered to do so by a style of musicking that does not assume that there is any necessary antithesis between the two. In jazz a soloist appears at his or her best (which is not the same as "most virtuosic") when collaborating with equals, the composer realizes his or her compositions most fully when they are taken up and developed by fellow musicians, the individual realizes his of her gifts best in the company of a committed group. Thus the notion found in many histories and other studies of jazz, of the great individual artist-hero—Charlie Parker, John Coltrane, Miles Davis for instance—creating out of his own nature and genius, has to be treated with great caution.

Of course, there have been many outstanding artists over the history of jazz, but we should beware of treating them as great isolated originators, as the classical tradition today treats Beethoven, Mozart and J. S. Bach (it is strongly arguable that the way they are treated is a gross distortion of the real nature and achievement of *those* artists also) or indeed, as the world of commercial entertainment—show-biz—treats its stars. In so far as the jazz musician's world perforce overlaps with and partakes of the nature of both those worlds it is understandable that this should happen—and of course it does pay the musicians, who after all have a living to make in that world, to go along with it as far as they can—but it should never be forgotten that those who stand out as the "great names" in histories and other studies of jazz are no more than first among equals, and owe at least a part of their eminence to the labors of many other musicians. To say this is not in any way to detract from their gifts or their achievements, but simply to point out that the nature of jazz performance requires that performers, whether famous or obscure, function in skilled and close collaboration, and that they depend on one another in everything they do.

The words "composer" and "composition" therefore have a very different significance in jazz from classical musicking; in jazz, as in the great age of classical music, to be a musician is primarily to be a performer, and those who compose regard composition simply as the creation of material for themselves and their colleagues to play. It is rare, though not unknown, for what is created to be a fully worked-out composition; more usually it is a springboard, which may or may not be notated, from which all the musicians may take off into collaborative creation. Many of these "compositions," such as Thelonious Monk's *Round About Midnight*, Charles Mingus's *Goodbye Pork Pie Hat*, and Charlie Parker's *Parker's Mood* are beautiful in themselves, but they reveal, and are meant to reveal, their full character only when the composer and his colleagues have played with them, in all seriousness and all fun (the two are not incompatible). The composer's gesture to his fellow musicians is one of love and trust in giving them a part of himself to make of it what they will, and it calls from those musicians a greater sense of responsibility and involvement than does the realization of a fully notated score. And in so far as there can be as many versions of the "piece" as there are occasions of its performance, the place and the listeners also make their contribution, just as in African musicking.

All too often, of course, the place is a sleazy nightclub with a minuscule bandstand, a tinny beat-up piano, and a dressing room that is no more than a cupboard next to the gents' toilet, while the listeners are a crowd of drunken businessmen and their wives on a night out, but the musicians' loyalty to one another and to their musicking can still make the performance transcend the limitations of the occasion. And when the place is suitable (not necessarily either grand or luxurious), the listeners committed and the dancing skilled (for does not dancing reveal a deeper involvement with the musicking than just sitting still and listening?) the performance, for as long as it lasts, can transform the participants into a society of mutual love and responsibility, of deep and multivalent relationships, that reveals the poverty of the affluent European society of a concert hall.

For a jazz performance is not as much about the *rejection* of European values as about *transcending* them, and about the incorporation of the oppositions of classical music into more realistic unities. Jazz musicians have always been concerned with classical music, not as representatives of an inferior culture trying to latch on to the superior, but as natural heirs who are claiming it as their birthright—or, rather, as a part of their birthright—and building it into their own synthesis. It is a dangerous game; the musician is constantly on both a musical and a social tightrope in attempting to reconcile the two sets of values. It is for this reason that, for all the excitement that can be generated by a jazz performance, the quality most valued by the musicians themselves is "cool"—that coolness of mind and clarity of musical judgment, which together enable them to keep their balance while on the tightrope. The history of jazz is littered with, on the one hand, fine and even great musicians for whom the responsibility was too great, and, on the other, with musicians who have given in to the pull of one or the other culture.

There is a stereotype of a black jazz musician who, brilliant as he or she may be as performer, is nonetheless inadequate or worse in everyday relationships and the business of life, who is killed by drugs, alcohol, and the appurtenances of high living; Charlie Parker and Billie Holiday are two often-quoted examples. They could not, we are led to believe, live out the ideal relationships that they brought into being with their music. This dissonance between the actual world and its relationships, and the ideal world, which they have not just imagined but actually experienced, has always placed highly creative musicians in danger;

Mozart, who died only two years older than Parker, was clearly overwhelmed by it, while even the archetypal artist-hero, Ludwig van Beethoven, managed somehow to survive twenty years more without ever coming to terms with the world in which he lived, or even being able to form a mature relationship with another human being. In the case of black artists the dissonance is intensified, only they know how deeply, by the racism of the society that they are obliged to inhabit, and for which they are creating their model of a community held together, not by coercion, but by love. The marvel is not that some succumb, but that so many survive, and survive triumphantly, with that ideal still alive, if not unscarred by their experiences. And that even those who, like Parker and Holiday, did succumb, continued to affirm their "philosophies of beauty and ethics" for as long as they were physically able.

The relative pulls of the two cultures spanned by jazz are not symmetrical, owing to the far higher social and financial rewards that the classical culture is able to offer to most musicians. A musician who accedes to the pull of the Afro-American culture will be found playing blues or gospel, in a musical ritual of a community that remains largely isolated from the mainstream of American society, and which continues to find within itself the resources for survival. For black musicians such a step is to move back into the maternal culture, a recharging of the batteries perhaps, which many, if not most, seem to do from time to time, while for white musicians, on the other hand, it is a venture not merely into a culture that still remains exotic and mysterious, not merely an adventure, but almost also a homecoming, an acknowledgment of one's real ancestors. For the musician playing jazz, it is the pull of the European classical culture that represents the greater threat, since as the dominant and socially superior culture it has more to offer. It can co-opt musicians almost without their realizing what is happening to them—a not infrequent happening in the history of Afro-American music as a whole. For the black musician it tends to be a no-win situation, as the guardians of the classical culture are liable to pat him on the head and make it clear to him that he is getting ideas above his station. Every so often there appears on the scene a young lion who is intent on storming the classical-music citadel; I cannot help wondering whether what is in that citadel—the approbation of white middle-class audiences and critics—is really worth his effort.

The history of jazz can be seen as a struggle between the two sets of values, expressed in musical terms as a to-and-fro between solutions to the problem of freedom and order. Unlike the situation in classical music, the struggle presents us with no final solution, only with a constantly changing series of accommodations; perhaps the only conclusion to be drawn is that no conclusion is possible—something with which Africans would no doubt concur. It should, of course, not be assumed from this that relations between white and black musicians within jazz have been of hostility or even of opposition; the history of the art abounds with shining examples of amicable, even loving collaboration. But it is easy to understand that because a black musician is staking more on his musicking than a white one, it has been black musicians who have been mostly the leaders and innovators, since genuine musical innovation, as we have seen, is a matter not just of new sounds or techniques but of new forms of relationship. This has been a more urgent quest for blacks than for whites—though, God knows, the white majority is in more desperate and urgent need than it knows of what it can learn from its black compatriots. Albert Murray expresses it memorably when, writing in praise of certain white musicians, he says that they "eagerly embrace certain Negroes not only as kindred spirits but as ancestor figures indispensible to their sense of romance, sophistication and elegance as well. Negroes like Duke Ellington, Louis Armstrong, Bessie Smith, Billie Holiday, Chick Webb, Coleman Hawkins and others too numerous to mention inspire white Americans like Woody Herman, Gerry Mulligan and countless others to their richest sense of selfhood and their highest levels of achievement."[1]

"Ancestor figures," we notice—that is to say, models not only of music but also of values and conduct, and it can be said, not only that the most creative periods in the development of jazz have been those in which black musicians moved to throw off white domination of their art, but also that those same musicians have at those times quite consciously and deliberately chosen to re-assert the traditional social as well as musical values of their culture. At such key moments, it has been to the sources of black music, much of it outside the experience of whites, that they have turned for renewal; if, as is sometimes said, jazz should be called "Afro-American classical music," it is in the sense that Haydn, who was well in touch with the vernacular sources of his art, would have understood, while Boulez or Cage, to whom such nourishment seems to be inaccessible, would probably not. Murray does in fact, in his book *Stomping the Blues*, refer to the major figures of such moments—Louis Armstrong, Ornette Coleman, Charlie Parker and others—as bluesmen *tout court*, which is fair enough in a way, and does enable us to recognize the vernacular roots of their art but at the same time it ignores the important factor of cultural tension, which is far stronger in jazz than in blues and is not only a principal source of its creative energy but also a key to its human importance in our time.

For jazz is not a comfortable form of musicking to live with; as Frederick Turner says: "It is as if we hear an interior sound in jazz that prevents us from embracing it in the ways we obviously have its derivatives, pop music and rock. Jazz, we obscurely sense, is hard to take at the level of pure entertainment, because however little we may know of it, of the history that went into its sound, we know enough to feel that it cuts too deeply into some unresolved national dilemmas to be casually accepted or lived with comfortably on a daily basis. We hear in the interior sound an intensity of purpose and aspiration that fends off easy familiarity . . . Jazz is the sound of life being lived at its limits, dangerous as an element that can burn."[2]

It is true that there is in jazz a quality of sound that is unique in western music; it is not exactly austerity, but a lean, stripped-down quality that makes no concession to conventional notions of beauty, and certainly resembles very little the smoothly blended sound of the symphony orchestra. But there is also a playful, ironically teasing quality about most jazz performances, which by no means negates their intense seriousness but has misled many, who are accustomed to the solemnity of classical performances, into dismissing it as frivolous. The tensions that fuel the performance are real enough; the humor is one way, not only of rendering them bearable, but also of subverting the values of the dominant society. It is probably for reasons such as these that jazz has been a really popular music (by which I have to mean, popular among whites, for that is where the purchasing power lies that determines popularity in today's society) for only brief periods, and it is significant that those were periods in which white cultural values were dominant, and the tensions resolved, at least for the time being.

Rather than attempting an historical survey of jazz, I intend to examine some phases of that history, to see how these accommodations between black and white values have taken place at specific points. It is proverbially difficult to say just when jazz first emerged as a recognizable style. It is possible to imagine a number of ways in which it might have taken place, and the prehistory of jazz, as of many cultural styles (style being defined precisely by Charles Keil as "a deeply satisfying distillation of the ways a very well integrated human group likes to do things"),[3] contains many such distillations, taking place in many different parts of the United States, according to the cultural mix of influences that happened to be around at the time. Ragtime was one such distillation, as we have seen, black minstrelsy and vaudeville were others, established on well-organized circuits by 1900. It is possible to see, even in the work of musicians as early as Francis Johnson, a similar cultural work taking place, while the very large number of black, and the smaller number of white wind bands in which European marches, dances and entertainment music were "ragged," all over the United States, testify to the continuing experimentation that was taking place. In New York, for example, we know that James Reese Europe, conductor of the famous orchestra of the Clef Club, the center for black musicians in the years before the first world war, and of the Hellfighters Band in France during the war, had a difficult task keeping his black musicians to the written notes: "I have to call a daily rehearsal," he wrote, "to prevent the musicians from adding to their music more than I wish them to. Wherever possible they all embroider their parts in order to produce new, peculiar sounds. Some of these effects are excellent and some are not, and I have to be continually on the lookout to cut out the results of my musicians' originality."[4] Despite Europe's keeping the lid firmly on the improvisational pot, the Hellfighters caused a sensation when they were sent to Paris in August 1918 to give a single concert and stayed for eight weeks. As Europe said later, "Had we wished we might be playing there yet." It might have been instructive, and perhaps chastening, for some of today's virtuoso conductors and orchestras to hear how the Clef Club Orchestra handled those works of the classical tradition that their repertory included as a matter of course; but, alas, no records were made of them.

But these and countless other ways of musicking, fascinating and rewarding as they were, did not add up to a single and unified way of doing things. The one exception, ragtime, paid for its undoubted coherence with a narrowness of range, too close an identification with European classical techniques, too complete a reliance on notation, too highly developed a set of technical procedures, all of which left little room for a contribution by the performer, to make it usable as a vehicle for further developments. A style is a curious affair; it is like rain, which needs, in addition to a saturation of water vapor in the air, a focal point on which the vapor can begin to condense. The "vapor" was heavy in the air between 1900 and 1905 everywhere in the United States where there was a sizeable black population, but only in one location were there conditions where the blackest of black musicking were brought into contact with the whitest of white; that was New Orleans.

New Orleans is unique among the cities of the United States. Its French origins, its cession to the United States as part of the Louisiana Purchase of 1803, its wealth and corruption, its cosmopolitanism and devotion to pleasure and the arts at a time when other American cities were still dominated by Puritan influence, are all part of legend, and the legend, for once, is substantially true. By 1840, for example, there were three more or less full-time opera companies in the city, whose population, including blacks, was a mere one hundred thousand. These companies, moreover, were no third-rate colonial imitations of metropolitan French culture but were described by knowledgeable European visitors as the equal of all but the finest European houses, and they performed works by the greatest names of the day, from Mozart to Rossini, Donizetti and Meyerbeer, as well as by competent local composers. Blacks as well as whites attended; even slaves could sit in the amphitheatre of the opera, and we have already seen that the Negro Philharmonic Society had its own orchestra and engaged visiting soloists. And of course blacks dominated the city's bands, for which the citizens had a passion; the famous slow march to the graveside at funerals and the return, playing lively music, was a feature of the city's musical life which a visitor noted as early as 1819.

The interplay was thus two-way. As blacks heard and used white styles, so the musicking of the blacks was picked up and used by the whites; the lower classes, as we have seen, picked it up directly, while the upper classes did so through the medium of the ubiquitous minstrel shows. That was only an extension of what was taking place wherever blacks and whites encountered one another musically. But there was another factor: miscegenation. Since the days of French sovereignty, it had been a custom among the old Creole (that is, of French or Spanish descent but born in the New World) aristocracy to keep a black mistress in a separate establishment. Unlike those who were fathered by Anglo-Saxon Americans, the offspring of these unions were generally acknowledged by their fathers, and often well provided for, some even receiving a Parisian education, so that there grew up in the city a class of "Creoles of colour," who regarded themselves as to all intents and purposes as white, and who absorbed European rather than Afro-American culture.

With the racial blacklash after Emancipation, however, the Creoles of color found themselves, along with all who had the slightest known or visible trace of African ancestry, reclassified under the city's notorious Legislative Code 111 of 1894 as black, and subject to all the legal and social disabilities of that status. Try as they might to hold on to their European ties, they found themselves driven out of employment in white areas and forced to associate, willy-nilly, with the despised blacks. A large number of professional and semi-professional musicians, trained in some cases in Europe but anyway in the European style, found themselves forced, if they were to earn a living at all, to play in the company of Afro-American groups, with their ragged rhythms, their blues-like melodic inflections and their "dirty" and highly individual instrumental tone. As the Creole musician Paul Dominguez said, many years later, "They made a fiddler out of a violinist—me, I'm talking about . . . If I wanted to make a living I had to be rowdy like the other groups."[5] It seems that it was this forced association, with all the hardship and real suffering that it caused, that brought about exactly the right combination of social and musical interaction to cause the condensation of a new style of playing among the large number of musicians who were capable of playing in any style that was asked of them.

The versatility of black and Creole musicians was another specific feature of the New Orleans scene that was a consequence of the large number of Creole musicians who, in an attempt to retain their European standards, became teachers of music. Frederick Turner tells of one Professor Jim Humphrey who would take the train out of the city once a week in the 1890s to teach talented plantation children, always in the "correct" European style; his pupils later formed the nucleus of New Orleans' famous Eclipse Brass Band.[6] Many of the early "greats" of New Orleans jazz passed through the hands of such teachers, having become skilled not only in playing, in the European manner, more than one instrument but also in reading and writing music; Bunk Johnson, Freddie Keppard, Louis Armstrong, Sidney Bechet and Jelly Roll Morton all had a training of this kind, or something like it. The legend of "primitive" or "unschooled" jazz musicians does not stand up to close examination; indeed, the nature of jazz would have been very different had they not had contact with European as well as Afro-American styles.

It seems to have been between about 1900 and 1905 that the new style crystallized. As it developed, it gradually absorbed into itself the diverse elements of other "proto-jazz" styles, and its eventual naming as "jass" around 1910 (the word seems to come from the same source as "jissom," revealing a disapproving attitude to the music's assumed sexual content) showed that the dominance of the new style was recognized; as Charles Keil says: "the very naming of musics . . . is a declaration of consolidation." Keil goes on to describe exactly the kind of process that must have taken place in the early years: "An exclusion principle or focus on a sharply limited set of forms marks the beginning of a style, but it grows by inclusion, assimilating to its purposes the instruments, techniques and ideas of significant other styles within earshot."[7] To see this process at work it is instructive to examine the work of two important figures in New Orleans music between 1900 and 1905.

The cornettist Charles "Buddy" Bolden (1877–1931) is generally regarded as the first major performer and bandleader of New Orleans jazz. He was taken to a state mental institution in 1906, in circumstances that remain obscure, and never emerged alive, so that it is not surprising that legends proliferate around his name. No recordings of him or his band exist, but he was by all accounts a phenomenally powerful player (the phrase "five miles on a clear night" was coined to describe his carrying power) and, if not the originator, at least an early protagonist, of jazz horn sound. He is usually thought of as the archetypally rough "gutbucket" player, and, indeed, it is clear that he could play wildly exciting blues and other black-style dance music, but, on the other hand, those who heard him attested to his ability to play very sweetly also; as one player said in later years: "When it came to playing sweet music, waltzes, there was nobody in the country who could touch him . . . Everybody was crazy about Bolden when he'd play a waltz, schottische or old low-down blues."[8] And he could not only read music, as could most of his sidesmen, but he could write it too. His early professional experience had been in a small band for society dances and parties where he would have had to play in a "refined" style. As his biographer Donald Marquis says: "Bolden played both by note and by ear, and he liked to please the audience. Having a good ear he could hear another band play and . . . was able to duplicate it by the end of the evening. As he matured musically, he would listen to a number, memorize it instrument by instrument, and then teach the part to the others."[9] Clearly no "primitive" cornet player, then, but a musician whose skills and imagination were considerable, and whose rough and riotous playing was the result not of unschooled technique but of self-identification and of conscious artistic decision.

Bolden's chief rival in that period of headlong development and consolidation, John Robichaux, was, as his surname suggests, a Creole of color. He had received a formal musical training, and his band, playing always in the literate mode, had, before the advent of Legislative Code 111, been employed in some of the most elegant halls and ballrooms of the city. After they found themselves forced to associate with black musicians, Robichaux adapted his style and held the band together in the rougher environments where they had to work; some of his players even moonlighted with black street bands. And, as Marquis says, "The two pioneers cared enough about music to recognize the skills the other possessed and the contributions each was making. Bolden was known to have used ideas from the Robichaux band; some of Buddy's fans remembered seeing Robichaux seated by himself at the back of a hall where Bolden was playing . . . And the two bands, Bolden's and Robichaux's, provided the earliest and most clear-cut examples of the two types of music, Uptown and Downtown, that simultaneously borrowed from each other and hastened the development of jazz."[10]

The Bolden band was essentially one of improvisers, whose performances were held together by a minimum of prearranged material, which may or may not have been written down, while the Robichaux band based its performances on written arrangements, which allowed minimal space for improvisation. Borrow from each other they may have, but finally it was the Bolden style that expanded at the expense of Robichaux's, assimilating the latter's ideas and techniques into the kind of synthesis that the community, who were the final arbiters, required. It was Bolden's, rather than Robichaux's, solution to the problem of musical, and thus of social, order that the community wanted. But then, as far as those musical solutions were concerned, we need not imagine that the community of listeners and dancers were unaware of the problems, or of the solutions arrived at, then or later; there is a transparency about the procedures adopted by jazz musicians which make it quite clear to those who care to notice it what is going on within the performing group, both as a musical and as a social entity.

The early New Orleans bands set a pattern for musical order which was to be followed for over half a century of musicking, through the simple expedient of using the harmonies, the "changes" of the tune being played, whether popular song, blues or original composition, as the unifying element over which each musician was able to improvise as he liked provided he observed the changes and remained faithful to the idiom, that is, to the community. As with those seventeenth-century Italian orchestral musicians whom I discussed earlier, playing "as he liked" meant for a good musician not only performing his part with idiomatic correctness but also taking due regard both for what the other musicians were doing and for the over-all effect; despite the power of the rules and the skill of the individual players, it was, finally, mutual human care and consideration that would enable the ensemble to give a performance that would satisfy the community of listeners and dancers. Behind the wild and often dissonant interplay of melodic lines in those early New Orleans bands, there is a deeper human harmony that still appeals, an informal collaborative society whose model is more African than European. We can never recapture the atmosphere of those early jazz performances, of which present-day "traditional" or "Dixieland" bands give only the palest shadow; I sometimes wonder if the present-day popularity of "Dixieland" among white audiences, especially in Britain, is not in part due to its evoking the society of that time in which blacks were kept firmly in their place and entertained the whites. Those who took part in those early jazz performances left little record of their thoughts on such matters, but it is hard to believe that performers, listeners and dancers had not, in that time of brutal repression and seemingly endless economic deprivation, given some thought to their relationship to the dominant Euro-American culture. The gaiety of the music we can still hear today is *not* mindless but that of serious and thoughtful musicians exploring their identity within the larger society and affirming and, above all, *celebrating* that identity in a way that was to make the whole world listen and dance.

The dispersion of the musical style from New Orleans took place partly through riverboat musicians on the big rivers, partly through the migration of blacks to northern cities in the years after about 1915, and partly, after 1917, through phonograph records. New Orleans, for all its French origins and relatively relaxed racial atmosphere, was still a southern city, and had its population of poor whites living close to the blacks; these would have been the first whites to absorb the new musical style and make it their own as part of everyday experience, rather than being filtered through the dance halls and brothels in a way which colored the perceptions of those upper-class whites who heard it on their low-life excursions into the fabled Storeyville (and which continue to color white perceptions of jazz even today). It was a band of those white musicians, mostly of Italian immigrant stock, the Original Dixieland Jass Band, who happened to be on the spot in New York when the chance to record came, and seized it. Their first two sides were an immediate success, selling over a million copies—probably as much for the animal imitations of *Livery Stable Blues* as for any genuine jazz quality.

As the first jazz band to record and to become widely known both in the United States and in Europe, the ODJB, as it has been known to succeeding generations, did much to set the climate for jazz as far as its wider, white public was concerned. In the first place, they simplified the idiom of the black musicians, substituting crude melodic formulas for their often subtle and flexible improvised melodic lines, and mechanical patterns for their vigorous rhythms. As Gunther Schuller says: "In its rigid substitution of sheer energy for expressive power, of rigid formula for inspiration, the ODJB had found the key to mass appeal." And, secondly, the members of the band promoted assiduously the idea that they were all untutored musicians who just played whatever came into their heads. Schuller tells us that the leaders even "kept bombarding the public with provocative statements such as 'I don't know how many pianists we tried until we found one that couldn't read music.'" "But," says Schuller, "their playing belied the myth of total anarchy such statements were designed to create. Contrary to being improvised, their choruses were set and rehearsed, and they were unchanged for years."[11] The ODJB, in fact, solved the problem of order by pretending that there was no problem, and like all such solutions, it could not last; the band was defunct by 1924. But the fiction of total anarchy served its purpose for them and for their successors and imitators; even today it remains an important factor in the public perception of jazz musicians and of their mode of performance. There is a sizeable proportion of the public who sees jazzmen as jolly, irresponsible fellows, not over-intelligent, who have a good time playing the first thing that comes into their heads. The fiction continues to be encouraged especially among the musical "establishment," serving as it does to defuse the challenge posed by jazz.

That jazz served well enough the spirit of revolt in the 1920s is clear from the electric effect that bands, both black and white, had on the young (black bands did not get to record until 1923 and did not until much later gain the amount of exposure offered to white bands, while racially mixed bands were unthinkable until the 1930s), especially on young middle-class whites and, perhaps even more explosively, on young middle-class blacks such as Edward Ellington in Washington, D.C., Fletcher Henderson in Georgia, and James Lunceford in Fulton, Missouri. As the carrier (one might say, the embodiment, since the values were embodied in the ways in which the music was played and responded to) of values that called into question those of white American culture of past and present, jazz was the natural medium of rebellion against the standards of prosperous middle-class America, which had given the young everything except what they really needed: communality, warmth, and emotional honesty. James Collier describes the differences in the attitudes of black and white musicians towards jazz in that period, differences that have not completely disappeared today even if the two groups are not quite so separate as they were then: "A black jazz musician was among his people a star, a hero, who held a place something like the place held by a basketball star today. But for the young white players, playing jazz meant entering a hidden world . . . As a result, these [white] youngsters, most of them teenagers when they started, came to jazz with the sense that they were a group of elect outsiders who had devoted themselves to a high truth."[12]

What is implied here is that what attracted the young white musicians, and their equally young audiences, to jazz was not just new sounds and rhythms, but new relationships, those of the hitherto inaccessible culture. It does not matter too much that the whites' perceptions of black culture were colored by a great deal of romanticism and wishful thinking (we must remember that the society that was brought into existence in a jazz performance was, for blacks no less than for whites, an ideal, a potential rather than an actual society); what people believe affects what they do no less than what actually is, and the important thing was the view that jazz seemed to offer of an alternative set of values and relationships. Their elders, who remained apparently satisfied with white America as it was, felt otherwise, and social leaders—politicians, clergymen, teachers and medical men—thundered about the mental, physical and moral damage inflicted by jazz (the fulminations against rock 'n' roll in the 1950s had a familiar ring to those who had lived through the 1920s). The vehemence of the denunciations suggests an appreciation, even if it was not fully conscious, of the challenge offered to conventional assumptions about the nature of human societies by the music and the manner of its performance, but, given the preoccupations of white culture at the time, it is not surprising that most of the alleged dangers of jazz boiled down to the usual brew of sexual and racial fears. As in the 1950s, the outrage at the flouting of familiar values was compounded by fear disguised as contempt for the mysterious foreigners in their midst, who seemed to have access to pleasures and to sources of power denied to themselves. "The consensus of opinion of leading medical and other scientific authorities," wrote the medical officer of a leading Philadelphia girls' school, "is that its influence is as harmful and degrading to civilized races as it has always been among the savages from whom we borrowed it."[13]

There is a sad little story, which illustrates for me the gulf that existed at that time between respectable white society and jazz. It is said that Bix Beiderbecke, who is generally regarded today as the first major white soloist in jazz, used to send proudly home to his parents, prosperous German-American merchants in Davenport, Iowa, copies of all his records as they were issued; on a visit to his home he found them all stowed away in the back of a cupboard, their postal wrappings still unbroken.

Beiderbecke spent a large part of his brief career in the big orchestra of Paul Whiteman, the self-styled "King of Jazz." The orchestra, excellent as it undoubtedly was, only intermittently even sounds anything like jazz as we would recognize it today. In the 1920s—notwithstanding its nickname, the "jazz age"—not many people had even heard those artists who today figure as jazz masters of their time, since their performances were generally in small night clubs and speakeasies where relatively few people went, and their records were mostly available only on the "race" labels aimed at the black market and sold only in ghetto shops. The high performance standards of the Whiteman orchestra were achieved at the cost of a denial of that freedom within the ensemble, which had been the essence of jazz performance up to that time. Although a number of later-to-be famous musicians passed through the orchestra in its fifteen-year history, between 1920 and 1935, they were permitted only the briefest of solos, and improvisation was practically nonexistent. Authority was centralized in the arrangers, who were often brilliant by any standards, and in the conductor; the problem of freedom and order had been not so much solved as closed off. It was the first, but by no means the last, attempt to produce the sounds and rhythms of jazz through the techniques and disciplines of the symphony orchestra. The closeness of the link with contemporary symphonic music is emphasizes by the use not only of "symphonic" dramatic introductions, often leading, anti-climactically, into perfectly ordinary dance tunes, but also of harmonies and orchestral devices derived from the "impressionist" composers of the time, notably Ravel and Delius. It is easy to sneer at the Whiteman orchestra today, but Whiteman was undoubtedly a good musician who did his best for the music as he perceived it; if his aim was, as he once put it, to "make a lady out of jazz," and to make jazz accessible to those white Americans for whom in its undiluted form it was too alarming, then in that aim he succeeded. It was he, too, who as part of that aim commissioned *Rhapsody in Blue* in 1924 from George Gershwin, for which we can be grateful. But the fact that he should have thought it necessary in the first place to make jazz respectable has much to say about the social and cultural divisions in our society.

The tendency to drift into easy solutions, based on imposed authority, to the problem of musical order was to recur frequently in the ensuing years, and, indeed, is still with us. The temptation to do so grew greater over the 1920s as the size of bands increased in response to the need for bigger sounds to fill the ever-larger ballrooms without the aid of electronic amplification, and to the desire for a greater range and variety of instrumental color. We see it occurring to various degrees in the big white, and some black, swing bands from Benny Goodman and Fletcher Henderson to Artie Shaw, and culminating in the relentlessly rehearsed arrangements of the Glenn Miller Band, whose ideals of instrumental blend are remarkably similar to those of the symphony orchestra, and whose working practices allowed no room for the uncertainties of improvised solos. There were other pressures on those bands, too, not only the demand by audiences in the big ballrooms and, from the 1930s, in the radio shows with which they lived symbiotically, to hear the songs "just like on the record," but also the need of a large and expensive organization to cater for the paying white audience and its desire for comfortable and not too demanding entertainment music. This was the same audience that the Broadway Masters catered for in musicals and individual songs, and, indeed, it was the latter who wrote most of the songs which arrangers arranged and the bands played, in ballrooms and nightclubs (places into which, since the end of prohibition, respectable people could go), on radio and records and in film and stage musicals. Jazz became during the 1930s and 1940s a popular music for the first and last time; the big bands appeared regularly in Hollywood films, and bandleaders were stars whose activities, and especially their sex lives, were reported and commented on as avidly as those of film stars—or, indeed, of rock and pop stars today. Jazz and jazz musicians had been co-opted to serve the values of white society, and its challenge had been defused.

This kind of jazz survives today, in showbands and backing bands, its style changed remarkably little since the 1940s. It survives also, interestingly, in educational institutions, whose "Jazz Ensemble," "Jazz Band," or "Showband," usually under the baton of the Director of Music, can form a showpiece for the school's or college's progressive image. Such ensembles, however, are generally dependent on scores, usually commercial arrangements, which leave little room for either individual or group improvisation (they sometimes include fully notated "improvised" solos) and leave the conductor firmly in charge of everything that takes place. There is no conflict here with the values of the school, or of the centralized industrial state whose interests, as we have already noted, the school is designed to serve.

That such a solution is not inevitable even when a large number of musicians are involved can be seen from the history of jazz in the midwest and southwestern United States, especially in those blues-based bands, climaxing in the long-lived band of Count Basie, which sheltered from the Great Depression in the relative prosperity of the corrupt but freehanded Prendergast administration in Kansas City. Basie, like many of the Kansas City bandleaders of the day, led from the piano; as one commentator has said: "He sat at the piano, smiling modestly, giving out the occasional tinkle with so little fuss that a stranger might have asked what he *did*. Yet he was the leader of a band full of brilliant, individual soloists who swung together with a unique lift and power, a rhythmic unity that seemed like second nature. And almost all of those individualists would have agreed that Basie was a great leader, though none could explain exactly why."[14] The same writer said of the band: "The standing repertory consisted of head arrangements worked up at rehearsals from . . . the store of sketches and rough charts. In the main the band's style depended on its collective spirit and the flow of ideas from soloists, brought about to a singular degree of unity by Basie's quiet, musicianly leadership and orchestral deployment of the piano."[15]

The Basie band consisted of individuals each of whom was in his or her own right a musician of superb skill and musical intelligence, who realized those qualities to their fullest by placing them at the service of the common enterprise. It was a remarkable social, no less than musical, achievement, not the least of which lay in the realization that the problems can never be solved once and for all but must be solved again and again every day and require constant vigilance and diplomacy to keep the need for order and the need for freedom in harmony with each other. But the rewards were commensurate with the effort; judging from their recordings, I do not know of any of the major bands of the time, not even that of Duke Ellington himself, that could play with such power and such delicacy and with such evocation of the spirit of joy and of love as the Count Basie Orchestra. Those fifteen or so musicians, constantly free to create something new, must have felt most fully themselves when building their commonwealth of the spirit in collaboration with their listeners and dancers (we recall that it was Lester Young, the band's great tenor saxophonist of its peak years, who liked to play for dancers because "the rhythm of the dancers comes back to you"). Even if a large proportion of those listeners were just the proverbial tired businessmen on a night out, all but the most insensitive must have perceived, however faintly, the outlines of that commonwealth and have been touched, if not fully knowing why, by its values. In its later years, it is true, the band succumbed to some extent to pressures for a more smoothly complete product and became more dependent on written arrangements, with a consequent loss of the players' improvisatory freedom, but it remained a powerful and beautiful group right up to Basie's death in 1984.

The group that perhaps shows most clearly how delicate is the balance between improvisatory freedom and audible order is that of Duke Ellington. When the orchestra began playing, in 1923, it was a co-operative group, of which Ellington gradually assumed command, more, it seems, through a talent for leadership than through his musical skills, which were at that time somewhat sketchy. The orchestra's performances initially evolved on a collaborative basis, with all the musicians making creative contributions, and as Ellington began to take control it became simply a matter of his having a veto over those suggestions and ideas as they were tried out. The conditions under which they worked from 1927 to 1933, at Harlem's Cotton Club, where they were required to provide music not just for the patrons to dance to, but also for the lavish and often fantastic floor shows, demanded a type of composition that could be coordinated with choreography and repeated on successive nights—which meant using notation. It was under these conditions that they developed a way of working in which ideas presented by the leader, or by one of the sidesmen, were tried over, added to, and placed within a framework in such a way as to allow a considerable degree of improvising freedom to the various brilliant soloists in the orchestra. Only after this process had been gone through would the arrangement come into being and be written down—and even then it was possible for it to go on developing as it was performed. This way of working still left the soloists with considerable responsibility for the performance, and there are instances in the orchestra's recorded legacy, for example in the *Black and Tan Fantasy* where, as Gunther Schuller says, "Through the dominance of one soloist, [the trumpeter Bubber Miley] the collective equilibrium that was such an integral part of jazz was temporarily disturbed."[16] That such a disturbance was possible, however, shows the vitality of the idiom and its openness to whatever may happen.

We are told that Ellington was not very interested in contemporary classical music, that the "impressionist" harmonies which abound in his orchestra's performances come not directly from Ravel, Delius, or Stravinsky but rather from other black arrangers, notably Will Vodery, who was chief arranger for the Siegfeld Follies, and Will Marion Cook, as well as from the big orchestras such as that of Paul Whiteman. But although over the years the balance between improvisation and composition remained remarkably open (the orchestra was always capable of making superb improvised performances from simple "head" arrangements) we find Ellington in later life being increasingly drawn to the kind of fully composed large-scale work for his orchestra that is usually thought more appropriate for the concert platform than for the bandstand—pieces such as *Black, Brown and Beige, Liberian Suite, Deep South Suite* and the three *Sacred Concerts* intended for performance in church. These works have been variously praised and damned, the former often by those who like to hear something they can recognize as compositions in the classical sense, the latter equally often by those who say that they are not jazz (neither verdict has much to do with their real qualities); an interesting comment is that of the critic Francis Newton in the London *New Statesman*, quoted by Schuller, that Ellington had "solved the unbelievably difficult problem of turning a living, shifting, and improvised folk music into composition without losing its spontaneity."[17] That a musician of Ellington's kind, and his proven stature, should want to do such a thing testifies to the continuing attraction exerted by the respectability of the concert stage. He lived to perform the Sacred Concerts in London's Westminster Abbey, where English monarchs have been crowned for centuries, and one cannot get much more respectable than that; the pieces are to my ears less immediate, less involving than the less formally composed pieces, and can perhaps be heard as the work of a musician who has lived dangerously and now feels the need to relax from the tension of reconciling two sets of values. But they can also be seen as representing a victory for "classical" respectability.

The Ellington Orchestra always stood aside from the rest of the history of jazz, paying only superficial tribute to successive styles as they came and went. I referred in a previous chapter to the renewal of the encounter between values, after the closure brought about in the era that was dominated by the big white swing bands, which took place with the style that was known as bebop in the 1940s and 1950s. As with many stylistic revolutions, the passing of time enables us to recognize the continuities as well as the breaks, and we can now see that these musicians were returning consciously to a reaffirmation, in a new and sophisticated way befitting the generation of the reopening of the civil rights struggle, of the values that had animated the older jazzmen. This continuity is emphasized by the fact that not only did many of the principal musicians of that revolution came from the midwest, where the older musical values had survived better than in the very commercial New York scene, but also that the rhythmic revolution that underlay bebop was a development of what the Kansas City bands, notably Count Basie's, had been doing for a long time.

Thus the dialogue was reopened and has continued undiminished over the subsequent years. A reaction in the 1950s towards the forms and techniques of classical music was led by a number of classically trained white musicians, who attempted a fusion, by the use of classical forms such as fugue and of asymmetrical rhythmic patterns (Dave Brubeck's *Take Five* is a famous example) and by the cultivation of the refined atmosphere of a chamber-music concert. None of this had much lasting effect on the art itself, but, as James Collier says, "Cool music . . . was popular for the simple reason that the European elements in it made it comprehensible to audiences raised in the European tradition . . . For the white majority, before 1950, jazz was a hobby for a handful of eccentrics; by the 1950s, especially on college campuses, it was an accepted part of the cultural scenery, something one knew about in the way that one knew about Freud, Beethoven, and Van Gogh. For jazz, before rock swept everything away, the 1950s were a relatively good time."[18]

For white musicians with a college degree, at any rate; I shall leave the reader to ponder the implications of that paragraph in the light of the earlier discussion. For the rest, things were not much different from what they had always been. The succeeding generation of musicians, coming to maturity in the 1960s, brought, as we saw in the previous chapter, a renewal of concern for the enduring resources and values of black culture, in folk music, the music of the churches, and of course the blues. This renewal was, wrongly, dubbed by certain critics "the new thing" or "the new jazz," since it was neither new nor a thing, but an attempt to shake off the restraints imposed by European harmony and even those of the tempered scale, using instead an interplay of melodic lines built often enough on ancient modes—an old idiom representing an old community. Those same critics also attempted to set up a rivalry along Brahms-Wagner lines between certain musicians of the time, but there was in fact no necessary antithesis, rather a different approach towards a common cultural pride and a common desire for independence of European cultural norms. Today there seems a more cautious spirit abroad, and a move towards European high culture and the avant garde—which may represent not a capitulation but simply a striving to take possession of its forms and to turn them to the musicians' own purposes. The danger of capture has never retreated, however, and is indeed perhaps even stronger than ever in the social and political climate of the 1980s. We can only, from a distance, wait and hope.

None of this, I hope, should suggest that jazz as a way of musicking, or the issues that it raises, concerns black Americans only. For generations now there have been white musicians for whom jazz is a natural way of playing, who are motivated by nothing more or less than a need to affirm, explore, and celebrate values to which they feel closer than to the official ones of western society as embodied in classical music, and more profoundly than popular music permits. On the other hand, jazz will in all probability never again be a popular music; it is too uncomfortable for that. But those who are prepared to allow themselves to go with the tensions generated by that way of musicking can be rewarded with some of the most heartening musical experiences possible in western society today. Players and listeners are taking part in a process, which at any point can end in disaster; the musicians have chosen to place themselves in the most delicate, subtle and dangerous relationship with their listeners, while the listeners have the responsibility of feeding back to the players the energy that they have received from them, so that when the performance is going well it resonates back and forth, to create a community in which at the same time all can feel fully realized as individuals. Contrary to what is often said, the excitement generated by a good jazz performance is not just physical, although the part played by bodily response and bodily movement must not be denied; it is the exhilaration of finding oneself, to use Albert Murray's words once more, raised "to the richest sense of selfhood and to the highest level of achievement." There is no product, no final solution to the problems, only the unending process of exploration, affirmation, and celebration. The magic does not happen with every performance, even with the finest and most devoted performers and the most sympathetic of audiences and the most skilled of dancers; there are too many workaday pressures that militate against it, not least of which are the pressures on the musicians to produce a saleable and consistent product and to ease tension by submitting to routine. But the ideal remains, and is realized sufficiently often to make the enterprise worthwhile for both players and their listeners ("Once a year, if I'm lucky," said Dizzy Gillespie[19]).

I conclude this chapter with some remarks by musicians, all quoted in Nat Hentoff's *The Jazz Life*, which illuminate the musicians' task better than any words of mine. First, the drummer Jo Jones to a beginning professional musician: "You're a musician. Don't ever forget that. You can do what very few other people can do. You can reach people, but to move them you have to be all open. You have to let everything in you out. And you have to be in a condition to play what you hear."[20] Second, Charles Mingus, "I play or write *me*, the way I feel, through jazz or whatever, whether it's hip or not. Music is the language of the emotions. If someone has been escaping reality, I don't expect him to dig my music . . . my music is alive and it's about the living and the dead, about good and evil. It's angry, and it's real because it's angry."[21]

And, finally: "Some years ago, a quartet had just completed a particularly exhilarating set, and its young Negro drummer came off the stand grinning with satisfaction. 'You sure sounded good,' said a listener. 'Yeah,' said the drummer, 'there was a lot of loving going on up there.'"[22]

NOTES

1. Albert Murray, *The Omni-Americans: New Perspectives on Black Experience and American Culture* (New York: Outerbridge and Dienstfrey, 1970), 102.

2. Frederick Turner, *Remembering Song: Encounters with the New Orleans Jazz Tradition* (New York: The Viking Press, 1982), 3.

3. Charles Keil, "People's Music Comparatively: Style and Stereotype, Class and Hegemony," *Dialectical Anthropology* 10 (1985): 122.

4. James Reese Europe, "A Negro Explains 'Jazz' (1919)" in *Readings in Black American Music*, ed. Eileen Southern (New York: Norton, 1983), 239.

5. Quoted in Jack V. Buerkle, and Danny Barker, *Bourbon Street Black: The New Orleans Black Jazzmen* (New York: Oxford University Press, 1973), 10.

6. Frederick Tuner, op cit., p. 70

7. Charles Keil, op cit., p. 126.

8. Donald M. Marquis, *In Search of Buddy Bolden: First Man of Jazz* (New York: Da Capo Books, 1978), 100.

9. Ibid., 47.

10. Ibid., 81–82.

11. Gunther Schuller, *Early Jazz: Its Roots and Musical Development* (New York: Oxford University Press, 1968), 180.

12. James Lincoln Collier, *The Making of Jazz: A Comprehensive History* (London: Granada Publishing, 1978), 127.

13. Quoted in Neil Leonard, *Jazz and the White Americans: The Acceptance of a New Art Form* (Chicago: University of Chicago Press, 1962), 39.

14. Ross Russell, *Jazz Style in Kansas City and the Southwest* (Berkeley: University of California Press, 1971), 258.

15. Ibid., 135.

16. Gunther Schuller, op cit., p. 350.

17. Ibid., 350.

18. James Lincoln Collier, op cit., p. 436.

19. Quoted in Geoff Wills, "Under Pressure," *International Musician* (October 1984): 46.

20. Nat Hentoff, *The Jazz Life* (New York: Da Capo Press, 1978), 24.

21. Ibid., 45.

22. Ibid., 74.

Whose Music Do We Teach, Anyway?

FOR MENC [MUSIC EDUCATORS NATIONAL CONFERENCE, NOW KNOWN AS THE NATIONAL ASSOCIATION FOR MUSIC EDUCATION], WASHINGTON, D.C., MARCH 28, 1990

First of all I have to declare an interest—or rather a lack of interest. I'm not interested in music at all. That's to say, it's a matter of indifference to me what happens to those great musical objects that are performed with such regularity in concert halls and opera houses, not to mention recording and broadcasting studios, and I don't much care whether or not they survive the twenty-first century. And it doesn't seem to me of the least importance whether or not the children in our schools get exposed to them—and I'm sorry, but that word "exposure" used in this way always conjures up for me a ridiculous cartoon image of a man opening up his dirty raincoat and flashing the Ninth Symphony or the B minor Mass at startled passersby.

Mind you, you mustn't think I don't love those great musical objects—well, some of them, anyway—after all, I grew up among them, and I've come to feel about them as I used to feel about elderly relatives before I became one myself—but there's a lot of them, some of them generally considered to be masterpieces, to which I just want to say, Oh go away and take your ego someplace else. Anyway, in the first place, I believe that either they will survive or they won't, and nothing that any of us in this room can do is going to make the slightest difference to that, and in the second place I think there is something to be treasured even more than the B minor Mass or the Ninth Symphony.

What I believe we shall be treasuring above all is not so much any music objects, however splendid they may be, as the music act, musicking, that remarkable form of human encounter in which people come together to make meanings, to explore and affirm and, yes, celebrate for a while their common humanity and their sense of who they are and of where they belong. Because that's what seems to me the real nature of what is called music, and that's what its function is in human life.

Music, in fact, isn't a thing, or even things, at all. It isn't symphonies or concertos or operas or lieder or pop songs; it isn't even melodies and rhythms. It's an action; it's something people do. All those music objects are to be understood as concretions of the human activity, and it is as activity first and foremost that we need to understand music. The trouble is that we get so misled by the tendency of our language to turn ideas and actions into nouns that we come to think of them as things in themselves, and then we attribute to them a life of their own, independent of ourselves, which they don't in fact have. And I believe that it's to a large extent the befuddlement induced by this reification of music that brings us together today to worry over what it is we think we ought to be doing in schools. Music teachers aren't alone in this, of course; the whole of Western education is befuddled by reification, the reification of knowledge, but we can't cure that today, and I'm not sure we ever can.

As an antidote to reification, and to help us think a little straighter, I offer you a simple conceptual tool. It's a word you may have noticed I used just now, the word "musicking," spelled with a *ck*, which is the present participle of the verb "to music." You won't find the verb "to music" in any English dictionary that I know of, but I'm determined to will it into existence. And since I coined the verb I claim the right to define it, which I do as follows: to music is to take part in a musical performance, not just as performer but also as listener, or as provider of material for performance—what we call composing—or in any other way, dancing, for example, should anyone be dancing, or even perhaps taking the tickets at the door or shifting the piano around. "Musicking" is thus not the same as either "making music" or "performing," since both those words apply only to what the performers are doing.

If we think a little about what the word means, we shall find that it's quite rich in its implications. Musicking is something that people do together; all those present are taking part in it, and the fact that the one verb covers everything that is going on in the performance space means that it recognizes no essential difference between what the performers are doing and what the rest are doing, and makes no essential separation between them. So that musicking isn't a matter of composers, or even performers, doing something to, or for, the rest of us, but rather it's all of us doing something together.

What it is we're doing, I believe, is making meanings and giving structure to our experience. As I said just now, a musical performance is an encounter between human beings, and like all human encounters it takes place within a physical and a cultural setting, and those settings have to be taken into account when we ask what meanings are being generated. Musical meaning is thus to be found not just in those musical objects that the Western tradition teaches us are its sole repository but also in the act of musicking itself. What is being performed is of course significant, but it does not determine the meaning of the event as a whole.

What it is that musical meaning is concerned with is an interesting question. I haven't time to argue the case now—you can read it if you're interested in my book *Music of the Common Tongue*—but I believe that it's centered on relationships, relationships between person and person, between person and society, between humanity and the natural world, and even between humanity and the world of the supernatural, should that be an element in the lives of those present. Through the act of musicking we affirm, we explore, and not least, we celebrate those relationships which we believe hold our universe together, we experience them as we feel they ought to be, and since how we relate is who we are, in doing so we are affirming, exploring, and celebrating also our sense of identity, of who we are, and of where we belong.

During a musical performance we don't just learn about those relationships but actually experience them through the power of the human and musical relationships that are established in the performance space. That, I believe, is the reason why when we have been present at a good and satisfying musical performance we feel more fully ourselves, more fully realized, and more in tune with ourselves and with our fellows. We feel we have been afforded a glimpse of how the world really is.

To oversimplify a little, but not a lot, we could say that those who are musicking are saying to themselves, to one another and to anyone else who is listening, THIS IS WHO WE ARE. And that applies no less to those performers and listeners who take part in symphonic and chamber-music and opera performances than it does to those enslaved Africans and their descendants throughout the Americas for whom musicking has always been more than a source of pleasure or even of comfort but, quite literally, a weapon for survival and for the affirmation of humanity and community in the face of a society that has denied both. A symphony concert is in this respect no different from a blues performance or a rock concert, or for that matter a performance by a Balinese gamelan or a West African drum ensemble; each is a ritual which for the members of a specific social group serves to affirm their identity and to reinforce the group's solidarity, and the values a symphony concert embodies are no more and no less universal than those of any of the others.

All this means that if we want to discover where musical meaning resides we have to ask not, What does this musical work mean? which is the question to which the overwhelming majority of modern Western musical criticism, esthetics, and theory is devoted—and, for that matter, modern music education—but rather, What does it mean when this performance takes place at this time, in this place, with these participants? To answer that question we have to explore those extremely complex sets of relationships that are established in the performance space in the course of the performance. We should notice, by the way, that the second question, What does the performance mean? doesn't negate the first but rather subsumes it, into a larger and more comprehensive—and much, much more interesting—question. And of course, in much human musicking there isn't a written-down or even a fixed musical work at all, in which case the first question is meaningless.

What we experience during a musical performance, in fact, is a complex set of human interactions and relationships of which the composer's intention is only one element, and not necessarily the most important one. To narrow the experience down to a mere matter of some kind of communication from the composer to each individual in the audience via the supposedly neutral medium of the performance is to do grave violence to the human complexity of musicking, and even to trivialize it. Likewise to assume that a "work" of music possesses a built-in and stable meaning that is always the same no matter where and when it is performed is to ignore the fact that meaning is created anew every time a musical performance takes place, and that it is created, as I have already suggested, by the interaction of all those who are taking part. I am certain, for example, that to perform the Eroica Symphony in a concert hall today is to create a very different set of human meanings from those that were created when it was first performed in Vienna in 1804. The patterns of organized sounds may be the same—well, more or less—but the meaning of the musicking has changed enormously.

It's not only questions of musical meaning that I believe can be approached by thinking of musicking rather than of musical objects; we can consider also in this way the very closely connected question of musical value. Thus, our question ought to be not, What is the value of this musical work?—which leads us straight into those sterile arguments of classical versus pop and finally involves us in such nonquestions as, Which is better, a Mozart symphony or a pop song? And it doesn't help matters any to turn the argument on its head and assert, as do some musical liberals, that John Lennon and Paul McCartney, or whoever, are the greatest songwriters since Schubert. Both are concerned with the wrong question, the question, What is the value of this piece of music?

A piece of music, whatever that may be—and the only thing that we can really be sure of as a permanent and stable object is the paper that bears the composer's notations—has no value in itself, or rather, it has value only insofar as it makes possible good performances. Only performance, or to be more correct, only musicking, has value in itself. The question that can help us in our quest for value is, What value has taking part in this performance—musicking—at this time, in this place, and for these participants? And that's a question to which only the participants themselves can possibly know the answer for sure. The outsider can make some informed guesses, however, provided that he takes the trouble to acquaint himself with the participants' values and is prepared to empathize with them at least a little. Thus, it might be useful to ask the question, Which is better, to take part in a performance of a Mozart symphony or to take part in a pop concert?—but we should have to be extremely cautious in proposing an answer. Certainly I don't believe there can be any permanent answer, either one way or the other.

In other words, there is no absolute or eternal or unchanging value in musicking; there is only value as it is perceived by the participants at the time—although that in itself represents what seems to me a permanent and unchanging value, which is the value that we put on human beings and on their ability to make up their own minds. The principal criterion of musical value is of what use is the musicking to the participants in affirming, exploring, and celebrating their sense of how the universe is organized and of how they relate to it. And that means there is no one kind of musicking—no one musical tradition, if you like—that is inherently superior to any other. All are to be treasured to the extent that they serve that important human purpose.

Please don't mistake what I'm saying. I'm not saying there is no place for judgments of quality in musicking, that anything goes. On the contrary—only the most subtle and imaginative and comprehensive exploration of the relationships between the sounds will do to form a focus for the occasion, and that's a task that calls for all the skill, clearheadedness, and devotion that both performers and listeners can bring to it. I've never yet heard of any musical culture that failed to distinguish sharply between what's good musicking and bad, between who musics well and who badly.

And speaking of devotion, we mustn't be misled by the conventions of the concert hall into thinking that anyone who isn't sitting still and quiet isn't devoted, or that musicians who clown around as they play aren't playing with seriousness and concern for what they do. You can be just as devoted to the musicking when you're dancing to it—an African, as well as many Afro-Americans, would say there was something missing if you weren't—or even if you're screaming at the musicians or just boogieing around and having a good time. It all depends on what the participants want from the musicking. A gospel singer in a black Sanctified church would wonder what he or she was doing wrong if the congregation sat still and quiet, and I saw just that happen to Ornette Coleman some years ago in the beautiful Palace of Music in Barcelona, when a packed and enthusiastic audience of reserved Catalans sat still and quiet throughout his performance—they just didn't know how to respond, and his performance suffered for it.

The point is that every musical tradition, every musical culture, every musical genre, whatever you want to call it, but every distinct way of approaching musicking, has developed around the needs of its participants to affirm, explore, and celebrate their sense of relationships, their sense, in fact, of who they are, and every performance must be judged according to how well it fulfills that function—and that includes even the most apparently frivolous and commercial brands of Western popular music. If making music purely for money automatically resulted in bad musicking we'd have to send Mozart's Requiem to the trashcan for a start.

That means also, of course, that no one can tell anyone else what kind of musicking they ought to be engaging in. Well, people can try, and often do, most notoriously of course in schools, but it's rare indeed to find that they can make it stick; much more likely is that they will end up by having a destructive effect on the musicality of the victim. That's because of a hidden syllogism that classically trained music teachers can practice on their pupils if they're not extremely careful. It goes like this: This—meaning "our" music, classical music—is the only real music. You're not interested, or proficient, in our music. Therefore you're not really musical. As I said, it's very destructive, and if you believe, as I do, that everybody, every normally endowed human being, is born with the gift of music no less than with the gift of speech, then you will find such practices reprehensible, to say the least.

So if you ask me, What is good music? I can only reply that it is music that is played and listened to with the utmost skill and devotion that players and listeners and dancers can bring to it, while bad music is that which is not.

All musicking is serious musicking when it is engaged in seriously, and those who use the term "serious" music when they mean "classical" or "concert" music should be made to stay after school and write out five hundred times "I must not confuse solemnity with seriousness." I have been to concerts that featured some of the greatest works of the symphonic tradition, given by superstar orchestras, conductors, and soloists, that to me, for all their solemn gestures of profundity, were as empty and as frivolous as anything by Wham! or whoever is currently top of the peanut league. I am tempted to say, more so, because at least with honest, good-time musicking there is a good time to be had, which is a serious and important human activity. And at least Wham! don't compound their commercialism with hypocrisy. And conversely, any performance in which the performers are doing their honest best, no matter how elementary their level of skill may be, can give us a glimpse of beauty and put us in touch with that pattern that connects the whole of the cosmos.

If you ask me what ought to be the content of public school music, I am tempted just to say "musicking" with an enigmatic smile and cop out at that. But I really can't leave it there, because there is something that puzzles and worries me about the musical scene, and especially about musical education, in the United States as I have encountered it.

It's this. The United States and Latin America are the point of origin of one of the most powerful musical cultures in the world today. That culture comes from the crossing of two great musical traditions, or perhaps we should say, groups of traditions, those of Africa and those of Europe, as black and white musicians encountered one another in the Americas during and after the period of slavery. It has a respectably long history; for nearly five hundred years now, it has been a tool of survival for poor black and white people alike, and during the present century it has expanded and proliferated until today we can confidently claim that it is this, and not those testaments from the European past on which modern classical concert life is based, that is the major form of musicking in the modern West. Certainly it is within this tradition that the vast majority of Americans, black and white and all shades in between, find their means of affirming, exploring, and celebrating their sense of who they are. Its development has been a cultural achievement of the first order.

And it doesn't exist in straight opposition to the Western classical tradition but forms more of a continuum with it. This shouldn't surprise us, since what we call today classical music was among its many formative influences. What opposition there is comes from the other direction, from the school and the conservatory and the symphony orchestra. To the musician in the Afro-American tradition, Bach, Beethoven, and Mozart aren't the opposition but colleagues, perhaps more alive than they are to your average symphony orchestra musician. Why shouldn't they be?—after all they were great improvising musicians too. And when Chuck Berry told Beethoven to roll over and tell Chaikovsky [Richard Taruskin, who ought to know best, uses this spelling] the news, Beethoven would probably have been one of the first to appreciate the joke. Maybe he's getting a bit tired of hearing his symphonies endlessly repeated by bored orchestras before motionless and impassive audiences in sterile concert halls and would like to roll over and cede a little space to musicking of a different kind.

In any case, to this outsider it seems strange that in the very heartland of this powerful and endlessly varied musical culture he should find that those who are charged with developing the musicality of young people should place so little value on it and should cling instead, with a tenacity that looks a little like desperation, to the great works of the European past. I say this in no spirit of criticism but simply as an attempt to bring what I was saying earlier about meaning and about value in musicking into the realm of practical musical and educational politics.

Well, like the old song, this story has no moral, and it probably has no end. Maybe it only goes to show that you needn't worry too much about the fate of your beloved classical masterpieces. What is to be treasured is not so much created things aş the creative act, and human creativity is inexhaustible. I do not think our job as music teachers is to be guardians of past masterpieces but is rather to treasure and encourage that creativity and that musicality that is part of the universal human birthright, and you needn't be too concerned in what forms it manifests itself. Our charges will know, perhaps better than we do, what they need. But I think we should count ourselves lucky that there exists to hand an idiom for the creative work. If we take it and use it, we, our students and the idiom, will all be the richer for it.

SITGES, MARCH 1990

Introduction to *Musicking*

Prelude: Music and Musicking

(1998)

In a concert hall, two thousand people settle in their seats, and an intense silence falls. A hundred musicians bring their instruments to the ready. The conductor raises his baton, and after a few moments the symphony begins. As the orchestra plays, each member of the audience sits alone, listening to the work of the great, dead composer.

In a supermarket, loudspeakers fill the big space with anodyne melodies that envelop customers, checkout clerks, shelf assistants and managers, uniting them in their common purpose of buying and selling.

In a big stadium, fifty thousand voices cheer and fifty thousand pairs of hands applaud. A blaze of colored light and a crash of drums and amplified guitars greet the appearance onstage of the famous star of popular music, who is often heard on record and seen on video but whose presence here in the flesh is an experience of another kind. The noise is so great that the first few minutes of the performance are inaudible.

A young man walks down a city street, his Walkman clamped across his ears, isolating him from his surroundings. Inside his head is an infinite space charged with music that only he can hear.

A saxophonist finishes his improvised solo with a cascade of notes that ornament an old popular song. He wipes his forehead with a handkerchief and nods absently to acknowledge the applause of a hundred pairs of hands. The pianist takes up the tune.

A church organist plays the first line of a familiar hymn tune, and the congregation begins to sing, a medley of voices in ragged unison.

At an outdoor rally, with bodies erect and hands at the salute, fifty thousand men and women thunder out a patriotic song. The sounds they make rise toward the God whom they are imploring to make their country great. Others hear the singing and shiver with fear.

In an opera house, a soprano, in long blond wig and white gown streaked with red, reaches the climax of her mad scene and dies pathetically. Her death in song provokes not tears but a roar of satisfaction that echoes around the theater. As the curtain descends, hands clap thunderously and feet stamp on the floor. In a few moments, restored to life, she will appear before the curtain to receive her homage with a torrent of applause and a shower of roses thrown from the galleries.

A housewife making the beds in the morning sings to herself an old popular song, its words imperfectly remembered.

So many different settings, so many different kinds of action, so many different ways of organizing sounds into meanings, all of them given the name *music*. What is this thing called music, that human beings the world over should find in it such satisfaction, should invest in it so much of their lives and resources? The question has been asked many times over the centuries, and since at least the time of the ancient Greeks, scholars and musicians have tried to explain the nature and meaning of music and find the reason for its extraordinary power in the lives of human beings.

Many of these attempts have been complex and ingenious, and some have even possessed a kind of abstract beauty, reminding one in their complexity and ingenuity of those cycles and epicycles which astronomers invented to explain the movement of the planets before Copernicus simplified matters by placing the sun instead of the earth at the center of the system. But none has succeeded in giving a satisfactory answer to the question—or rather, pair of questions—*What is the meaning of music?* and *What is the function of music in human life?*—in the life, that is, of every member of the human species.

It is easy to understand why. Those are the wrong questions to ask. There is no such thing as music.

Music is not a thing at all but an activity, something that people do. The apparent thing "music" is a figment, an abstraction of the action, whose reality vanishes as soon as we examine it at all closely. This habit of thinking in abstractions, of taking from an action what appears to be its essence and of giving that essence a name, is probably as old as language; it is useful in the conceptualizing of our world, but it has its dangers. It is very easy to come to think of the abstraction as more real than the reality it represents, to think, for example, of those abstractions which we call love, hate, good and evil as having an existence apart from the acts of loving, hating, or performing good and evil deeds and even to think of them as being in some way more real than the acts themselves, a kind of universal or ideal lying behind and suffusing the actions. This is the trap of reification, and it has been a besetting fault of Western thinking ever since Plato, who was one of its earliest perpetrators.

If there is no such thing as music, then to ask "What is the meaning of music?" is to ask a question that has no possible answer. Scholars of Western music seem to have sensed rather than understood that this is so; but rather than directing their attention to the activity we call music, whose meanings have to be grasped in time as it flies and cannot be fixed on paper, they have quietly carried out a process of elision by means of which the word *music* becomes equated with "works of music in the Western tradition." Those at least do seem to have a real existence, even if the question of just *how* and *where* they exist does create problems. In this way the question "What is the meaning of music?" becomes the more manageable "What is the meaning of this work (or these works) of music?"—which is not the same question at all.

This privileging of Western classical music above all other musics is a strange and contradictory phenomenon. On the one hand, it is claimed to be an intellectual and spiritual achievement that is unique in the world's musical cultures (for me the claim is summed up by the reported remark of a famous scientist who, when asked what message should be included in a missile to be fired off in search of other intelligent life in the universe, replied, "We could send them Bach, but that would be boasting"); on the other hand, it appeals to only a very tiny minority of people, even within Western industrialized societies; classical music records account for only around 3 percent of all record sales.

We even see it in the way the word *music* is commonly used; we know what kind of music is dealt with in the music departments of universities and colleges and in schools and conservatories of music, and we know what kind of music an upmarket newspaper's music critic will be writing about. In addition, musicology is, almost by definition, concerned with Western classical music, while other musics, including even Western popular musics, are dealt with under the rubric of ethnomusicology (the real musical study of Western popular musics, in their own terms rather than those of classical music, is only just beginning and does not yet dare to call itself musicology).

The contradiction extends to the nature of the music itself. On the one hand, it is regarded as the model and paradigm for all musical experience, as can be seen from the fact that a classical training is thought to be a fit preparation for any other kind of musical performance (a famous violinist records "jazz" duets with Stéphane Grappelli, and operatic divas record songs from Broadway musicals, all without apparently hearing their own stylistic solecisms). And on the other, it is regarded as somehow unique and not to be subjected to the same modes of inquiry as other musics, especially in respect to its social meanings; brave spirits who have attempted to do so have brought the wrath of the musicological establishment down on their heads. Even those who try to right the balance by comparative study of other human musics most often avoid comparisons with Western classical music, thus emphasizing, if only in a negative way, its uniqueness and implicitly privileging it in reverse, although it is in fact a perfectly normal human music, an ethnic music if you like, like any other and, like any other, susceptible to social as well as purely musical comment.

So it is that while scholars of music may disagree on any number of matters, there is one matter on which there is virtually unanimous agreement, all the more powerful for being for the most part undiscussed and unspoken. It is that the essence of music and of whatever meanings it contains is to be found in those things called musical works—works, that is, of Western classical music. The most succinct modern formulation of the idea comes perhaps from the doyen of contemporary German musicologists, Carl Dahlhaus (1983), who tells us, flatly, that "the subject matter of music is made up, primarily, of significant works of music that have outlived the culture of their age" and that "the concept 'work' and not 'event' is the cornerstone of music history." Any history of music will bear out Dahlhaus's contention. They are primarily histories of those things that are works of music and of the people who made them, and they tell us about the circumstances of their creation, about the factors that influenced their nature, and about the influence they have had on subsequent works.

It is not only historians who assume the primacy of musical works but also musicologists, whose purpose is to ascertain the real nature and contours of musical works by recourse to original texts, as well as theorists, whose purpose is to discover the way in which the works are constructed as objects in themselves, and aestheticians, who deal with the meaning of sound objects and the reasons for their effect on a listener. All are concerned with things, with musical works. Even the recent area of study known as "reception history" deals not, as one might reasonably expect, with performance itself but with the changing ways in which musical works have been perceived by their audiences during the term of their existence. The part played by the performers in that perception does not come into consideration; when performance is discussed at all, it is spoken of as if it were nothing more than a presentation, and generally an approximate and imperfect presentation at that, of the work that is being performed. It is rare indeed to find the act of musical performance thought of as possessing, much less creating, meanings in its own right.

The presumed autonomous "thingness" of works of music is, of course, only part of the prevailing modern philosophy of art in general. What is valued is not the action of art, not the act of creating, and even less that of perceiving and responding, but the created art object itself. Whatever meaning art may have is thought to reside in the object, persisting independently of what the perceiver may bring to it. It is simply there, floating through history untouched by time and change, waiting for the ideal perceiver to draw it out.

It is for the sake of that unchanging, immanent meaning that paintings, books, pieces of sculpture and other art objects (including musical works and the scores that in some not quite understood way are supposed to be the bearers of them) are cared for, lovingly exhibited in air-conditioned museums (and concert halls), sold for exorbitant prices (the autograph score of Schumann's Piano Concerto in A Minor was sold in London in 1989 for nearly one and a half million dollars), printed in luxurious editions, pursued to the creator's manuscript (and performed in "authentic" versions). The critic Walter Benjamin encapsulated the idea in one memorable sentence: "The supreme reality of art," he wrote, "is the isolated, self-contained work."

This idea, that musical meaning resides uniquely in music objects, comes with a few corollaries. The first is that musical performance plays no part in the creative process, being only the medium through which the isolated, self-contained work has to pass in order to reach its goal, the listener. We read little in music literature about performance other than in the limited sense of following the composer's notations and realizing them in sound, and we are left to conclude that the more transparent the medium the better.

There are even those who believe that, since each performance is at best only an imperfect and approximate representation of the work itself, it follows that music's inner meanings can never be properly yielded up in performance. They can be discovered only by those who can read and study the score, like Johannes Brahms, who once refused an invitation to attend a performance of Mozart's *Don Giovanni*, saying he would sooner stay home and read it. What

Mozart, the supreme practical musician, would have had to say about that one can only imagine. We note the corollary to *that* idea, which is seriously held by many musical scholars and even musicians: only those who can read a score have access to the inner meanings of music. One wonders, in that case, why we should bother performing musical works at all, when we could just sit at home, like Brahms, and read them as if they were novels.

As for performers, we hear little about them either, at least not as creators of musical meaning. It seems that they can clarify or obscure a work, present it adequately or not, but they have nothing to contribute to it; its meaning has been completely determined before a performer ever lays eyes on the score. Composers, especially in the twentieth century, have often railed against the "liberties" taken by performers who dare to interpose themselves, their personalities and their ideas between composer and listener. Igor Stravinsky (1947) was especially vehement in this regard, condemning "interpretation" in terms that seem as much moral as purely aesthetic and demanding from the performer a rigidly objective approach called by him "execution," which he characterized as "the strict putting into effect of an explicit will that contains nothing beyond what it specifically commands." The eagerness with which many composers took up electronic composition from the 1950s onward was motivated at least in part by the prospect of dispensing altogether with the services of those troublesome fellows.

The second corollary is that a musical performance is thought of as a one-way system of communication, running from composer to individual listener through the medium of the performer. This is perhaps just another way of stating the first, though it brings a change of emphasis, for it suggests that the listener's task is simply to contemplate the work, to try to understand it and to respond to it, but that he or she has nothing to contribute to its meaning. That is the composer's business.

It suggests also that music is an individual matter, that composing, performing and listening take place in a social vacuum; the presence of other listeners is at best an irrelevance and at worst an interference in the individual's contemplation of the musical work as it is presented by the performers. A flowchart of communication during a performance might show arrows pointing from composer to performers and a multitude of arrows pointing from performers to as many listeners as are present; but what it will not show is any arrow pointing in the reverse direction, indicating feedback from listener to performers and certainly not to composer (who in any case is probably dead and so cannot possibly receive any feedback). Nor would it show any that ran from listener to listener; no interaction is assumed there.

A third corollary is that no performance can possibly be better than the work that is being performed. The quality of the work sets an upper limit to the possible quality of the performance, so an inferior work of music cannot possibly give rise to a good performance. We all know from experience that that is nonsense; performers are always capable of turning trivial material into great performances. Adelina Patti could reduce an audience to tears singing "Home Sweet Home," while the wealth of meanings that Billie Holiday was able to create with her performances of the tritest of popular songs is both legendary and documented on record. Were it not so, then much of the culture of opera would collapse, for who would tolerate the musical and dramatic absurdities of *Lucia di Lammermoor*, for example, or of Gounod's *Faust* if it were not for the opportunities the old warhorses give singers to show off their powers?

But I should go further and shall argue later that it is not just great performers who are capable of endowing such material with meaning and beauty. However trivial and banal the work may be that is the basis of the performance, meaning and beauty are created whenever any performer approaches it with love and with all the skill and care that he or she can bring to it. And of course it is also possible to give a beautiful performance without any work of music at all being involved, as thousands of improvising musicians have demonstrated.

A fourth corollary is that each musical work is autonomous, that is to say, it exists without necessary reference to any occasion, any ritual, or any particular set of religious, political, or social beliefs. It is there purely for what the philosopher Immanuel Kant called "disinterested contemplation" of its own inherent qualities. Even a work that started its life as integrally attached to a myth and to the ritual enactment of that myth, as, for example, did Bach's *Saint Matthew Passion*, which was intended as part of the Good Friday obsequies of the Lutheran Church, is today performed in concert halls as a work of art in its own right, whose qualities and whose meaning for a modern listener are supposed to depend solely on its qualities "as music" and have nothing to do with the beliefs that Bach believed he had embodied in it.

My musical friends scoff at me when I say I can hardly bear to listen to the piece, so powerfully and so cogently does it embody a myth that to me is profoundly antipathetic. "Don't bother about all that," they say, "just listen to the marvelous music." Marvelous music it is indeed, but marvelous for what? That is a question that seems never to be asked, let alone answered. Other musical cultures, including our own past, would find such attitudes curious; Bach himself, could he know about them, might well feel that his masterpiece was being trivialized.

Neither the idea that musical meaning resides uniquely in musical objects nor any of its corollaries bears much relation to music as it is actually practiced throughout the human race. Most of the world's musicians—and by that word I mean, here and throughout this book, not just professional musicians, not just those who make a living from singing or playing or composing, but anyone who sings or plays or composes—have no use for musical scores and do not treasure musical works but simply play and sing, drawing on remembered melodies and rhythms and on their own powers of invention within the strict order of tradition. There may not even be any fixed and stable musical work, so the performer creates as he or she performs while the listeners, should there be any apart from the performers, have an important and acknowledged creative role to play in the performance through the energy they feed (or fail to feed), selectively and with discrimination, back to the performers.

But even within a literate musical culture such as the Western classical tradition, the exclusive concentration on musical works and the relegation of the act of performance to subordinate status has resulted in a severe misunderstanding of what actually takes place during a performance. That misunderstanding has, as we shall see, had in turn its effect on the performance itself—on the experience, that is, of the performance, for both performers and listeners—an effect that I believe to have been more to impoverish than to enrich it. For *performance does not exist in order to present musical works, but rather, musical works exist in order to give performers something to perform.*

That being so, a musical performance is a much richer and more complex affair than is allowed by those who concentrate their attention exclusively on the musical work and on its effect on an individual listener. If we widen the circle of our attention to take in the entire set of relationships that constitutes a performance, we shall see that music's primary meanings are not individual at all but social. Those social meanings are not to be hived off into something called a "sociology" of music that is separate from the meaning of the sounds but are fundamental to an understanding of the activity that is called music.

The fundamental nature and meaning of music lie not in objects, not in musical works at all, but in action, in what people do. It is only by understanding what people do as they take part in a musical act that we can hope to understand its nature and the function it fulfills in human life. Whatever that function may be,

I am certain, first, that to take part in a music act is of central importance to our very humanness, as important as taking part in the act of speech, which it so resembles (but from which it also differs in important ways), and second, that everyone, every normally endowed human being, is born with the gift of music no less than with the gift of speech. If that is so, then our present-day concert life, whether "classical" or "popular," in which the "talented" few are empowered to produce music for the "untalented" majority, is based on a falsehood. It means that our powers of making music for ourselves have been hijacked and the majority of people robbed of the musicality that is theirs by right of birth, while a few stars, and their handlers, grow rich and famous through selling us what we have been led to believe we lack.

This book, then, is not so much about music as it is about people, about people as they play and sing, as they listen and compose, and even as they dance (for in many cultures if no one is dancing then no music is happening, so integral is dance to the musical act), and about the ways in which they—we—go about singing and playing and composing and listening. It is also about the reasons we feel the urge to do these things and why we feel good when we do them well. We could say that it is not so much about *music* as about people *musicking.*

So far as I know the word *musicking* does not appear in any English dictionary, but it is too useful a conceptual tool to lie unused. It is the present participle, or gerund, of the verb *to music.* This verb does have an obscure existence in some larger dictionaries, but its potential goes unexploited because when it does appear it is used to mean roughly the same as "to perform" or "to make music"—a meaning that is already well covered by those two words. I have larger ambitions for this neglected verb.

I have proposed this definition: *To music is to take part, in any capacity, in a musical performance, whether by performing, by listening, by rehearsing or practicing, by providing material for performance (what is called composing), or by dancing.* We might at times even extend its meaning to what the person is doing who takes the tickets at the door or the hefty men who shift the piano and the drums or the roadies who set up the instruments and carry out the sound checks or the cleaners who clean up after everyone else has gone. They, too, are all contributing to the nature of the event that is a musical performance.

It will become clear as we go along how useful this verb—and especially its gerund—is (the added *k* is not just a caprice but has historical antecedents), and I shall use it from now on as if it were the proper English language verb that I hope it will become.

I have to make two things clear. The first is that to pay attention in any way to a musical performance, including a recorded performance, even to Muzak in an elevator, is to music. The second is related but needs to be stated separately: the verb *to music* is not concerned with valuation. It is *de*scriptive, not *pre*scriptive. It covers all participation in a musical performance, whether it takes place actively or passively, whether we like the way it happens or whether we do not, whether we consider it interesting or boring, constructive or destructive, sympathetic or antipathetic. The word will remain useful only for so long as we keep our own value judgments clear of it. Value-laden uses that I have heard, such as "Everyone ought to music" or "You can't call listening to a Walkman musicking," distort its meaning, weaken its usefulness as an investigative tool, and plunge us back into futile arguments about what music or musicking is. Value judgments come later, if they come at all.

Apart from favoring the idea that music is first and foremost action, the word has other useful implications. In the first place, in making no distinction between what the performers are doing and what the rest of those present are doing, it reminds us that musicking (you see how easy it is to slip into using it) is an activity in which all those present are involved and for whose nature and quality, success or failure, everyone present bears some responsibility. It is not just a matter of composers, or even performers, actively doing something to, or for, passive listeners. Whatever it is we are doing, we are all doing it together—performers, listeners (should there be any apart from the performers), composer (should there be one apart from the performers), dancers, ticket collectors, piano movers, roadies, cleaners and all.

I am not, of course, so silly as to see no distinction between what the performers are doing and what the cleaners are doing; they are obviously doing different things, and when we want to distinguish between the two sets of activities we already have adequate words with which to do so. In using the verb *to music*, on the other hand, we are reminded that all these different activities add up to a single event, whose nature is affected by the ways in which all of them are carried out, and we have a tool by means of which we can begin to explore the meanings that the event as a whole is generating. We take into account not just what the performers are doing and certainly not just the piece that is being played or what the composer, should there be one, has done. We begin to see a musical performance as an encounter between human beings that takes place through the medium of sounds organized in specific ways. Like all human encounters, it takes place in a physical and a social setting, and those, too, have to be taken into account when we ask what meanings are being generated by a performance.

That being so, it is not enough to ask, *What is the nature or the meaning of this work of music?* To do so leaves us trapped in the assumptions of the modern Western concert tradition, and even within those limits, so narrow when one considers the whole field of human musicking, it will give answers that are at best partial and even contradictory. And of course, if there is no fixed and stable musical work, as is true of many cultures, then the question cannot even be asked. Using the concept of musicking as a human encounter, we can ask the wider and more interesting question: *What does it mean when this performance (of this work) takes place at this time, in this place, with these participants?* Or to put it more simply, we can ask of the performance, any performance anywhere and at any time, *What's really going on here?* It is at that point, and not before, that we can allow our value judgments full rein—if we wish to do so.

In framing that question, I have placed the words "of this work" in parentheses to remind us that there may not necessarily be a musical work but that when there is, then the nature of that work is part of the nature of the performance, and whatever meanings it may in itself possess are part of the meaning of the event—an important part but only a part. I do this in order to reassure those who fear that I am going to ignore the part that the nature of the work plays in the nature of the performance or even that I am going to deny its existence altogether. Of course not; those set sequences of sounds we call works, or pieces, of music form an important part of the musical economy of the modern world, from the Ninth Symphony of Beethoven to "Rudolph the Red Nosed Reindeer."

But they are not the whole of musicking and in fact are not even necessary for it to take place, as can be seen from the large number of human musical cultures in which there is no such thing as a musical work, in which there are only the activities of singing, playing, listening—and most probably, dancing.

Thus we see that the second question does not exclude the first but rather subsumes it, into a larger and more comprehensive question. In addition, if the definition of musicking I have offered takes in all the activities that affect the nature of that event which is a performance, then that must include preparing for it. That means that composing, practicing and rehearsing, performing, and listening are not separate processes but are all aspects of the one great human activity that is called musicking. And if the meaning of the work is part of the meaning of the event, then the opposition between "work" and "event" expressed by Carl Dahlhaus does not exist.

By expanding our questioning to the total performance we can escape from the assumptions of the Western concert tradition as it exists today, which continue to dominate the ways in which we think about music; and we can see that tradition, as it were from the outside, as a small and these days (it was not always so) tranquil (some might even say stagnant) lagoon of the great restless ocean of human musicking. We may see also that, when viewed from outside, it is less isolated from that great ocean than those who look only from inside may think and perhaps also that whatever vitality we can continue to find in it today is, as it always has been, produced by the quickening effect of the life-giving water of that great ocean.

Any theory of musicking, which is to say any attempt to explain its meaning and its function in human life, that cannot be used to account for all human musicking, no matter how strange, primitive or even antipathetic it may seem to our perceptions, is not worth the paper it is written on. It is not just a question of why the *Saint Matthew Passion* of J. S. Bach and the Ninth Symphony of Beethoven are great works—which they undoubtedly are, once we accept the premises on which they were composed. It is not even just a question of why people like to sing and to hear "Rudolph the Red Nosed Reindeer" or "Does Your Chewing Gum Lose Its Flavor on the Bedpost Over Night?" or why drunken ol' pals like to gather around the piano and sing bawdy songs together in rustic harmony. It must also explain why it is that taking part in a performance of the *Saint Matthew Passion* or the Ninth Symphony or "Rudolph the Red Nosed Reindeer" arouses in some a powerful and joyful emotional response while in others it induces only boredom and irritation.

But the theory must go further, and be able to explain why Indonesians enjoy taking part in performances of gamelan music, why the Ewe of Ghana like to play, sing and dance to Afro-Cuban popular music as well as the *adzida* dance, and why many, but by no means all, African Americans like to sing and to hear gospel songs. It must also be able to explain why so many white people go for African American blues, some of them even becoming successful and admired practitioners, why rap has become an important and influential way of musicking on both sides of the American color barrier, and how it is that reggae got big in Japan.

It must be able to explain, in fact, not just why members of one social and cultural group differ in their ways of musicking from members of another group but how it is that members of one culture can come to understand and to enjoy, and perhaps creatively misunderstand, the musicking of others. It must explain also how some musical cultures become dominant, sometimes across the whole world, while others remain confined to the social group within which they originated. And of course it must be able to explain why people like to music at all.

There is no dearth of studies, many of them brilliant and illuminating, of musicking's social function, that show the ways in which musicking functions as a social and even a political act. Nor do we lack for studies of the dazzling series of interactions, fusions, crossovers and hybridizations that are taking place today between musicians the world over. In this book there is no way in which I could possibly deal with all these phenomena even if I had the knowledge and experience to do so. Nor am I trying to give an account of what musicking has become in our time or of how it got to be that way; I shall have little to say about recording, broadcasting or what has become known as the music industry.

My purpose here is different—at the same time more modest and more ambitious. It is to propose a framework for understanding all musicking as a human activity, to understand not just *how* but *why* taking part in a musical performance acts in such complex ways on our existence as individual, social and political beings. What I am proposing is a way of interpreting what we already know about human musicking, a *theory of musicking* if you like.

Who needs a theory of musicking? Surely, such a thing is too academic to be of either interest or use to ordinary people?

Everyone, whether aware of it or not, has what we can loosely call a theory of musicking, which is to say, an idea of what musicking is, of what it is not, and of the part it plays in our lives. As long as that theory remains unconscious and unthought about, it not only controls people and their musical activities, limiting and circumscribing their capabilities, but also renders them vulnerable to manipulation by those who have an interest in doing so for purposes of power, status, or profit. It is one of my aims in this book to make readers more aware of the nature of their "theories" of musicking and thus be in a better position to take control of their musical lives. A theory of musicking, like the act itself, is not just an affair for intellectuals and "cultured" people but an important component of our understanding of ourselves and of our relationships with other people and the other creatures with which we share our planet. It is a political matter in the widest sense.

If everyone is born musical, then everyone's musical experience is valid. That being so, a theory of musicking, if it is to have any basis in real life, must stand up to being tested against the musical experience of every human being, no matter who he or she may be or how the experience was acquired. For that reason

I shall write in terms that are as closely tied to concrete musical experience as I can make them, and I ask in turn that every reader test everything that I have to say against his or her own experience.

So if the meaning of music lies not just in musical works but in the totality of a musical performance, where do we start to look for insights that will unite the work and the event and allow us to understand it?

The answer I propose is this. The act of musicking establishes in the place where it is happening a set of relationships, and it is in those relationships that the meaning of the act lies. They are to be found not only between those organized sounds which are conventionally thought of as being the stuff of musical meaning but also between the people who are taking part, in whatever capacity, in the performance; and they model, or stand as metaphor for, ideal relationships as the participants in the performance imagine them to be: relationships between person and person, between individual and society, between humanity and the natural world and even perhaps the supernatural world. These are important matters, perhaps the most important in human life, and how we learn about them through musicking is what this book is about.

As we shall see, the relationships of a musical performance are enormously complex, too complex, ultimately, to be expressed in words. But that does not mean that they are too complex for our minds to encompass. The act of musicking, in its totality, itself provides us with a language by means of which we can come to understand and articulate those relationships and through them to understand the relationships of our lives.

That being so, we need to look as well as listen around us during a performance, to find out what relationships are being generated in the performance space. To show the kind of questions we might ask of a performance, I shall be examining carefully an important event in Western musical culture, namely, a symphony concert as it might take place in a concert hall anywhere in the industrialized world. I am going to try to deconstruct it, which is to say, to decipher the signals that are everywhere being given and received, and to learn the meaning not just of the musical works that are being played there but of the total event that is a symphony concert. I have three reasons for taking this event as an example.

The first is that it is likely to be an experience that most readers of this book will have undergone at least once, and you will therefore be able to check my observations against your own.

The second is that a symphony concert is a very sacred event in Western culture, sacred in the sense that its nature is assumed to be given and not open to question. I know of few writings that so much as attempt to describe it in detail, let alone question its nature. I shall therefore, and I cheerfully admit the fact, find it a pleasurable task to examine it and to ask the forbidden question, *What's really going on here?*

I have to pause here, remembering the response of some critics to my earlier attempts to deconstruct a symphony concert. It seems that I need to explain that to do this is not to anathematize or in any way pass judgment on either the event or the works that are played during its course. To try to tease out the complex texture of meanings that a musical performance—any musical performance, anywhere, at any time—generates is *not* reductive or destructive. Quite the contrary; it is to enrich our experience of it. And after all, at the very least, the ceremonies of the concert hall must, to the unbiased eye and ear, appear as strange as did those rituals of Africa and America which the first European travelers encountered and just as much in need of accounting for. As I said earlier, it is an ethnic music like any other.

Nor, in asking of a symphony concert the question *What's really going on here?* am I suggesting, as some critics seem to think, that what is going on is something sinister, something "dehumanizing" or "authoritarian" (two words recently used in this regard by a critic). It is no part of my purpose to characterize symphonic or indeed any other performance in such crude reductive terms. I simply want to show the kind of questions that we might ask of it, and I cannot help wondering if those who show such resistance to asking questions of a symphony concert might not themselves be a little afraid that they will uncover meanings they would rather not know about.

Another caution that I have learned from my critics is that I am not making the logically quite unjustified jump from deconstructing a symphony concert to characterizing (and apparently, by implication condemning) classical music as a whole. As those critics have kindly pointed out to me, there are other kinds of events within the classical music culture: chamber music concerts and opera, for example, as well as solo recitals and record evenings; and while they clearly possess many features and meanings in common with symphony concerts, they also differ from them, as can be seen from the fact that their respective audiences, while they overlap, are not identical. To those critics I can only repeat that my intention is not to give a blanket characterization of classical music but simply to show the kinds of questions one can ask of a particular kind of musical performance.

All that said, I have to confess that there is a third, more personal reason for taking the symphony concert as example. It arises from my own continuing ambivalent relationship with the Western classical tradition, with the works that are assumed to comprise it, on the one hand, and, on the other, with the institutions through and in which it is disseminated, performed, and listened to today. Despite the fact that I grew up half a world away from its heartland, I was brought up in that tradition. I learned to play its piano repertory, I listened to records and went whenever opportunities presented themselves (very rarely up to my twenties) to attend performances of the symphonic and chamber repertory; opera did not come my way until I was too old to succumb to its charms. I still get a feeling in the seat of my pants every four minutes or so when I play my magnificent new CDs of wonderful old warhorses like the *Emperor* Concerto or the Rachmaninov Second Concerto, when I used to have to get up and turn over the twelve-inch, 78-rpm record.

It is my heritage and I cannot escape it, and I understand well the continuing urge on the part of performers, as well as of musicologists, theorists, and historians, to explore those repertories and learn their secrets. I myself continue to love playing such piano works of that tradition as are within the reach of my modest technique and take every opportunity to do so, both in public and in private.

But from the moment when I began to attend large-scale public concerts, I have never felt at ease in that environment. Loving to hear and to play the works but feeling uncomfortable during the events at which they are presented has produced a deep ambivalence that has not lessened over the years. Now, in my seventy-first year, I have come nearer to pinning down what is wrong. I do not feel at ease with the social relationships of concert halls. I can say that they do not correspond with my ideal of human relationships. For me there is a dissonance between the meanings—the relationships—that are generated by the works that are being performed and those that are generated by the performance events.

I have no desire to impose these feelings on anyone who might read this book, and I hope that by acknowledging them right at the start I can avoid even the appearance of wanting to do so. I strongly suspect, however, that I am not alone in feeling as I do; if so it may be that my exploration of my ambivalent feelings might be of use to others besides myself, including perhaps, mutatis mutandis, those who feel at ease in the concert hall environment but not in certain other musical environments—a jazz or rock concert, for example.

In any case, I do not regret the dissonance, which has over the years been a rich source of feelings and ideas, nor do I feel any resentment against the culture for what is apparently my own self-exclusion from it. It is this continuing ambivalent fascination with the culture of the concert hall that leads me to frame

Neville Braithwaite in London, c. 1980.
Photographer unknown.

a question—a subquestion, if you like, of that which I framed a few pages back: *What does it mean to take part in a performance of Western concert music in a concert hall in these closing years of the twentieth century?* I shall be devoting a substantial part of this book to an exploration of this question.

There must be a link between the nature of symphonic works and the nature of the events at which they are played. That link is flexible, as we can see from the fact that most of them were first played to different audiences and under different conditions from those under which they are played and listened to today; but it must, on the other hand, exist, since only works from a certain specific repertory are displayed at modern symphony concerts. One does not hear "Rudolph the Red Nosed Reindeer" there, or "Black and Tan Fantasy" or "Please Please Me"; they are heard in other places, under other conditions. That leads me to a difficult question, which I hesitate to ask but must ask: *Is there something built into the nature of the works of that repertory that makes performing and listening to them under any circumstances go counter to the way I believe human relationships should be?* Do they sing a siren song? Or to put it in newspaper headline terms, *Was even Mozart wrong?* Many people whose views I respect would answer those questions with a firm yes.

Nevertheless, I feel the case for the prosecution has yet to be proved. The various counsels for the defense, in schools, music colleges, and universities, may be overemphatic in defense of their client and overeager to claim privilege for it, but we are not in a court of law, and an adversarial stance does little good for either side. Besides, as long as they center their argument on music objects and ignore the music act, centering on music rather than musicking, the cycles and epicycles keep spinning merrily, and the question can never be answered. Maybe that is why they do it. In any case, that is one reason the question must be asked in a new way.

It seems obvious to me that performing these works under certain circumstances generates different meanings from performing them under others. For instance, when I, an amateur pianist using material provided by Josef Haydn under the name of Piano Sonata in E-flat and charging nothing for admission, play the piano to a couple hundred of my fellow citizens of the little Catalan town where I live, people from a variety of occupations that could be called working class as well as middle class, most of whom I know and who know me, at least by sight in the street, I think we are together making different meanings from those made when a famous virtuoso pianist performs from that same material to an anonymous paying audience in a big concert hall. At the same time, since we are both playing from the same material, making more or less the same sounds in the same relationships, there must also be a residue of meanings that are common to both performances. Maybe if we knew completely where the differences and the similarities lay, we should understand completely the nature of musical performance. In any case the first step is taken when we ask the question *What's really going on here?*

But do not expect from me any final or definite answer to that or any other questions that I may raise in this book. In the first place, I do not think there *are* final and definite answers to any of the really important questions in human life; there are only useful and useless answers—answers, that is, that lead in the direction of enrichment of experience or of its impoverishment. And in the second place, it is one of the assumptions on which I write that you, the reader, are perfectly capable of coming up with your own answers, just as you are capable of doing your own musicking. All I hope to do is help frame the questions, for if questions are not framed properly, then there is not much hope of coming up with right, or useful, answers.

There will be times when, in order to make a question clear, I have to propose an answer—and I do have answers of my own, many of them strongly felt, that I do not intend even to try to keep under wraps. But as I used to say to my students, I don't care whether or not you agree with my answers, so long as you see that there are questions to be asked.

The majority of this book, then, will be taken up with a description, as fine-grained as I can make it, of the ceremony in Symphony Hall and of the human and sonic relationships (and the relationships between those relationships) that are being generated there. I wish it were possible to run at the same time, in counterpoint as it were, a parallel text that explains why I believe it is important to understand the nature of these relationships. But (and it is one of the themes of this book) while the gestures of musicking can articulate many kinds of relationship at once, words, on the other hand, can deal with things only one at a time, and there is no way they can be made to bear the cargo of multiple simultaneous meanings that the gestures of musicking can do. I shall therefore be obliged to pause from time to time in my description and to interpolate three interludes, which I hope will give a more theoretical understanding of my search for the meaning of a musical performance. They are only loosely attached to the description that precedes them, and readers who wish to continue following the description uninterrupted could leave them to one side and come back to them later.

So let us begin by looking and listening carefully around us at this symphony concert. It does not matter too much where it is taking place, for it is an international ceremony; that is part of its nature. It might be taking place in New York, London, Tokyo, Wellington, Taipei, Minsk, Reykjavik, or Denton, Texas. Wherever the Western scientific-industrial culture has gone and wherever a middle class has grown prosperous from its activities, there we shall find symphony concerts taking place and concert halls built to house them.

BIBLIOGRAPHY

Dahlhaus, Carl. 1983. *Foundations of Music History.* Translated by J. B. Robinson. Cambridge: Cambridge University Press.

Stravinsky, Igor. 1947. *Poetics of Music.* Cambridge, MA: Harvard University Press.

From *Musicking*

A Solitary Flute Player

(1998)

(I have to come clean about the following chapter and say that it is here against the advice of some of my friends who have read my manuscript. They caution me that the solitary flute player appears too much like a totalized representation of the "other" that has beset European thinking about the rest of the human race—one thinks of Edward Said's eloquent protest [1978]—and that he appears to be an idealized and interchangeable creature who has no real existence as a human being.

I bow my head to such comments and have to concede that they may well be right. But I am very fond of that flute player; to me he is no created "other" at all but a friend and respected fellow musician. If he appears in my account of him to resemble that "other," the fault lies not with him but with the imperfection of my representation. If we listen carefully and sympathetically, we shall find that he does have something to tell us about the nature of the musical act and about its social nature, and I cannot allow myself in all conscience to silence him.)

A herdsman is playing his flute as he guards his flock in the African night. Alone with his flock, playing his flute with no one but himself and his animals to hear him, what relationships could he possibly be conjuring up, when there is no one within earshot to whom he might be relating? Surely, there is nothing there but his own solitariness?

But let us look and listen more carefully.

First let us look at the flute he is playing. Technologically speaking, it is a simple affair, made of cane or hollowed-out wood, with maybe three or four burned-in finger holes, capable of producing only a few notes. It is end-blown, and the flutist holds it angled slightly to one side as he blows against a notch in the end of the tube. He may well have made it himself, or perhaps someone in his village, known to him, made it for him. Although one of a type, it is a unique individual because every piece of wood or cane is unique, and it has been fashioned into an instrument by following the natural shape of the material. Its individuality may be emphasized by carved, painted, or burned decoration. Like all wind instruments it is animated into life by the breath from his body, the most intimate relationship one can have with a musical instrument. He may well feel it to be a valued friend and colleague rather than an inanimate sounding object.

Simple it may be in its construction, but primitive it is not. Rather, it is the outcome of constant experimentation through generations, of choosing the right kind of reed tube, cutting it at the right time of year, burning out the finger holes in exactly the right places, and cutting the notch to exactly the right size and shape. Nor is the technique of playing it primitive. We should remember that the elaborate key and valve mechanisms of Western orchestral instruments are there to make them easier, not harder, to play. The simplest instruments are often the hardest to play, needing constant care if the sound produced is to be properly under control.

So between the herdsman and his flute there already exists a complex set of relationships before he ever uses it to make a note of music. Like all musical instruments it does not exist in a social vacuum, but in its design and making, its tuning and sound quality, it is a product of the society of which he is a member. It represents in tangible form the society's technology and its ways of thinking and especially its concepts of human relationships.

This flute, in fact, is as much a product of technology and of technological attitudes and choices as is the Western orchestral instrument that goes by the same name, and it is as finely adapted as the Western instrument to the musical and social purposes for which it is intended. Neither flute is a better or worse instrument than the other; each is the result of different technological and musical choices. This flute is made from what lies to hand, keeping as nearly as possible the natural forms of the wood, with a minimum of shaping. The technology that made it is not crude or underdeveloped but is the result of an attitude toward the natural materials that is the opposite of what is generally found in industrial societies. The one likes to disturb the natural materials as little as possible, while the other prefers to transform them.

What is the flutist playing on his instrument? We hear an endless stream of tones, many of them sounding out of tune to our ears, accustomed to Western tempered pitches, and the number of notes the instrument makes available may seem pitifully small. It will produce, of course, only one note at a time, but the player does not seem to feel the need for more because he has learned to hear in the melody and its intricate rhythms enough complexity to satisfy him. It is a different style of complexity from that which musicians in Western industrial societies enjoy, which tends to involve a large number of tones sounding together.

If we listen carefully, we shall hear delicate inflections in the sounds. By changing his embouchure, by varying the power of his stream of breath, and by small movements of his fingers over the finger holes he can change the pitch of the notes, sliding and smearing them as well as changing their quality in subtle ways. We shall hear also curious inflections on the beginnings and ends of tones and phrases, as well as hesitations, hiccups, arabesques, and graces, gestures that are full of meaning in his musical universe if not in ours.

The rhythms he is playing are enormously complex, too complex at times for us to follow, but we may be sure that they are always being measured against a rhythm that is going on in his head, which he may even be tapping out with one foot as he plays. That rhythm is almost certainly not a procession of equally spaced pulses such as Western musicians use to guide their performance but may be a repeated twelve-beat cycle of 2, 3, 2, 2, 3 beats, against which he pits the rhythms of his melodies, for he needs a clash of rhythms as much as a Western musician needs harmony and its tensions.

We cannot, of course, know what he is thinking as he plays or what he imagines he is doing. He may be inventing a new melody, trying it over and over until its sound relationships are coherent and satisfying to his ears, and also perhaps practicing getting his fingers around a tricky passage, for musicians the world over like to set themselves technical problems. It is quite likely that the shape of the melody he is making will be owed at least in part to the way his fingers move over the holes, and that its phrase lengths and its rise and fall will come at least in part from the way he breathes.

He may be playing a familiar melody, one composed perhaps by someone in his village or by someone whose name is forgotten in time. Or he may just be letting his fingers and his breath wander over the instrument, thinking with his muscles, guided by impulses whose nature neither he nor we can fathom, forming melodic and rhythmic shapes that appear and disappear, as ephemeral as smoke.

But whatever it is he is playing, it will not be invented from nothing. No human being ever invents anything from nothing but is guided always in his invention by the assumptions, the practices and the customs of the society in which he or she lives—in other words, by its *style.* A person may rebel against the assumptions of the society, but the style of the rebellion will inevitably continue to reflect those assumptions. It is inescapable. And since style is concerned with the way in which things relate, it is itself a metaphor for the way in which the society conceives of the pattern that connects.

So the way in which the flutist brings the sounds into relation with one another as he plays is in a general way determined by the set of ideal relationships that he holds in common with the other members of his social group, whether village, tribe or nation. How he plays will be within the limits of the style he has received from the group, and in playing in that style he will be exploring, affirming, and celebrating the concepts of relationship of the group, as well as his own relationships within it and with it.

Relationships, of course, can be of many kinds. They range from love to hate, from dominance to submission, from dependence to independence, from respect to contempt, and any of those in complex combinations. The flute player might play entirely in the received manner, perhaps a received melody played entirely in the manner in which he received it. Or he may use the melody as a basis for innovation in small ways, ornamenting it with graces and variations, or he might reconstruct it completely but always within the limits of the style. Or he may launch out in new ways, which, by violating the norms of the style, will criticize it while still relating to it.

Thus, his relationship to the style, which is the community's way of doing things, may be respectful, submissive and dependent or disrespectful, dominant and independent—or more probably, it will be somewhere on a scale between one extreme and the other, perhaps even both at the same time, for human beings are rarely clearly one thing or another but are contradictory and paradoxical. Through musicking, humans have the power to explore and articulate those contradictions and paradoxes simultaneously, in ways that verbal language cannot.

The flutist's way of playing, then, will contain within itself ways of mediating change with continuity, stability with instability, stagnation with renovation, in complex relationships with one another. So it is that he will be articulating not just his solitariness but his relationships with the entire population of his conceptual world. Although physically alone, he is surrounded as he plays by all the beings that inhabit that world, not only humans, animals and plants but also the land itself, the ancestors and the yet unborn, and even the illimitable population of the spirit world; and through the sounds he makes he is exploring, affirming and celebrating the ways in which he relates to them.

Because his world is not a literate one, his relationship with the ancestors and the past of his people is mediated not through written records, with their fixity, their appearance of objectivity and the distance they place between the reader and the subject of the writings, but through the recollections of older people, through stories and myths that have been told to him, and through dances, songs and melodies passed down to him by elders. Some of the songs of the ancestors have to be carefully learned and repeated exactly if their force is to be retained, but others are flexible and can be changed, added to and varied. And of course, because there is no fixed written record of those songs any more than there is of the people's history, and because people's memories are fallible, even those songs that are supposed to be fixed are subject to constant drift. They can even be forgotten, leaving space for new creation. The ancestors, though respected and frequently summoned for consultation through musicking and dancing, are not allowed to dominate the present generation, which has to be free to work out its own destiny.

Nor does the flutist live in an isolated, self-contained society. Those of us who live in modern nation-states isolated from one another by passports, quotas and visas may welcome, for every good reason, the kind of international musical "dangerous crossroads" described by George Lipsitz (1994); but in fact, over the course of human history there have been few human groups, however small and remote, that have not been in regular contact with members of other groups, that have not interacted and spoken one another's language. The self-inflicted isolation of modern nation-states, each within its own frontiers, is a recent phenomenon; Benedict Anderson (1983), in his analysis of nationalisms, calls them "cultural artefacts of a particular kind" and dates them from no earlier than the late eighteenth century.

The flutist's world is much less circumscribed than members of literate societies like to think, and because it is not literate, it is flexible. He is free to absorb directly from those outsiders with whom he is in constant contact what he needs to make his own life, and his musicking, more interesting and satisfying to himself. He may even master the styles of one or more of his neighbors, becoming musically multilingual (after all, bi- or even multilingualism is the rule rather than the exception among most of the human race), as long as he can find in those styles musical relationships with which he can empathize.

All human beings are about as complex as one another. We speak verbal languages that linguists assure us are all about as complex as one another, and we all live within networks of relationships that are as complex as one another, even if they are not all complex in the same ways. The networks of functional relationships in the industrialized world may well appear brutally simple, if not crude, to those who are accustomed to the subtle and complex patterns of a village society. Wherever they have gone, human beings have used the language of sonic gesture to articulate those relationships, to model the pattern that connects, and have developed that language in ways that can deal with the pattern's complexity. Even to play a homemade flute, alone, with no one but oneself to hear, is an act that can define relationships that are just as complex as that of taking part with two thousand others in a symphony concert.

As he plays, the flutist is bringing into existence a sonic space that is defined by the limit of audibility of his flute in each direction, upward toward the skies as well as outward on the earth around him, into which he is projecting himself. It is his own sonic territory, in which his ideas of relationships are valid. And because how we relate is who we are, he is in effect saying, to himself and to anyone who may be listening, *Here I am, and this is who I am.* Who that "I" is, is complex and even multiple, endlessly developing and unfolding, as are the sonic relationships that the lone herdsman, with no one but himself to hear, is creating in the night.

BIBLIOGRAPHY

Anderson, Benedict. 1983. *Imagined Communities: Reflections on the Origin and Spread of Nationalism.* London: Verso and NLB.

Lipsitz, George. 1994. *Dangerous Crossroads: Popular Music, Postmodernism and the Politics of Place.* London: Verso.

Said, Edward. 1978. *Orientalism.* London: Routledge and Kegan Paul.

Interview by Robert Christgau

(2000)

Christopher Small is one of the surprisingly small number of classically identified commentators to suggest any kind of parity between popular music and the operatic-symphonic tradition. In England he was preceded by composer-academic Wilfrid Mellers (*Twilight of the Gods* and *Music in a New Found Land*) and critic Henry Pleasants (*The Agony of Modern Music* and *Serious Music and All That Jazz*). In America he was followed by Susan McClary, who eventually won a MacArthur Fellowship for championing what is called the new musicology, an endeavor influenced by Small's first book, *Music, Society, Education*, which explored many of the ideas she'd been thinking through in the early eighties. Small has also been a close long-distance associate of radical American ethnomusicologist Charles Keil, whose *Urban Blues* was the first book of rock criticism ever published.

Never what you'd call an academic powerhouse, Small published only one book while he was still teaching at the Ealing College of Higher Education in London. The other two—1987's *Music of the Common Tongue*, an utterly original history of African American music, and 1998's *Musicking*, an analysis of an imaginary symphonic performance that climaxes with the highly unorthodox speculation that the root subject of music isn't time, as is so often held, but relatedness—appeared after he'd retired with his companion, Jamaican-born music and dance educator Neville Braithwaite, to Sitges, Spain, a beach town outside Barcelona. There we undertook this conversation in July. I wanted to talk to Small because

I sensed that, although he and I shared many ideas and attitudes, there were ways in which my feelings about such matters as the autonomy of the aesthetic had become more conventional than his. Since I have no classical training whatsoever and regard myself as a populist radical in artistic philosophy, I thought this anomaly worth airing out. In addition, I just wanted to talk music with the man—because few have thought more deeply or unpretentiously about music than Christopher Small.

Robert Christgau is a senior editor at the *Village Voice*. His latest book is *Christgau's Consumer Guide: Albums of the 90s* (Griffin). His previous book, *Grown Up All Wrong* (Harvard University Press), is now available in paperback, and his first book, *Any Old Way You Choose It* (Cooper Square Press), has just been reprinted.

RC: You were born in New Zealand in 1927. Where in New Zealand?

CS: Town called Palmerston North.

RC: What did your parents do for a living?

CS: My father was a dentist, and my mother was an ex-schoolteacher. They were both keen on music. My father was quite a good pianist. My sister Rosemary and I, she's older than I am, both became sort of good child pianists, you know—lots of mistakes but lots of expression—and he rather gave up and I'm always sorry about that, looking back. I remember him singing and playing sort of hearty songs.

RC: And was your mother musical?

CS: My mother came from a musical family, yes. My grandfather used to conduct a choral society in Wellington in the 1890s. I have a presentation baton that his choir gave him, made of oak, weighing half a ton. They were giants in those days.

RC: Was Palmerston in rural New Zealand, or was it an urban center?

CS: It was about ninety miles north of Wellington. For the time it was quite a big town.

RC: But that's still pretty isolated.

CS: No, it was a dump. We all hated it. It was a boring town by any standard. People think New Zealand is boring, which it is not and never was to my mind. But Palmerston North was a boring town. It had no real sort of social-cultural life. And it was very snobby, sort of nouveau riche snobbish. And we all hated it. But my father had settled there and made his practice there, so . . .

RC: Your undergraduate studies were in the sciences?

CS: My parents wanted me to be a doctor.

RC: What was your major?

CS: What happened was I started in a medical course. And it was the year all the soldiers came back from the Second World War and I couldn't get into the medical school because they were all given preference and quite rightly so. So I switched to a science degree, thinking that I would enter the medical school by the back door. I majored in zoology. By the time I finished the degree in 1948 I decided I didn't want to be a doctor anyway.

RC: And then you went on to study music?

CS: They had just established a new department of music in Victoria University in Wellington for, I suppose, the first professionally trained composer, a man called Douglas Lilburn. He had studied in England with Vaughan Williams, and he was the first New Zealander really to come back with a professional composing technique. The music department consisted of one lecture hall over the chemistry labs; it always stank of hydrogen sulfide. It doubled as a recital room. They put a standard lamp in there at night. One office, a record player, and a piano, and that was it.

RC: You got a bachelor of music. What does that mean in American terms? Is that like a master's?

CS: It really doesn't figure particularly with anything. It was fairly unspecialized, and you could get it without being able to play a note on any instrument. No instrumental tuition was included at all. It was rather like an old-fashioned English degree. But the one thing they did expect and that is that every student compose—automatic, to get your degree; you had to compose a large work for chorus and orchestra. And I think that was a good thing. It made me take a fairly casual attitude toward composition. I never thought of myself as . . . well, after the initial time . . . I never thought of myself as a composer.

RC: Your teaching career?

CS: I taught in secondary schools in New Zealand.

RC: Starting when?

CS: '53. And at the same time I was working with a small company trying to establish itself making animated films. That was an interesting, not very good experience. But still, I learned a lot—composed for films of all sorts.

RC: You were teaching in a secondary school, which in the end proved to be more significant for your thinking.

CS: Yeah, I suppose so. But I was still very much tied up with the venture.

RC: You were teaching music?

CS: Well, no, but it was a small country school and I had to teach anything, practically—I was doing sixth-form chemistry, French, English . . .

RC: And then you moved to London?

CS: Yeah, well, I was invited to write the score of a ballet, which was going to be the first ballet ever totally created, choreographed, [and] designed by New Zealanders as far as we knew. So I did the score for that. And it was produced in Wellington. It was quite successful—amateur dancers; there was no professional theater in New Zealand at all at that time. It won me a scholarship, a New Zealand government scholarship to study composition, and I went to Priaulx Rainier in London. That was in 1961.

RC: But pretty soon there you also were teaching.

CS: No, no, not for a long time, because I had a two-year scholarship and then I knocked around for about two years, two, three years after that. I'm not quite sure what I did with myself. I suppose looking back I was assimilating a whole other thing. I worked for a publisher for a while.

RC: As an editor?

CS: Well, editing and on the production side. And then finally I decided this wasn't my métier and I applied for a teaching job. And they wouldn't take me as anything but a rookie teacher so I had to go back to and take a rookie's job. Taught in a marvelous school in Wembley. And then I got a job in this teacher's college.

RC: And so you were teaching secondary school in those first four years. But this teacher's college was a little beyond that.

CS: And then I came back to London, to Ealing, where I was teaching at the undergraduate level. As I was doing for the rest of my teaching days.

RC: Ealing College of Higher Education. And you did that for about twenty years.

CS: Well, '71 to '86.

RC: And you were a music teacher solely at that time? When you were teaching from '64 to '68 were you a music teacher as well, primarily?

CS: Not quite. Primarily, not quite.

RC: And at the same time you got caught up in the avant-garde scene? Cornelius Cardew and . . .

CS: Yeah, I knew him slightly. Bernard Rands was the . . . I haven't heard from him in twenty years or more. I don't know where he is now. Last I heard of him, he was in Boston.

RC: Let me backtrack just a little bit. When you first got interested in music as a child, how would you describe what you were attracted to?

CS: Well, I loved playing the piano. Didn't like practicing [*chuckles*].

RC: Is there a child who does?

CS: I remember long before I ever had my first lesson I would sit at the piano and just pretend to be a virtuoso although I'd never heard of the word. And of course it was a musical environment and we were encouraged. My older brother played the fiddle.

RC: It seems unlikely to me that you were merely being dutiful or going along with the family flow.

CS: Oh no, not at all. I loved it. And they had whole sets of records, 78s of course, which they bought. I remember they had a set of the Beethoven Fifth Symphony, black label HMV Records proudly proclaiming the new electrical process. And we had a set of *The Gondoliers*, Gilbert and Sullivan; we had a set of the Schubert "B Flat Trio," various pieces like that, and all sorts of bits and pieces. God knows where all the records came from. Old popular songs. Dame Clara Butt's "Land of Hope and Glory."

RC: What I'm really driving at, although I probably shouldn't be revealing it, is whether it was the relationships and the secondary and tertiary relationships which you describe so vividly in your most recent book, or whether there was some more fundamental or—I don't know, that's not the right word—more purely sensual or . . . it's a very mysterious . . .

CS: It's a very mysterious thing, I . . .

RC: I know that. But you've thought about it a lot, so I'm asking you to unravel the mystery.

CS: I haven't really thought about it with regards to myself.

RC: Um, I thought perhaps you hadn't. That's one reason I wanted to ask [*laughs*].

CS: When I was a kid I had quite a lot of illness—when I was very young, four, five, six years old—and we had one of these big old-fashioned HMV gramophone consoles with Grand Rapids–style machine wood carving all over it. And they used to put this beside my bed, and I can still remember my bed covered with these records. God knows where these records came from. All sorts of comical records. There was a piece I remember which I thought the most beautiful piece in the world; it was called "Herd Girl's Dream." And I can still play it; it was by a trio. All this stuff I remember . . . someone singing, I don't who the hell it was, singing Negro spirituals.

RC: Yes I did the same thing. I mean, I'm younger than you by fifteen years, but I did have the same. My parents were not musical the way yours were, but they had a piano and both played piano a little bit and had records and I loved to listen to them.

CS: And then my brother who was eight years older, quite a lot older than I was, he went off to university and came back with some Duke Ellington and a whole lot of music by these British bands like Harry Roy and his Tiger Ragamuffins, who were trying to get jazz established in England in the thirties. They were much more serious musicians than they were given credit for. And my parents wouldn't let him play them on the big gramophone.

RC: The records in my house were all popular records—*South Pacific* and Bing Crosby singing "Swinging on a Star," and there was a Fats Waller record that I loved. It was different things that attracted me. But I loved music. I loved to sing although I never wanted to play the piano. I never learned to play an instrument; I've tried a couple of times as an adult. I didn't have the time to practice.

CS: I never knew what was classical and what wasn't. It was nothing of that at all. But jazz apparently was not allowed in the house. I remember my brother Larry bought himself a little portable record player. He brought his records up to his room, and I used to listen to them up there. My parents relented after a while. I still remember he had "The Blue Room," Duke Ellington.

RC: There's one more general thing I'd like to ask: how you would describe your political orientation and history, which is clear enough but never exactly explicit or programmatic in your books.

CS: Well, I was always inclined toward the left.

RC: Your family is not? Your family is liberal?

CS: Yeah, sort of, I suppose.

RC: But you were inclined toward the left?

CS: Yes.

RC: And this is true even in the forties?

CS: Oh yes, very much so. Well of course, in those days, New Zealand was a very left-wing country. The 1935 Labour government introduced the first comprehensive social security system in the world, and we took all this for granted. And when the British elected the Labour government after the Second World War in 1945, it all seemed a sort of natural continuity. We were very naive, of course. And this is why when I encountered the horror of Thatcherism, I was horrified perhaps even more than most people because it just seemed as if, suddenly, at a stroke, she was able to completely destroy everything that had been carefully built.

RC: It's been terrifying for all of us.

CS: I remember that in my primary school days, our teachers—we had a map of Spain up on the wall, and we were following the course of the civil war, and my teacher shouting, "If there's a God in heaven why isn't he stopping this?" And we knew something about Hitler and the Jews and all that. I mean, teachers today would be sacked if they carried on the way ours did.

RC: Right.

CS: I mean, we just took it for granted. The whole orientation was like that.

RC: So that's your initial orientation, but there's clearly some time—I don't know when, after you leave New Zealand, perhaps, or earlier—when you move further left than that?

CS: I don't know, it doesn't seem like it.

RC: You think you have exactly the same—look, I don't want to argue with you, I'm asking because you're the one that knows.

CS: Mutatis mutandis, of course, but I don't feel any different politically than I did.

RC: Well, can you label yourself with any comfort whatsoever?

CS: It's very difficult.

RC: I'm sure.

CS: Some sort of liberal socialist, I suppose. But I wouldn't like to, um, pin a label [on] myself at this point. Socialism has become such a dirty word.

RC: Well, that's all right, it's not a dirty word with me. I'm quite stalwart about using it unpejoratively in my prose. I come from at best a centrist background myself, and a nonprofessional background, so it's a little different for me. But in any case—I mean, I would say, all the references to Ivan Illich in the first book, and the analysis of the evolution of African American music, references to the Society of the Spectacle, to me, place you in some sort of anarchist tradition, I would—infer. But as I say, you're never explicit about it, and maybe that's wrong.

CS: Yeah, there was a time when I thought of myself as an anarchist, that's true.

RC: But no longer?

CS: I don't know anymore.

RC: When was the time?

CS: Not so long ago, actually.

RC: Till when?

CS: It still strikes a chord. But there's so much science and pseudoscience produced that I don't know where I stand anymore.

RC: Explain to me what you mean by that.

CS: About evolution . . .

RC: You've lost me, and I think that's because you know about things I don't know much about. So try to explain.

CS: The whole issue of sociobiology, for example. I try to tell myself that I don't believe a word of it. Nevertheless, it's unsettling.

RC: Which would suggest to you that the anarchist model isn't altogether appropriate to what human beings actually are.

CS: Yes, I don't see that we can actually do it, lovely idea though it is.

RC: Can you place when you began to feel that way? Because it makes a difference in terms of your work.

CS: Yeah, I think it's in the last few years.

RC: Since *Musicking*?

CS: Oh, no, no, because *Musicking*'s only a couple of years ago.

RC: I know, but then it was written before then, so I assume it was done by '96 or so, right?

CS: Yeah, it was done, '97.

RC: So you would say sometime in the nineties.

CS: Sometime in the nineties I would say, yeah. And of course the other thing, as I said, is the speed and the ease with which all this was able to be undone. This whole triumph of this . . . a term I like is totalitarian capitalism. It just appalls me, and sometimes I think, "Thank God I'm on my way out," because I hate to think what the next decade is going to be like.

RC: I must say I don't feel that way. I think it's conceivable we've bottomed out. I mean, I have some hope. Okay, I'm very glad I asked you that, because it's not altogether clear in your work.

CS: No, I didn't even ever try to voice political opinions—explicitly political opinions.

RC: I wouldn't say that.

CS: [*chuckles*]

RC: I would call many of the opinions in your books explicitly political.

CS: Well, okay.

RC: Now I want to move on to explicating your ideas about music, and the first question I would like to ask is a question that you ask at the beginning of *Musicking* but didn't answer in a way that I fully understood what you thought, put it that way. You say, "How do musical cultures become dominant?" You said that was one of the questions you were going to address. And I didn't feel that the question was addressed.

CS: Did I say that?

RC: I'm afraid you did. I'm not gonna try and hold you to it if you feel you didn't answer it and don't really know yourself; I have no problem with that. To me, it's a very interesting question and one I'd be curious to know your thoughts on. Apparently you feel that it's pretty complex as well.

CS: Yes, it is. I certainly know that I didn't answer it, even if I did pose it. And it's something that I've been thinking about, the whole business of the relationship between music and power and who has the power to say what and who has the power inside a musical ensemble as well as in relation to . . .

RC: The reason it seems to me like a complex question is that there are two fairly obvious but not especially consistent answers, one of which would be that the Western classical tradition has spread in the way you say it's spread—I don't think it's spread quite as much as you think it has, but nevertheless it has—because it mirrors the patterns of industrial capitalism as industrial capitalism spreads. It could be said that those values have been imposed by the power of the West, which is where the music originates. But the odd thing is that the same thing can be said about the other tradition you write about, which is, in many respects, as you say many times in many different ways, a rather different tradition. And people would say that that the popularity of the African American tradition, which is also very widespread, is an imposition of capital, an imposition of American power specifically. And I'm not sure either of those things is true. I'm not convinced either is true.

CS: I'm not so sure if I mean—maybe I said it—about the word "imposed."

RC: That's my word and not yours. You said, "How do musical cultures become dominant?" I'm saying, these are the commonplace answers, and the word "impose" is used in those commonplace answers.

CS: I'm not sure it can—I'm not good at thinking on my feet. It can't do it unless to some extent it reflects something of the way people think reality is structured. And that can be imposed.

RC: Yes, that's right.

CS: That can be imposed—just think of the way over twenty years people have accepted the destruction of their lives, thinking that this is all for the good. People can be . . .

RC: Brainwashed.

CS: Brainwashed, persuaded against their own interests.

RC: But on the other hand?

CS: But on the other hand, no.

RC: Is there another hand? I thought there was going to be. Well, let me give you another hand and ask what you think of it. Is it possible that people are not entirely brainwashed and respond in a relatively autonomous and felt way to specific organizations of sound, and that some of them, perhaps, have more easily assimilated—to avoid the word universal—usefulness than others?

CS: Yeah, I would go with that, yeah. That's something like what I was trying to say at the end of *Music of the Common Tongue*. There's obviously a push-pull between dominance and resistance, which is both expressed and structured by musical action and activity.

RC: Okay, let me jump a little bit to deal with the classical tradition, which is the main subject of *Musicking*. You're very critical of the classical music audience, I would say.

CS: I didn't mean to be.

RC: Is that true?

CS: That's true.

RC: It isn't how it reads.

CS: I meant to simply look at it as objectively as I could. I had no intention—reviews have said this, about how I tear it apart, and I didn't really mean to.

RC: It may be true that you didn't mean to. Do you think it's conceivable that you did anyway? I believe you didn't mean to. If you say so, I believe you.

CS: My intention was to say, Now look—let's have a look at what's really going on here.

RC: Perhaps your intention was to subject them to the same sort of scrutiny to which they regularly subject their Other, and they didn't like it one little bit.

CS: Well, I was trying to turn as nearly as I could a sort of ethnographic eye on them.

RC: Right! And they found it very insulting.

CS: You see, I found right from the start, right back in *Music, Society, Education*, I got this response: Oh, you're trying to destroy Beethoven. Well, I said, I'd look fucking silly if I tried [*laughter*]. No, really, I never—the new edition of *Music of the Common Tongue*, they allowed me to write a new preface. And could I just read you a little bit of it?

> Somehow I seem to have given the impression that I think of African American and European classical music as being entirely separate streams, and that like Mowgli's four-legged friends I make a clear-cut distinction which somehow

carries a moral or ethical load: African American good, European classical bad. Further (and in spite of what I thought was an explicit denial), I was maintaining that the former was in a state of perfect health while the latter was degenerate, its "ossification," as one critic put it, "contrived by a threatened if not willfully malign Establishment." It is true that I devoted a chapter to the "Decline of a Music." I see no reason today to modify my opinion on that; the decline has become if anything even more obvious in the ten years since I first remarked on it. But I did not welcome the news then, if news it was, and I do not rejoice over it now. I certainly did not and do not subscribe to any mind-boggling conspiracy theories to explain it, and I continue to listen to performances in the European classical tradition no less than in any other tradition and to play as many of the works of that tradition as my modest piano technique permits.

RC: Okay, fine, but the question I wanted to ask is actually to proceed from that, to go a little further. That is, there are certainly many members of the industrial ruling class and their lackeys—which some would say include you and I—that have no interest whatsoever in classical music. Would you be able to make ethnographic distinctions between these two subgroups?

CS: No, I've puzzled about this myself.

RC: Well, I'm glad to hear it.

CS: There's obviously nothing automatic or one-to-one about this. There's some people seem to have different ways of structuring reality that either converge or diverge. I don't know an answer to that.

RC: Well, do you think that it might be possible that for all their failings, for all their inability to understand exactly the ritual in which they're engaged, put it that way—and I don't know what I think the answer to this question is either—that their mere active involvement in any realm of the aesthetic would render them more humane? Is it possible? In other words, given among ruling-class people with oppressive tendencies there are many different kind of oppressors. Do you think it's possible that in general the bell curve would fall over a little further towards humanity for this group of people? Or do you think there's really no way to know?

CS: I think there's no way to know. You've got the famous example, of course, of Nazi concentration camp doctors getting together to play Beethoven string quartets after days of doing unspeakable things.

RC: This is obviously true. Nevertheless, I wonder, even though I'm essentially hostile to that world in a way that I don't believe you are. It's not my world, I don't come out of it, I've been taking shit from those people for my entire life, and I've really got no use for them. Nevertheless, I wonder, whether they aren't better people in some way.

CS: I don't really think so. I don't think one can make that kind of a statement. After all, there are too many bastards even among the great musicians of the tradition.

RC: Indeed, of the African American tradition too. Being a great artist doesn't make you a nice person; it makes you a not-nice person.

CS: It's a question of how you learn to structure reality and how the structuring of reality reflects back on the musicking. There's a constant to and fro. That's true with all forms of music, not just classical. And something like that I was trying to say with the whole question of the audience, when I talk about the members of the audience being solitary and all that sort of stuff, I was not attempting to criticize or to be nasty about it. It just seems to me . . .

RC: . . . a fact that ought to be noted.

CS: Yeah. And I think there's a case for representing these things in a neutral way if you can do so. I have rows with Charlie Keil over this. As I said in *Musicking*, if you're going to use the word "musicking," use it in an ethically neutral way, whether you like the way it's being done or you don't. Charlie won't have this. He talks about, this is musicking and that's not musicking.

RC: Well, Charlie's a convinced anarchist.

CS: I love Charlie dearly, he's a wonderful man.

RC: I do too.

CS: I've been on the advisory board of his MUSE [Musicians United for Superior Education] outfit.

RC: I give them money myself. It's a wonderful idea. And of course that wonderful phrase of his, "paideia con salsa" [spicy education] sums up something we all believe in, I think.

CS: But I think that I really have tried not to take a critical stance about this. I make my observations, and take a point of view if you like, but I have no desire to demolish it. And to be honest, I don't much like the classical music culture at present. I don't feel comfortable in a concert hall.

RC: Well, you said that, which is one reason people might think you're hostile to it.

CS: Yeah, but that doesn't mean I'm hostile. And I also say I make no complaint about this fact, that maybe I'm just cutting myself off from something.

Maybe you'll find it's a distinction that's impossible to hold. But I'm not trying to attack it.

RC: I don't know whether it's possible. I honestly don't know. As I say, I do have a hostility toward it—that's a fact that ought to be noted. I have it. But it is a sufficiently insular and smug world—its smugness is certainly the most infuriating to me, and most infuriating thing about it. And that means that anybody who looks at it with anything less than a completely . . .

CS: Approving eye

RC: . . . approving eye is liable to be seen as a dastardly interloper.

CS: There's another thing here too, and that is, it seems to me that the classical musical scene in the United States is far more elitist, far more . . .

RC: Oh, that's probably right.

CS: Far more smug, far more enclosed in itself than in Europe. And also—I think I said it somewhere in *Music, Society, Education*, I certainly meant to—that you get this hostility. I remember now that the editor took it out . . .

RC: [*laughs*]

CS: Because I was talking about scenes in like *Night at the Opera*.

RC: Oh some of that's there. I just saw that a couple of weeks ago.

CS: There's real hostility there, in a way that you wouldn't get, at least not so vehemently.

RC: Did you ever read Lawrence Levine's book about Shakespeare and opera in the nineteenth century?

CS: Yes, yes, *Highbrow/Lowbrow*. And I think there is more of a dichotomy. And I got this way, way back, even when I was a twenty-year-old science student. I used to read *Etude* magazine, which I now realize was the sort of bastion of those attitudes. I used to think the sun shone out of it, you know, simply because it was high culture and I was ignorant, a backwoods boy. But there is in America this much, much stronger hostility between popular and classical musical audiences and musical societies than there is Europe. I don't hear much of the kind of hostility that you just voiced, for example. People will say, Oh well.

RC: Well, my hostility is unusual.

CS: No, it's not, not in my generation.

RC: It's unusual among people who could be called intellectuals, put it that way.

CS: I get it all over the place. Charlie for one, Charlie hates it. I mean, Charlie's Charlie. But all sorts of other people I run up against, there is a great degree of hostility. And I'm not surprised. When I first went teaching in an American university, I was amazed at some of the attitudes, when I actually ran up against them in this college department, the smugness and the absolute resistance.

RC: Well, it's a little less pronounced these days.

CS: That was only five years ago.

RC: Really?

CS: [*chuckles*]

RC: Well, I'm told it's gotten better. I wanted to ask one more question about the symphony orchestra, and it's mainly because it's something that's always interested me. In addition to the story that the symphony tells and the social relationships embodied by its performance, do you think there's anything about the symphony orchestra in terms of its literal sound, its physical sound, or of the kind of precision and uniformality and discipline it requires of its members in addition to the structural and relationship questions?

CS: Oh, I think that in the social structure . . .

RC: Beyond the social structure, I'm asking if there's a strictly aural, A-U-R-A-L, element to it.

CS: Oh yes, there is, the precision of pitch that's demanded, for one.

RC: And the notion of sweetness, too, perhaps?

CS: The notion of sweetness, the eschewing of attack sounds, the search after smooth attack, the general need for total precision, and also uniformity of sound between the players. Each string player makes approximately the same kind of sound.

RC: And how would you say that signifies, just in a few words, if you can?

CS: Well, to put it crudely . . .

RC: Yes, please.

CS: I would say it's industrial discipline.

RC: Thank you. Now I'd like to ask another question. Somewhere, I think it's early in *Common Tongue*, you say that the African American tradition fulfills a need in white culture. You said there's a felt need in white culture for this. Can you try to describe, briefly and crudely, what that need would be?

CS: Well, I thought I did.

RC: I think it would be useful for our purposes for you to sum it up.

CS: Well, it's the acting out of visions of communality, intimacy. Will that do?

RC: Yes it will, but let me ask you this . . .

CS: Again, of course, one has to remember that these aren't necessarily absolute directions, that a lot of people will run a mile from a small town because of its communality and intimacy.

RC: Okay.

CS: And these values are not necessarily absolute goods, but they're just things that people seem to feel are missing from their lives.

RC: In one of the places that you talk about this, you say, in addition to the rhythmic and sonic—can you talk a little about how that attraction works? In other words, is there an intrinsic attraction to the rhythmic sophistication—that's not the best word—complexity, development, of African-based music that draws people on its own?

CS: I can only speculate.

RC: Of course.

CS: It has to do with a kind of multilayered concept of what reality is. To get access to structures of feeling that are more than monovocal or univocal—the way notes get approached suggests a more sidelong look at things, a more . . . not subtle, because . . .

RC: Oblique—well, that goes without saying.

CS: Yes, oblique would help too, yes.

RC: Playful?

CS: And playful.

RC: Well, I'm going from sidelong to oblique and trying to see where it takes us.

CS: Of course, Mozart can be very playful.

RC: I was going to say that devotees of the European tradition would say that none of these things are absent. But what you're saying is that the rhythm conveys it in a different way. I mean, I thought the sidelong—not knowing the classical tradition I can't be certain that this is right—was getting at something that I thought was quite brilliant, frankly. It's obviously a deep conundrum.

CS: And there's another thing: that we're talking about classical music as it is today, which isn't necessarily . . . take Mozart, as Mozart was in Mozart's day, or even as Mahler was—we know that, for instance, violinists in Mahler's day [*hums, first in strict meter and then more supplely*]

RC: But even so, in that period there were also people being drawn to African-derived music, and there must have been a reason for that. While there was clearly more rhythmic freedom—I mean, you establish that, you're not the only one to talk about it, and there's no doubt that you're right. "Ossified" is not such a terrible word for what's happened to this tradition; I'm sorry, it's just not. But even a hundred years ago, when that tradition hadn't yet ossified, that attraction still existed, and there must have been something else going on. Or was there? Was it purely that it was an imaginative realm in which you can imagine freedom that you incorrectly attributed to this dark-skinned Other and that was all it was about? Or was it sonic as well?

CS: Yes, it must have been built into the sound as well. All this is built into the sound.

RC: And there's something about the way rhythm works, or African rhythm works. Maybe it's about the foregrounding of rhythm. That's a relatively obvious concept that's only occurred to me recently. It's more where it goes in the music and that in itself . . .

CS: But however you slice it, it is there in the actual sound. In Susan McClary's new book, *Conventional Wisdom*, she talks about this a lot, with blues and so on, and also with Vivaldi and with Mozart—the sound quality. She's quite subtle in some of her analysis of the way in which the sound quality figures in the overall social structure that's being articulated. Yes, sure. And again with Mozart, one of the things that upsets whatever certainties I have had is that in recent years I've been practicing the Mozart sonatas, and the further I get into them the less sure I am of anything [*chuckles*] except that they're wonderful and that they keep on beckoning, "Come on, come on, come on, come on," and you never quite get them right. There are rhythmic subtleties which are not notated at all, and I don't think that when you listen to most performances; I think there's a whole culture in Mozart which is being lost in the public classical tradition.

RC: Did you ever listen to Wynton Marsalis's classical trumpet records?

CS: Not very carefully, no.

RC: I don't think very much of Marsalis in many respects, but it is amazing how both the sound and the flow of that music, even to a completely untrained person like myself, to me it seems completely obvious that this is a different sensibility that's attacking these works, just because he's grown up in a tradition in which a different notion of rhythm is taken for granted. So I'm sure you're right.

CS: On the other hand of course we also have to remember that African Americans have been strongly attracted to classical music, and if that hadn't been so we wouldn't have the music—Handy, for example—and the sort of bands and the orchestras that used to play, you know?

RC: I would like to move on to another issue. It seems to me that there are two what seem to me to be contradictory tendencies in your work. In the "Solitary Flute Player" chapter, which is clearly where you go furthest with this way of doing things, to use that as an example, there is a tendency to make all music, all musicking, equal. But there are other places if you look for them, which I then did, where you're not averse to making value judgments. You say, talking about Beethoven—you used "power," "authority," "complexity," "subtlety." I was struck that two of them were really about power, though, power and authority. Or you talk about Aretha Franklin's version of "Amazing Grace" on the live gospel album, and you talk about these being titanic creations. So on the one hand we have a solitary flute player; on the other hand we still have you making value judgments all over the place.

CS: Two questions: one, what do you think I think of Aretha Franklin doing "Amazing Grace"?

RC: I think you think it's great, and you probably think it's as great as Beethoven in its own way or something like that.

CS: I wouldn't . . .

RC: Something like that. I understand you're not making that comparison, but still you have enormous respect for it.

CS: Yes, of course I'm not averse to making value judgments, in their place. But the flute player, I've got into a lot of trouble over that flute player.

RC: I know you have, and I'm basically in favor of it. But I do see it being contradictory.

CS: I don't see why. I can't see any reason why it's contradictory.

RC: Oh, that's interesting to me. Let me see if I can articulate that. Because that isn't some special flute player; that's any flute player. It seems to me you did more than say, he has a right to do this, it's valid in its own terms, [and] it requires creativity in its own way. You don't say that. You say the kinds of creativity it achieves are commensurate with the kinds of creativity in any Western music, either the black or the classical tradition, and while I personally—I mean, I make value judgments for a living, so I'm sensitive on this issue. I don't claim they're absolute, but I don't believe they're arbitrary either. I believe it's possible to talk meaningfully about what's better and what's worse.

CS: Of course.

RC: You really don't see?

CS: I don't think I ever said that the flute player is as good as Beethoven or anything of that kind. What I did try to say is that all ways of musicking are approximately as complex as each other. And that the—I wasn't setting that poor little guy up against Beethoven, or even Aretha Franklin, or even anybody. I was just saying, "Look, this guy may be in his level of skills anything from elementary to . . ."

RC: Let's make him fiftieth percentile, just for the sake of argument.

CS: All I was trying to say, maybe I didn't say it, was that there is, no matter how primitive it may appear to ears attuned to other kinds of complexity, there is sufficient complexity in any way of musicking to keep anybody happy and also of course to make it possible if not necessary to say he's doing it well, or he's not, or he's doing it absolutely fantastically. He may be playing the same damn flute. This is what I was driving at, not trying to abolish all ideas of—I mean, I've said it repeatedly, within any division there are people who do things well and people who don't do them quite as well.

RC: The Ben Ratliff piece about you in *Lingua Franca* said sometimes that he thought your ideas worked best for self-contained musical subcultures.

CS: Yeah, I was quite cross about that.

RC: Well, but . . .

CS: I suppose I'm not cross . . .

RC: I don't know if you know exactly what it is I do. I'm best known for something called the Consumer Guide. I listen to music fourteen hours a day. I come from my own sensibility, which is, basically, Chuck Berry at the very heart and then it exfoliates everywhere. And I rate records—every year I find eighty to one hundred A or A minus records, and there's a small cabal of people all over the world who make it their business to buy every goddamn one of them. Basically what I believe and what my own listening experience suggests is that it's possible to spend your entire life listening to nothing but great music in a fairly wide variety of traditions. So that's where I'm coming at this from. I guess it seems to me that this is a big advantage of industrial capitalism. It's industrial capitalism that lets us do this, and I think this is positive. And so the reason I'm asking about value judgments is that I'm very attached to this way of hearing music. Do you think that people are just as well off being in one tradition?

CS: I've thought about this, and I don't really know the answer. I can just kick the thing around a bit. In some ways I can answer yes. After all, that's where most people have been.

RC: But you wouldn't do it yourself.

CS: No, I have my central tradition.

RC: You certainly would feel impoverished if you didn't have much of what you've learned.

CS: I, yeah—less and less, I listen to music less and less. I play an awful lot. But I listen less.

RC: We're going to get to that.

CS: I think it's obviously a good idea if you at least have an idea that there's something else beside your tradition going on. I mean, this is what's the matter with the classical tradition, maybe. But I don't know what the, not to say natural, the traditional position would be; probably in most cultures there's a great deal of overlap between traditions, and they're not usually behind one. It's a bit like languages. Bilingualism, if not more, is the common condition of most people in the world today.

RC: Yeah, but I'm suggesting that something like tourism—and I use that term knowing it's a pejorative term—has its own particular rewards, and they're rewards that are actually appropriate to the technological and political conditions under which we live. And I wish more people could live, and without being too stringent an economist, would like to believe it's possible they will live.

CS: It's certainly nice to be able to listen to all these other musics [*slowly*]. But I don't find it necessary.

RC: Because?

CS: Wait a minute, I'm not sure what I even mean there. I'm sorry, I'm not a good interviewee because I'm not . . .

RC: You've said this, but you've been fine.

CS: I'm not good at . . .

RC: Thinking on your feet.

CS: . . . and I forget things. Where were we, tourism? It's okay, and it's obviously—not obviously, but I suppose it's a good thing to be aware of other musical traditions. But there's so many different human conditions. I can think of so many ways in which it would be a good idea and so many ways in which it wouldn't be a good idea. I can't feel any answer to that question.

RC: Well, I think that's because—let me move on to another contradiction that I hope to explore with you. In *Musicking*, you're very explicit very early about saying that musicking includes listening. And late in the book, when you're talking about examples of musicking, in one series you quite explicitly and I'm sure self-consciously include a girl walking with a Walkman in the list. And I think that a part of you really believes this, but that there's another part of you that definitely valorizes performance over listening. That the ability to play an instrument—at any level, I'm not saying you're being elitist about any of that stuff, or the willingness to sing or even dance, to you seems more important, a better kind of musicking—at some level, even though you say, no, I shouldn't be making these judgments, there's something in you that tugs you in the other direction. You think that there's some truth to that?

CS: I do . . . yeah, I wouldn't be so coy about it, actually.

RC: Okay.

CS: I would like to say that everybody should be in a position to be some kind of performer. The person who is not able to perform at all is in some way deprived. Yeah, I would be quite explicit about that. That said, that doesn't mean we all need to be virtuosos.

RC: That's not an issue. It's quite clear that you don't feel that. That's no contradiction. I don't feel any inconsistency at all in your assertions about that.

CS: I'd actually put it this way, that performing seems to me, whether it's musical performing, seems to me a built-in human need of some kind. You know, all the usual sentimental things come to mind, mother singing to children. Down here, I saw an English dad singing to his little girl yesterday, horribly out of tune, and I thought, great. Performing is a dimension of human experience, which I do think would be lacking if one doesn't do it in some way or other.

RC: I take this seriously because I do not play any instrument, and as I've told you, I've tried a few times, basically because I thought it would be good for my writing, and I just never had the time to practice even enough to get there. I just didn't have those hours a week it would have taken for me to get the manual dexterity in my thirties, which is when I gave it a try. But I guess more than that I feel as if I am very actively engaged in music without performing at all. And I also—you know, I told you about these people who collect records, I think that most of them are just like me, only they don't write as well as I do. These are not collectors—there are collectors and they serve a function, but I think they're a little silly. These are people who love music. And I get these thank-you notes: You turned me on to Brian Eno's *Another Green World*, *The Indestructible Beat of Soweto*, whatever, something I never would have thought of, jazz, this that the other thing. And, I'm sorry, I believe those people are very passionate about music, and that music has great meaning in their lives, whether or not they play any instrument or not, and the ones I've met don't.

CS: That's fine. Certainly better with it than without it. But I still think that in the sort of fullness of musical experience, whatever it is, however basic, a little performing is necessary for a full understanding of the musical process. Performing and listening. And now I may be retreating at the moment, I'm getting old, from new listening experiences. Sometimes somebody comes along and kicks me out of it and I think, Great, thank you. And here the situation in Sitges—[people] aren't particularly interested in new music, and I tend to go around and around in the same thing. Yeah, it would be nice to have new listening experiences, which is something I am maybe deprived of. Maybe the answer is . . .

RC: For me, many people think that—I'm fifty-eight, and I love hip-hop, and

I always have. And certainly there are people who think I'm faking it, or—but I'm not. My only problem is that I don't have enough time to listen to the music I know I love, which is another question I hope we have time for. But I guess what I would say, is that that full understanding of the musical process? I don't believe that anybody is ever going to have a full understanding of the musical process. I mean, you know that too. Let's put it this way. There's no doubt in my mind that there are excellent performers that understand the musical process much more poorly than I do. I'm sorry—I have no doubt about that. I've met them. And they're narrow people. Classical musicians especially, in America are not people whose company I generally enjoy.

CS: Well, okay, I don't know what to say except that that's how I . . . Whatever your interests in the musical process, it's enhanced.

RC: That's the reason I tried to learn to play piano. And I just finally decided that I had to do other things with those hours.

CS: Well, maybe that wasn't the right performance for you, I don't know. Because I think anybody . . .

RC: Well, I'll sing to my daughter, but I do it very poorly, and I don't do it anymore. My wife is much better than I am. And my daughter much prefers having my wife sing [*chuckles*].

CS: I suppose in a sense I'm talking about an ideal social situation, where there's so many social factors against performing, including the uncharitable excellence of so many performers.

RC: The thing is, if pop is your basic orientation, that's simply not—clearly, there are many people in pop who have exactly the same attitude, but it's nowhere near as hegemonic as it is in classical music. And it's obviously true that many people of small technical accomplishment have done great things in popular music.

CS: Yeah, well, that's not what I'm talking about. I still think that the act of performing in whatever situation, however modest it is, is an integral part, an essential part of the musical experience. And one is poorer without it.

RC: Can I move on to a related matter? You still with me, or are you beginning to get tired? I'd like to talk about recording. Actually, you're quite explicit about it toward the end of *Music of the Common Tongue*, that it's a distortion of what you regard as . . . do you think distortion's too strong a word?

CS: Yes.

RC: Well, what word would you use?

CS: Well, it alters it.

RC: It's an alteration, there's no doubt, and for many of the reasons that you cite. I mean, for the very fact that there's no physical presence, there's no audience, it has to be intensified in other ways or it doesn't have the same sort of impact. But do you think it's possible that that alteration can be a completely viable alternative, or do you think it's always inferior?

CS: No, I'm not . . .

RC: I'm asking. That's not a leading question.

CS: No, no, I don't think so. It's a different kind of experience.

RC: Because one of the most interesting developments in the past fifteen years has been in hip-hop, where what's happened is that people who related to music almost entirely through records and were active listeners then began to take those records and create music out of them.

CS: Yeah, sure. And if you take the whole art of deejaying and all that stuff, it's taking something and giving another twist to the wheel. I'm with you completely. But just the act of sitting and listening to records is a different kind of experience, not necessarily inferior.

RC: Certainly it's a different kind of experience, and it has its drawbacks, which . . .

CS: . . . are obvious.

RC: . . . which are obvious. But also in some cases—I keep hearing these stories of young African American men, middle-class men, who have absconded with their fathers' record collections. I mean, there's twenty thousand, one hundred thousand, there's some vast number of people who are right now trying to figure out what they can do with this panoply of sound to make it some other kind of sound.

CS: Then that's becoming something different; then you're taking an active . . .

RC: I understand that it's different. But it begins with the listening, and then it moves on. All right, I have two more questions that I'd like to ask and then we can close it down. You say that musicking is one of the qualities that make us human. Do you think it's possible to be human without musicking?

CS: I think probably not—I'm hedging, but not as a fully developed human being. I mean there are so many people in whose lives music plays no part whatsoever, and I don't know what sort of people they might be. I've never met any.

RC: Oh, I have met some. But I'm like you—basically, almost everybody I know cares intensely about music one way or another, and that includes people who are not involved in the music world at all. But I guess I'm always a little suspicious, even when it's my own kind, when somebody asserts, Well, we are the human beings, and those other people are not. Do you understand why I would feel that way?

CS: Yeah, I wonder how it can be possible to go completely . . . It must be something got turned off at the very early stage of development. It does seem more and more that, speaking evolutionarily, that protomusic and protodance precede protospeech, by probably a long way, and how the music gets dropped out and this whole, what Gerald Edelman calls "neural Darwinism," neuropathways not taken up at an early age atrophy, and the same would happen with speech and occasionally does happen with speech, and how it's possible to become a functioning human being is something I find very hard to understand, but apparently it is. And I don't know the reason.

RC: I'm sure we can think of people we like more than Mrs. Thatcher.

CS: I don't know what happens, but I just feel that there must be some developmental lack there somewhere. I don't know if anyone's done any investigation into it. I do know people who claim to be tone deaf, for example.

RC: Yes, I know, there's a nice peroration on the term "tone deaf"; it's in *Musicking*, isn't it? I was very pleased to see it.

CS: But I just wonder what is the real status of this unmusicality. I don't know.

RC: Let me ask you just one more question to get back toward the beginning. How do you feel about the effectiveness of your work? It seems, as near as I can tell, it's people like me who respond most enthusiastically, that in the world that you come out of and which you still say you regard as your central musical orientation, do you feel you've had the effect you would like to have?

CS: I mean, if I go back to *Music, Society, Education*. I walked into John Calder's office in 1975 with a proposal that I should I do a translation of Henri Pousseur's book *Fragments théoriques sur la musique expérimentale*, which I'd done a large chunk of, because he had the reputation of being a very interesting maverick publisher who'd published Ives and the Cage books and those sort of things. I had no intention of writing a book when I walked in there. So after a while he said, "Well, when are you going to write your book?" Well, you know, every academic thinks he's got a book him. I said, "Well, I can have a go." He said, "You give me an outline, and we'll give you a contract," and that's how it happened. And to this day I am amazed at the book's reception, because I never imagined that anyone would take the slightest interest in it. I expected it just to sink from sight; it never occurred to me that there was anything out of the ordinary about it. When it got its first review, which was from Wilfrid Mellers in the *Guardian*, I couldn't believe it. And then suddenly there was a whole torrent of reviews all over the place. And then Calder started chivying me for another book. (Calder and I by the way have parted on not good terms at all. He owes me I should think somewhere near $2,000, which I shall never see.) But I never really thought of it as having a mission at all. I'm very gratified that people—one of the things that did happen with *Music, Society, Education*, I got a lot of letters from undergrads and schoolkids, several letters from schoolkids, and students in music college, and I suppose it began to occur to me that I did have a point of view. But I have really not much contact with the kind of effect it's had. Susan [McClary] keeps telling me about people picking it up and so on. It's interesting that for all we're saying about the States, that it's in the States that it's had the best reception. In Britain it's, "Oh, Chris Small, good knockabout stuff but not to be taken seriously."

RC: She knows more about that than I would, actually.

CS: Well, she's closer to it. Okay, I taught a semester in the University of North Texas, in '95, postgraduate students, and that seemed to provoke responses. I'm told that "musicking" has become a term that's just been bandied around, but I get the feeling that people are not understanding what I really mean by it.

RC: But basically you feel that you've done far more . . .

CS: I suppose I think that I've done more than I ever expected. I never thought of myself particularly of having a mission. You know, I had these ideas, all of which have come out of my experience of performing.

RC: And teaching.

CS: And teaching.

RC: The first book especially, I felt—that's the reason I asked you about your teaching experience, because it was a teacher's book, I thought. The last two chapters are about teaching.

CS: Oh yes, sure, that. I thought you meant that I had actually been teaching this.

RC: No, that it was a book that reflected your experiences teaching. And a lot of the feeling in it, it seemed to me, had to do with a feeling for young people.

CS: Oh, yes.

RC: Which I could see from the way Neville [Braithwaite] was talking, I wondered whether that was a feeling that had been developed in concert with him in some way.

CS: Well, a little bit, but we hadn't known each other that long. But yes, I tremendously admire his work, the work that he was doing. Yeah, it did obviously grow out of my teaching. I mean, I wrote that first book; it just came out like

MÚSICA per PIANO
MUSIC for PIANO

amb/with Christopher Small
accompanyat per/assisted by
Neville Braithwaite, tenor

Saló d'Or, Palau Maricel, Sitges

Diumenge/Sunday
10 juliol/10 July 1994
a/at 8 de la tarda/pm

Entrada lliure, amb col.lecta destinada a l'assistència dels malalts de SIDA de l':
Admission free, with collection for those suffering from AIDS in the:
HOSPITAL-RESIDENCIA SANT CAMIL

Col.labora: Juventuts Musicals i el Ajuntament de Sitges

PROGRAMA

Edvard Grieg	Mariposa Op 43 No 1
John Field	Nocturno No 5 en si bemol
Edvard Grieg	Procesión nupcial noruega Op 19
W. A. Mozart	Sonata en si bemol K570 Allegro Adagio Allegretto
Canciones:	
Edvard Grieg	I love thee (*Te quiero*)
Christopher Small	The lovely lass of Inverness (*La hermosa doncella de Inverness*)
Albert Malotte	The Lord's Prayer (*El Padrenuestro*)
Scott Joplin	Maple Leaf rag (*Rag del club Maple Leaf*)
Scott Joplin	Solace (*Consuelo*) — Serenata mejicana
Zez Confrey	Kitten on the keys (*Gatito en el teclado*)
	DESCANSO 10 min
Frédéric Chopin	Vals en do sostenido menor Op 64 No 2
Frédéric Chopin	Vals brillante en la menor Op 34 No 2
Frédéric Chopin	Vals en mi menor Op posth.
Canciones:	
Carl Böhm	Calm as the night (*Tranquillo como la noche*)
Trad. jamaicana	Liza
Trad. jamaicana	Linstead market (*El mercado de Linstead*)
Enrique Granados	Danzas españolas No 5: Andaluza No 2: Oriental No 6: Rondalla aragonesa
Louis Gottschalk	The banjo — Grotesque fantasie

Program of a recital given in Sitges, 1994. Photograph by Robert Walser.

that, you know. The second one, of course, took me six years, just about killed me. And the third one took a long time too. I ditched at least half. But [ad]mission—I've always been absolutely amazed at the attention these things have got. Keep saying, if I'm so famous why aren't I rich? [*laughs*].

RC: You have to be more famous than that to be rich. It's another level of fame.

CS: I don't know if that answers the question.

RC: It seems to me that I see two different strands here. One is that because you speak for progress and right reason, there are Susan McClarys today in the world of academic musicology, for instance, whereas there were no such creatures [before]. But it's conceivable that would have happened without you. You think alike, Charlie Keil thinks alike, and people have come upon these ideas separately, because there's this contradiction inherent in the way music is produced and people see it. On the other hand it looks to me as if the establishment, especially the one that is the central focus of this book, is completely impregnable.

CS: I don't see myself making much impression on them.

RC: I know, I don't either. And I just wondered, does that make you feel bad? I guess it doesn't. You just say, oh well.

CS: Well, of course it does. Not bad personally but to think that they aren't in touch with that situation. The only thing that's gonna make the bottom fall out of that world is lack of money. They stop getting supported, then—and I don't see that happening. I mean, the amount of money going through Covent Garden Opera House goes up and up and up and up and up and up and up and up. All these scandals erupt, and they just get their wrists slapped and they still get more money. Most of it goes straight into the pockets of these superstars.

RC: I find all that stuff really odious, needless to say—utterly odious, infuriating. If you feel up to it we can continue to chat for a few minutes. We come at things from opposite directions. I began by believing that the social was the source of meaning in the music I cared about, and after thirty-five years of listening to music in a critical, serious way, I'm not comfortable with that idea. I feel as if there's something else there. It's like a person who gets older and really starts to believe in God. Maybe that's what it is [*laughter*]. I grew up religious and became an atheist and I'm not quite as much an atheist as I used to be. I've come to be uncomfortable with the notion that there's no such thing as the realm of the purely aesthetic, which is an argument you make somewhere in *Musicking*. And the reason I asked these questions about sound and about whether the rhythm itself attracted people is because I can't believe that there's nothing intrinsic about those sounds, that has some sort of a physiological—or whatever it is, maybe it's spiritual, whatever that means—attraction, I'm not comfortable anymore thinking it's all socially determined and about social relationships, which definitely is where I began. And that even goes for the concept of beauty itself, which I used to believe was completely relative. And I believe this is just a matter of listening to music for so long, I can't quite believe anymore—it just seems too crude and simplistic to say that isn't a factor, that this thing that people always talk about is sheer mystification. And I'd be interested to know—in this book, you also speak quite negatively of your own attraction to the way of musicking that's the center of all your life, and I felt you were too hard on yourself. I felt, No, it isn't just because you're a pensioner living a comfortable life in Sitges that you like Beethoven.

CS: I didn't mean to say that.

RC: But that you identify with those values that you believe and articulate. Another question, you say all these symphonies tell basically the same story. That's a very important thing to say, and it's a provocative thing to say. The people who live in that world need to be told that until they finally can't get it out of their heads. They have to hear it a hundred times and maybe eventually it will sink in, because at some level it's absolutely true. But they tell different stories, and some of these stories probably shade these facts differently than others. You say that yourself when you talk about the Tchaikovsky that you analyze at the end. And there's also, once again, that sonic—I mean, melody itself, for instance, seems to me, as a musical illiterate, exerts an attraction that I find difficult to believe is simply a matter of how one is trained to hear when one is young and all of those things. They must inflect it, but I can't believe that's the only explanation, the only factor. I've talked for a long time, how do you feel about that?

CS: Well, as far as the whole question of relationships is concerned, I go back to Gregory Bateson, Bateson in what he calls "The Question of the Epistemology of the Sacred," he's on the right track. I got and get enormous faith from Bateson. Relationships are not just social relationships in the narrow sense.

RC: No, it's formal relationships as well.

CS: It's also how we relate to ourselves, and to the cosmos if you like, putting it in the windiest possible terms. And this whole notion of the pattern which connects which I keep bringing in, that our notion of music seems to be of something being beautiful, is in relation to what we think is the pattern.

RC: Do you think that maybe some of that isn't socialized, though?

CS: Some of it isn't. I don't think there's any way around it, finding out which is which, than setting out to find out if there are any human universals in reactions to this. Of course it's very difficult anymore to do this, because practically the whole world has got in on the act. And of course my African player never was untouched by outside influences.

RC: Oh no, you're very good on those. I mean, you do it in *Music of the Common Tongue*, too, that the whole notion of the unspoiled culture you're properly dismissive of, I'm very glad to say.

CS: It's obviously strongly socialized. But how much of it is really inherent in our sense of relationships I don't know.

RC: So, in other words, you're saying, Yes, you do believe in beauty in some way.

CS: Yes, essentially.

RC: So do I.

CS: Well, of course.

RC: Well, for to me that wasn't so obvious. I know I believe in it now. I wouldn't have said that twenty-five years ago.

CS: I did talk a little bit about it there. I didn't mean to be dismissive about it.

RC: I have to go back and look at it. Certainly the impression I took away was that you were—once again, you're being polemical here. You're speaking to a bunch of people for whom the notion of beauty is an absolutely sacrosanct, ossified concept which they never really ponder at all, and so you were challenging—and maybe because that was the thrust of who you were speaking to it sounded more that way than you thought it did.

CS: Obviously I'm very receptive and moved by beauty, which sounds like the lady who said, "I accept the universe." [Thomas] Carlyle said, "Madam, you'd better" [*laughter*]. Yeah, of course, I mean, there it is. I didn't mean to dismiss it, I was trying to probe into what it could possibly mean, and somewhere it means to me it's alive to this notion of the pattern of relationships.

RC: All right, which needn't be entirely a matter of your socialization, although your socialization certainly affects it. I could have misread you, but I understood you to say something a little more extreme than that. And I felt that you really had moved in a more extreme direction in this book than you had in the first two books.

CS: Well, that's what I was meaning anyway, and I hope to hell I didn't fuck it up. [*Everyone chuckles.*] I mean, what can you do, you can't scotch the notion, there it is. This sort of Grecian urn thing, you know.

RC: You're making general arguments, and so sometimes specifics do get lost too. It's good that you did what you did analyzing those two symphonies, because you quite clearly isolate that as a way of thinking. Which doesn't happen—well, I guess it does happen sometimes in *Music of the Common Tongue*, [and] it does about William Billings, for instance, very much. I was reading this stuff about the narrative, and I was thinking, well, there are different stories that I want to hear; they're not all exactly the same.

CS: Oh yeah, of course they're not exactly the same, and I hope I didn't . . .

RC: No, you didn't. But there is that moment when you say it can be reduced to three things in about ten words: "Order is established. Order is disturbed. Order is reestablished."

CS: But that's true of all narratives, well, all narratives that are familiar to us in any case. I'm not the first person to say this; it's a sort of commonplace in literary theory, I'm told. That is the structure of every novel.

RC: I relayed this to my wife. She wasn't so sure she agreed.

RC: There's one other thing, actually, if you don't mind backtracking. You say a great thing about how Beethoven couldn't have expected anyone to hear the Ninth Symphony more than eight or nine times in his life, and how you think that maybe its effect gets worn out, which I think possibly is true. But I have to say, that as a listener to much simpler works than that, I don't find that they get worn out after eight or nine times at all. There are certainly songs that one can hear hundreds or even thousands of times and get—now maybe it's because the effect is a simpler one that it's more easily repeated?

CS: I don't think I said worn out. I think there was something else, something about losing its ability to shock.

RC: Well, I think it was a little weaker than shock, what you said.

CS: There may be another thing too, which is that the popular song is designed to be played over and over and over and over and over again, whereas I don't think Beethoven intended the symphonies, and there are elements of surprise in Beethoven symphonies which there are not in popular songs, or very little of the deliberate waylaying which there is in Beethoven, like, for instance, the end of the third movement of the Ninth comes to rest so peacefully and so wonderfully you're in heaven, and then suddenly bah dah-dah-dah-dit-dah, all hell breaks loose. Jesus Christ, you know. That's deliberate. There's nothing of that.

RC: It's a different aesthetic experience too, I suspect. You know, there's something in pop songs called the hook, which I'm sure you've heard of. Now some hooks are just things you want to hear over and over again, but sometimes they are surprises of the sort you're talking about, and obviously they do cease to surprise. So what they do instead is that they please you by popping up at the very moment that you know they're going to pop up.

CS: Well, that's what I was talking about here. It's exactly the same.

RC: But the kind of enjoyment is much less pretentious. I mean, are the people who listen to the Beethoven, are they pretending?

CS: No, not necessarily.

RC: But many are just saying, "oh, here it comes, I can't wait." That seems okay to me.

CS: Yeah, okay. Like my father, who used to say, "Let's listen to the dear old Fifth Symphony." That's exactly what I mean. He was very fond of the Fifth Symphony. But it's not what Beethoven intended. He wanted a fist in your face.

RC: If artists got what they wanted, we wouldn't really like what they gave. We're able to use it for ourselves.

CS: Yeah we take it all and use it. I can't stop people from taking what they want from this.

RC: Correct. That goes for us too. Absolutely.

CS: And I'm absolutely astounded at some of the things that people have taken from what I've written.

RC: It's okay though.

CS: I suppose it's okay.

RC: I mean you just have to . . .

CS: Whether or not it's okay, it's there. Sometimes they're attributing to me more attacking attention than I had and I do think that's a misrepresentation and sometimes I think a willful misrepresentation. I never intended my books as an attack on anything.

RC: As polemics.

CS: Okay, an argument, to try and change people's—polemics to that extent, but not really as an attack on the classical tradition. I can give my opinion on it, which is another matter. I can't help my opinion showing, and much of it is because I care passionately about it. And the more I go on the more I feel that the trouble lies not in any inherent characteristic of the music so much as in the way it is being approached in our time. At the moment I'm putting a lot of energy into trying to find out as much as I can about the way Mozart sounded in Mozart's day, for example.

RC: Do you think you might write about this eventually?

CS: I don't know. I'm running out of energy. I've got to prepare a big lecture for next year in New Zealand. The International Society for Music Education asked me to give the keynote speech at a big conference in Auckland, which is lovely, because it's the first time in my life in my own country.

RC: Right. How can you say no?

CS: So I've got to put that together. And I think it may get me going again. After all, each of these three books took ten years' time.

RC: I know.

CS: You know, I probably won't be around in another ten years.

RC: So you were fifty when the first book was published?

CS: [*Pause*] I was a late developer.

The Sardana and Its Meanings

(2003)

If you should happen to be in Barcelona on a Sunday morning and find yourself in the big square in front of the cathedral, you will see a remarkable sight. A crowd of maybe a couple of thousand people will have assembled there, just milling around and strolling, a very ordinary-looking crowd of city dwellers in their Sunday leisure clothes—housewives, technicians, children, grandparents, shopkeepers and businessmen, students, hippies, and teenagers, all of them inhabitants of Spain's second city. I even once saw there the then *alcalde* or mayor, Pasqual Maragall himself, in jeans and a white open-necked shirt.

There is a band of a dozen or so musicians setting up on the cathedral steps, dressed in identical sober suits and ties. As they get out their instruments, we see that some are familiar to us but some aren't—there are not only orthodox brass, such as trumpets, euphoniums, and trombones, but also big shawms of various sizes with broad hard reeds, the largest of them about three feet long, and a small three-stringed double bass, which is the only stringed instrument. The leader has a tiny flute, called a *flaviol*, which he fingers with his left hand while with his right he strikes a tiny drum that is strapped to his upper left arm. It is the only percussion instrument. The leader plays a little flourish on the flaviol and the whole band enters, with a wham!—a big strident outdoor sound, mercifully without amplification (who needs it?), which is striking and strange in its combination of power and plangency.

If you are looking down into the square from the top of the cathedral steps, you see something that never fails to fascinate me. After the music starts, the crowd keeps milling around for a couple of minutes as if nothing were happening, and then little by little, circles of dancers with linked hands start to emerge from the randomly moving crowd, growing like organisms as more and more people join in. Coats, handbags, briefcases, and other accessories are put in a pile in the middle of the circle, safe from theft under everybody's eyes. There's always one circle that grows larger than the rest, but there may be any number of smaller circles on the periphery, some with only two or three people and others a dozen or so or bigger.

The dancers hold the upper part of their bodies relatively immobile, but their feet engage in some very fancy footwork. An important part of the dance is the counting of beats, so that you know when to change from the quite dainty pointed-toes step to vigorous jumping up and down, when to raise the linked hands above the head and when to bring them down. And although (because?) the dancers' hands are joined in the circle, the dancers don't dance *to* one another very noticeably; rather, each dancer is self-contained, facing the center, intent on his or her own steps and doubtless concentrating on counting beats.

It's not the most exciting dance in the world, certainly nothing like those fiery, graceful, and sensuous courtship dances one encounters further south in Andalucia, or even in the other Pyrenean provinces of Navarra and Aragon; there is nothing sexy about this dance. If one had to characterize it in a word, that word might be "dainty," or "finicky." The rhythms are all a bit downbeat—nothing of those fascinating twists of melody or of rhythm and harmony that make other Spanish dances so exciting for the spectator and so characteristically "Spanish" for the hearer. It's all a bit prosaic really, not at all romantic. It's only the striking sound of the shawms against the brass and the occasional hemiola twist to the rhythm that gives it any color at all.

But in a sense it's that very prosaic, unemphatic, everyday quality that is an important part of its meaning. And to myself, who has spent my life until fairly recently in English-speaking countries, the most remarkable thing about this dance is the fact of its being danced at all, not in some remote village but in the center of this great industrial capital city, every Sunday morning, by ordinary people—not folklore freaks like English Morris dancers—and certainly not like them regarded as a bit of a joke by the rest of the population. It's all intensely serious and quite unselfconscious. It is the sardana, the national dance of the Catalans.

I have the good fortune to live in a small seaside town a suburban train ride from Barcelona, and so I see the sardana danced often; you'll see it danced anywhere in Cataluña on feast days and holidays. The Catalans live in that Mediterranean coastal strip that straddles the Pyrenees, partly in France but mostly in Spain. They regard themselves as quite different from either the Spanish or the French; in the middle ages Cataluña was a considerable power in the Mediterranean, and it was only in the eighteenth century that the Catalan state was finally subdued and dismembered after taking the wrong side in the War of the Spanish Succession, the sector north of the Pyrenees going to France and in the south becoming subject to the kings of Spain. There are, as they like to remind us, about six million of them, so that there are more Catalans than there are Danes or Norwegians. They speak their own language, which they claim as the purest Romance language, unsullied as they say by the incursions of Arabic that the Moors brought into Castilian, and they continue to resent the dominance of Madrid in their affairs. Catalan independence has had many ups and downs, and under Franco it was ruthlessly suppressed, the language not permitted in schools or official business, the streets of towns renamed, and all-important power of decision making removed to Madrid. Oh yes, and the public performance of the sardana, while never actually prohibited, was strongly discouraged. Since Franco's death in 1975 and with the return of democracy under King Juan Carlos, Cataluña has received a measure of independence within the Spanish polity and today has a position not unlike that of a state within the United States of America.

In general the Catalans regard themselves as much more European, less cut off by the Pyrenees (the bitchy French have a saying that "Africa begins at the Pyrenees"). They're much more business minded—if you walk down the Paseo de Gracia, which is Barcelona's Fifth Avenue, it seems that every other building is a bank, and it's not surprising to learn that Cataluña is Spain's richest region. Nevertheless, there remains among the Catalans a similar feeling to that which one notices among the Welsh, of bruised nationhood and a need to assert that nationhood as a matter of identity and pride. They despise the rest of Spain as feckless, lazy, and backward, and the rest of Spain returns the compliment by regarding them as dour, money grubbing, and puritanical.

And that's where we encounter the sardana, the dance and its music; to take part in it is to explore, affirm, and celebrate an identity as a Catalan and to say to oneself and to anyone else who may be taking notice, THIS IS WHO WE ARE. We have to note, however, that the identity isn't exclusive; if I or any other foreigner want to join the dance, we are welcome to do so, provided we learn the steps. If we just join a circle and try to busk it we'll ruin the dance for everybody. But if we really wish to learn it, there are plenty of people who are willing to teach us.

Why Doesn't the Whole World Love Chamber Music?

(2001)

The following is the text of an address I gave to the annual conference of Chamber Music America in New York City, January 12, 2001. The audience consisted of some 400 musicians, both performers and composers, as well as chamber-music society administrators and sponsors, who received it politely, even warmly, and showed no sign of feeling under attack. Some readers of this journal [*American Music*] may well feel that this shows I did not hit hard enough at ingrained elitist attitudes. So be it; this is what I said. —CS

Many of you will have looked at the title I have given this talk, and wondered what an outsider like me can possibly have to say about that question. You yourselves will quite likely have already given the matter some thought and have wondered why it is that all the world should not be captivated, why all the world should not want to sit down and listen with you, when you are offering such rich musical treasures, some of the most refined and beautiful, most intimate and satisfying, and above all most spiritually elevating and intellectually stimulating of all works of music.

You would not be alone in this view. I received just the other day a brochure for a number of chamber-music groups that are touring the smaller towns of Catalonia in the coming months, including the one I live in. In its preface it has this to say, in somewhat pompous Catalan: "Chamber music is one of the most elevated manifestations of music. It is the one which can give most satisfaction to those who practice it and to those who listen. It is the most educative and formative of solidarity and discipline of character, of respect for others and the satisfaction of forming part of a collective enterprise."

Now even allowing for a certain rotundity of language, we can hear behind this kind of assertion a deep and genuine feeling, that chamber music is music distilled into its ultimate essence, with all the inessentials stripped away, leaving only pure musical thought and argument, a narration of the composer's innermost thoughts and feelings. Why then does not the whole world love chamber music?

It seems to me that to find a real answer to that question we have to dig into the nature of music itself. I'm going to have to take a massive detour around that topic before I can approach the question directly, and I'm going to have to ask your patience and assure you that we shall get there in the end. We might even find something of interest on the way.

The first thing to be said about music is that its nature and its meanings, whatever they may be, do not lie in musical works, however beautiful and wonderful they may be, however justly we may admire and love them. Whatever meaning music may have, whatever function it may have in human life, lies in an action, the act of taking part in a musical performance, whether as performer or as listener or indeed in any other capacity. Any yet that is exactly what Western musicology, music history and criticism, not to mention concert life itself, still fail to recognize. There is not even an entry under "Performance" in the *New Grove Dictionary*.

This curious neglect stems partly from the perennial tendency in European thought to create abstract entities from real actions and then to treat the abstractions as if they were more real than the actions from which they were derived. It is the trap of reification, which has been the besetting fault of Western thought ever since the time of Plato, who was one of its earliest perpetrators.

By this process of reification the basic musical actions of performing and listening, which won't hold still long enough for scholars to study in the manner to which scholars are accustomed, become the abstraction, music, which doesn't *do* anything but appears to be more real, more solid, than the acts of performing and listening. Then by a stealthy process of elision the abstraction "music" is taken to be equivalent to a musical text as it is to be found between the covers of a score, and bingo! We have an object that *will* hold still long enough to be studied at leisure, and it becomes assumed that it is there that musical meaning resides. The important question, What is the meaning of this musical act? becomes the more manageable, but more limited and less useful question, What is the meaning of this musical work as it appears in the pages of this score?

Each work gets to be thought of as a Platonic entity, existing prior to and transcending any possible performance of it, an entity to which all possible performances are only approximations, ephemeral and contingent to the existence of the work itself. The work itself floats through history, untouched by time and change, waiting for listeners to draw out its meaning, by a process which Immanuel Kant called disinterested contemplation. That meaning is permanent, possibly in cases of extreme greatness even eternal, transcending time and space, and it was created by a composer before anyone else laid eyes on the score. Listeners have nothing to contribute to it other than their disinterested contemplation. Their task is to seek out and respond to that meaning. As for performers, those troublesome but unfortunately necessary fellows, their task is to present the work to the listeners as best they can. They are merely the medium, the necessarily imperfect medium, through which the work has to pass.

I have been told that I'm out of date in presenting this schema, that musicians and musicologists and so on don't think like that nowadays. I wish I could believe it, but I don't. It persists as an unspoken assumption behind most contemporary discourse on music. Pick up practically any book on the theory, the aesthetics or the history of music, and ask yourself what it is that the author *really* means by the word "music." I read a month or so ago in a distinguished music-education journal a review of a new book, a short introduction to music. The reviewer tells us, with a straight face and without comment, what the author has to say on this very matter. The schema could not be set out more clearly or succinctly. He says: "The key personnel in musical culture are the composers, who are generating what might be called the core product. Performers are in essence no more than middlemen (apart from those exceptional interpreters who acquire a kind of honorary composer's status); and listeners are consumers, playing an essentially passive role in the cultural process that, in economic terms, they underpin." I thought at first the reviewer was joking, but he wasn't. An idea that has dogged us since Plato doesn't give up that easily.

Perhaps if Immanuel Kant had ventured out of his musty study and gone down the road as far as the nearest tavern he might have been forced to admit that the idea of music as objects to be contemplated, disinterestedly or not, bears little relation to music as it is actually practiced throughout the human race. In that real world where people actually make and listen to music, in concert halls and suburban drawing rooms, in bathrooms and at political rallies, in supermarkets and churches, in record stores and temples, in fields and nightclubs, discos and palaces, stadiums and elevators, it is performance that is at the center of music.

It is not true that performance takes place in order to present a musical work. That's the wrong way around. Musical works exist in order to give performers something to perform.

It is of course true that performance is ephemeral, but it is certainly *not* contingent, either to the musical process in general or to the meaning of specific works of music. On the contrary, performance is the primary process of all music, from which everything else flows. It can take place without an audience and it can take place without a fixed and stable work of music at all, and it frequently does so. Whole musical cultures get along very well without such things. Composing begins when a performer, liking what he or she has just done, repeats it perhaps many times, and works to improve it so that a more or less fixed sequence crystallizes out from the flowing stream of sounds in time. Composing evolved out of performing and flows back into it, and makes sense as an activity only in relation to performance. That is the purpose of composing: to facilitate performing—and of course listening.

Always, of course, when we talk about listening we have to include the performers themselves as listeners. They are the first people to listen to the performance, and are almost certainly the most involved and intense listeners of all, since they perceive not only through their ears but also through the bodily sensations of performing. And of course they are often enough the only listeners, playing for themselves.

Now if there is anything that is clear about performing and listening—and composing too for that matter—is that they are actions. They're something that people do. And if that's so, if the heart of music isn't things but actions, then perhaps the word "music" shouldn't be a noun at all. It ought to be a verb. The verb "to music." Not just to express the idea of performing—we already have an adequate vocabulary for that—but to express the broader idea of *taking part* in a performance. As those of you who have read my books *Music of the Common Tongue* and *Musicking* will know, I have taken the liberty of defining this verb, and I offer it to you now, the verb "to music," with its present participle "musicking," not as one of those gratuitous coinages that academics love but as a genuine tool for the understanding of the music act.

This is how I have defined it. It's quite simple. *To music is to take part, in any capacity, in a musical performance.* That means not only to perform but also to listen, to provide material for performance—what we call composing—to prepare for a performance—what we call practicing or rehearsing or woodshedding—or to take part in any activity that can affect the nature of that style of human encounter which is a musical performance. We should certainly include dancing, if anyone is dancing—and in some cultures if no-one is dancing then no musicking is happening—and we might even on occasion extend it to what the box-office clerk is doing when he sells tickets, and the person who tunes the piano, and the cleaners who clean up afterwards, since what they do certainly affects the nature of the event which is a musical performance.

Apart from favoring the idea that music is action, the verb has other useful implications. For one thing, it makes no distinction between what the performers are doing and what the rest of those present are doing. It thus reminds us that musicking—and you see how easy it is to slip into using it—is an activity in which all those present are involved, and for whose nature and whose success or failure all those present bear a measure of responsibility. It isn't just a matter of composers, or even performers, actively doing something for the passive listeners to contemplate. Whatever it is that is being done, we are all doing it together.

I hope you won't think that I'm so silly as to see no difference between what the performers are doing and what the cleaners, for example, are doing. They are obviously doing different things. But by using the verb "to music" in this way we are kept aware that all these activities add up to a single event, whose nature is affected by the way in which each activity is carried out, and we have a tool for exploring the nature and the meanings of the event as a whole.

If musicking is verb and not noun, action and not thing, then we should look for its meanings not in those musical objects, those symphonies and quartets and operas, or even those melodies and songs, that we have been taught to think of as the repositories of musical meaning. Those do have a potential for meaning, in fact for a range of possible meanings. But it's only when the work is performed and the performance interacts with the experience that the listeners bring to it, with their preconceptions and their mode of socialization—in a word, with their values, or sense of ideal relationships—that the potential is realized and meaning is created.

It is not only the sounds themselves that carry meaning. The setting where the performance is taking place will impose relationships between the participants and create meanings even before a note of music has been sounded. The behavior of those present, the physical gestures they make—or don't make—as they play and listen are also an important part of the meaning that is being created. We in the Western classical-music culture have minimized the use of bodily gesture in both performing and listening, and we do tend to disregard this aspect of the music act that is very important in other cultures, but even the fact that we do minimize bodily movement is in itself significant and has something to say about our relationship with our own bodies. Many people from other cultures feel that the minimizing of physical gesture in our musicking brings about an impoverishment of the musical experience for which no splendor of sound or intellectual force can compensate.

The listeners' responses—and, as always, we include that of the performers—and the meanings they make from what they hear depend as much on the values and the experience that they bring to the performance as on the objective sounds. Their concepts of ideal relationships are the parameters within which they respond—or fail to respond—to the sound-relationships of the musical work being played. Those concepts may be flexible, but they are not infinitely so, and on the other hand the potential for meaning can only come alive and make meaning to those listeners when there is a degree of congruence between the two sets of relationships. We don't expect to get up and boogie when Beethoven's *Heiliger Dankgesang* is being played.

Different listeners at different times and under different circumstances will bring to a performance different concepts of ideal relationships and so they will get different meanings from a performance of the same work. There may well come a time when a lack of congruence causes them to get no meanings at all from it, or none that they feel concerns them, and the work will drop from the repertory. There is nothing inherent, nothing permanent or transcendent about the value of an artwork. Any value it may possess is the outcome of choices made by the living. The fact that we choose to treasure the works of art that we do treasure says as much about us and our values as it does about the works themselves. That means that each question about the value of a work of art is in reality a double one. We ask not only what there is about the work of art that makes us want to treasure it but also what there is about us that we should want to do the treasuring. And conversely, when we reject an artwork or a performance the reason may well lie as much in ourselves as in the rejected work or action.

When any musical performance takes place there is created within the performance space a complex web of human relationships. At the center of the web are the sounds that the performers are bringing into existence and the relationships that they create among them. Radiating out from these, and feeding back to them, are the relationships among the performers, between the performers and the listeners, among the listeners and anyone else who may be present, and even between those who are present and those who are not. It is in those relationships, so rich and complex that they cannot be articulated in words, that the meaning of a musical performance lies. Those relationships within the space stand for, or model, ideal relationships as they are imagined to be by those taking part: between person and person, between individual and society, between humanity and the natural and even the supernatural world. These are among the most important concerns in human life, and whenever we engage in the act of musicking, even the most seemingly trivial and frivolous, we incur a responsibility towards them.

I want to make it clear what I mean. I mean that when we music, when we take part in a musical performance, the relationships that we collectively bring into existence model those of the cosmos as we believe they are and as they ought to be—what we might call our universe of values. I need hardly say that the relationships I am talking about are not those of the inanimate world that physical scientists try to measure and explain and control, but the relationships that all living beings from viruses to humans to sequoia trees need at some level to comprehend and to order if they are to survive.

When we music, we do not just *learn about* those ideal relationships, nobody is telling us about them. We actually *experience* them in all their marvelous complexity. The musicking empowers us to experience the actual structure of our universe of values, and in experiencing it we learn what our place is within it and how we ought to relate to it. Not just intellectually but through our bodily gestures and our emotions. We explore those ideal relationships, our values, we affirm their validity and we celebrate them, every time we take part in a musical performance. To borrow the words of the anthropologist Clifford Geertz, when we music the lived-in order merges with the dreamed-of order. The fact that Geertz used the phrase, not about musicking but about ritual, puts us on the edge of a fascinating thicket that I just don't have time to enter today: the idea that a musical performance, any musical performance anywhere and at any time, can be thought of as a ritual, and a ritual is a pattern of actions in which shared values—that is, shared concepts of right relationships—are affirmed, explored and celebrated. The ritual order enacts the vision of a social order. The relationships that compose that order will be found, not only in the internal relationships of the sounds being produced by the musicians, but also in the relationships between all those taking part.

That I could say is the main basis of this talk: that the order we create when we music is an enactment of our ideal social order, an order in which we can feel most completely realized, most developed and fulfilled. Musicking is a means by which we learn to interpret the world and its relationships, what they are and what they should be.

But we don't all interpret the world in the same way. Each one of us carries around our own way of making sense of it, our own values, our own concept of what are and what are not right relationships. We all tend to think of our own concepts, if we think about the matter at all—and most of us don't, much—as the really real ones. Naturally, that's why we value them. Those relationships that we consider to be good, valuable and treasurable in life—as well as those which we consider to be bad and worthless—have for us overriding importance, and we value other people to the extent that they share our values.

None of these concepts is absolute or inbuilt. They are, to use the sociologists' term, socially constructed. We learn them as a result of an active engagement with the world around us and our fellow beings. From the moment of birth we learn what relationships are of value and what are not, and in this way we learn to order our experiences of the world. We can thus expect that members of the same social group, whose experiences are broadly similar, will tend to order their experience in broadly similar ways, and to hold broadly similar values, which will tend to reinforce one another. It is in fact shared assumptions about relationships that makes social groups, from empires and nations to families and bonded pairs, and holds them together.

How those values are acquired is a dialectical process between, on the one hand, the experience and inborn temperament of the individual and, on the other, the shared perceptions of the various social groups to which he or she belongs. The sum of those shared perceptions is what is called a culture.

We naturally tend to hold values that make our own existence more meaningful and validate our feeling of our own worth. Whatever our position in society may be we shall espouse values that support our sense of worth and self-esteem. If that position is elevated or privileged our values will be those which justify that position. This is not necessarily a conscious choice, just our sense of the proper order of things. On the other hand, those in a lowly position may either espouse values that make them feel just as good as the elites, or else they may accept their position as part of the given order of things—which is what keeps the English, and to a lesser degree the American, class system alive.

Those who do hold social power—those who control the education system and the media of communication, and those who hold the purse strings for what is called cultural activity—are going to use that power in an attempt to impose their own version of ideal relationships throughout the whole society, to make people acknowledge that it is their version of reality, their culture, that is the *real* one. I used the word "impose," but that's too strong a word. Once again it's not necessarily done deliberately or by any orchestrated campaign or conspiracy. It's just the way the members of the group perceive their reality. After all, if our values and thus our culture are superior—and that's borne out by the fact of our elevated social position—then it must be in everyone's interest to partake of that culture. It's a neat circle, and it's what the sociologists call hegemony. Where "culture" ends and "hegemony" begins is hard to establish. What is just culture to me, and perfectly natural, may be hegemony to you.

We begin to see how it is that musicking has always functioned as a powerful means of definition, and especially self-definition, who we think we are socially. For if members of different social groups have different values, that is, different concepts of ideal relationships, then the kinds of musical performances that enact those relationships will differ from one another also. Each musical performance articulates the values of the members of a social group, large or small, powerful or powerless, dominant or oppressed, rich or poor, at a certain moment in its history, and no style of musicking is more universal or absolute in value than any other. I have to repeat: no way of musicking, no musical culture or tradition, is intrinsically superior or inferior to any other. If we ourselves do feel that some ways of musicking are superior and others inferior that is generally connected to our feelings about the social groups whose values are being articulated musically.

I have to make three comments on that idea. The first is that not any old performance will do. Quality of performance matters, of course it matters. I know of no musical culture in which no distinction is made between a good and a poor performance, according to the criteria of that culture. Only those performances will do in which all the performers are exploring the relationships of their universe of meaningful sounds as comprehensively and subtly and imaginatively as they are capable of doing—a process which always demands all the skill and care they can bring to it—and in which the listeners' response is equally imaginative and comprehensive.

Second, all musical cultures are more or less equally complex. Linguists assure us that there is no such thing on earth today as a primitive language and neither is there any such phenomenon as primitive music. All human beings are more or less equally complex in their relations to each other and to the cosmos as a whole, and all are capable of, and in fact *need* to be capable of, articulating those relationships. If *we* find only simplicity or primitiveness or even crudity in, say, the sound of an African herdsman playing his home-made flute to his beasts in the night, or of a folk singer as she sings an old familiar song in her own way, or even in the sound of the latest teenybopper band or rapper, that may well be because on the one hand our ears are not attuned to the complexities of the sounds being produced, and on the other because our minds are not attuned to the complexities of the conceptual worlds, the values and the relationships, or to the complexity of the mental and physical processes that went into the making of the sounds.

And third, if each performance articulates the values of a specific social group, then every musical performance is inescapably to some degree a political act. Politics, of course, is about power, and an important element of power is the power to define oneself and maybe to define others, to say, not only, This is who I am, or This is who we are, but also to be able to say to others, That is who you are. Much of the historic class struggle, not to mention the struggles against racism and sexism, consists in that struggle for the power to define oneself, to be able to say, This is who we are, against those who would tell you, That is who you are, or even, That is *what* you are—which is to say, less than fully human. Many kinds of musical performance can be seen as sites for contestation of that important human right. Volcanic struggles have taken place over it, especially over the last century or so when so many human groups have been struggling for the right to self-determination, not just as nations in the ordinary sense but also as human beings within a society that devalues or oppresses them. George Lipsitz's fascinating book *Dangerous Crossroads* is full of examples of this musical struggle from all over the world, from Haitians to Australian Aborigines to Native Americans to black South Africans to Czech intellectuals under communism, to unemployed rejects of rich industrial societies. He records the dangers that musicians face who dare to challenge through their musicking the values of those who rule them. The banning of live performance and records, imprisonment, burning of homes, even torture and murder are some of the threats under which thousands of musicians live today, simply because they assert the right to perform in a way that affirms and celebrates *their* ideal relationships. The right to perform is inextricably linked to the right of self-definition, and the right to self-definition is the first step on the long road to real political power.

Not only for performers, but for their audiences too, since the power to music in a way that articulates one's own values is the power to say, This is who we are, for listeners no less than for performers. And not only under governments that fall outside the democratic pale. All dominant groups, all ruling classes, even in societies that call themselves democratic, will encourage and underwrite styles of musicking that support their values and sense of inherent superiority and will disparage, discourage and even actively harass those performers and audience whose musicking challenges those values.

The history of black expressive culture in both the United States and Britain shows dozens of examples of this process, from the days of blackface minstrelsy right down to the present. Many of us will remember the scandalized reactions of white America and Britain to the eruption of rock'n'roll into the public—which is to say the white—domain in the early fifties—the radio bans, the campaigns of concerned parents, the harassment of performers and dancers. The history of jazz also teems with such reactions, from the earliest years of the twentieth century into the 1930s and even later. You can read some of them in Robert Walser's excellent collection of readings in jazz history, called *Keeping Time*.

In Britain the history of London's great West Indian Carnival at Notting Hill, the official attempts to suppress it, the oppressive policing, the arbitrary spoilsport regulations imposed by local authorities and the wildly exaggerated and even lying press reports of drugs, fights and robberies, is something I myself have witnessed right from its earliest days in the mid sixties.

Tricia Rose in her book *Black Noise* describes the indignities and humiliations that she and several thousand other young African Americans had to endure before being admitted to a big New York stadium in the early 1990s where a rap performance was taking place, including body pat-downs and metal detector scans and searches through pocket books and handbags. She reports also that the finding of venues for rap performances is becoming increasingly difficult for promoters, and she comments, "The struggle over context, meaning and access to public space is critical to contemporary cultural politics. Power and resistance are exercised by signs, language and institutions. Consequently popular pleasure involves physical, ideological and territorial struggles."

We in this room today are lucky. Context, meaning and access to public space are not matters that we have needed to bother ourselves with, and certainly don't have to struggle for. We can take them for granted. This is because the meanings and the ideal social relationships that we articulate through our own favored way of musicking are those that bear the stamp of approval from the sources of power and authority in the modern state.

The context of everything we do musically is one of social approval, not to say prestige. The access of both performers and listeners to public space is not only assured but paid for from public funds or from the largesse of the very rich. Even listeners are taught the skills of competent listening. They used to call it musical appreciation: I don't know what name it goes under today. The selection and training of performers takes places in state and privately funded institutions, which approve and certify their quality. They are not liable to have to pay exorbitant insurance on their transport, or to find themselves hassled by immigration and customs officers looking for illegal substances. As audiences we do not find our handbags and pocket books being searched at the entrance to Alice Tulley Hall, nor do security men patrol the aisles during a performance of Beethoven's Opus 132. It cannot be politically subversive or socially dangerous for anyone to take part in these performances.

A classical-music performance is in fact no longer a site for social contestation—if indeed it ever was. We practitioners of the music, performers and listeners alike, can afford to take its values for granted as lasting and universal, and our right to do so is unquestioned. This means that classical musicking can often function as a vehicle for the social aspirations of upwardly mobile people—This is who I am, which can easily slip over into, This is who I want to be, and even, This is who I want to be seen as being—which gets shorthanded, often unjustly, as snobbery and social climbing.

It seems to me, as an outsider to both Britain and the United States, that the American class system, perhaps for the very reason that it is more permeable than the British, generates more social tensions and resentments as people are able to move upward very much more easily and rapidly. This permeability, and again I have to qualify it with the phrase "It seems to me," is reflected in the greater hostility shown in the United States by those from outside the classical-music culture toward those on the inside. In Europe generally, if people are not involved in the culture they tend to shrug their shoulders and forget it, even if it *is* their tax money that is paying for it. But in America I have seen real resentment. It's not just that I have frequently heard expressed, often from intelligent and sensitive people, sentiments of extreme antipathy to the whole culture of classical music, including of course opera, but also that American popular culture teems with images of that resentment, from *Roll over Beethoven and tell Tchaikovsky the news* to the Marx Brothers' hilarious destruction of a performance of *Trovatore* in *A Night at the Opera*. There's real malice there. As for the final scene of *At the Circus*, with the symphony orchestra on its floating platform disappearing out to sea still furiously playing Wagner under the baton of its outrageously caricatured conductor, well, that's an archetypal image if ever there was one. If chamber musicking is a particular target of these resentments it must be at least to some extent for the very reasons that we its practitioners adduce to show its superiority to other ways of musicking. Social class and social aspirations, whether we like it or not, have a great deal to do with it.

Class of course is by no means the only determinant of our musical tastes, despite what some overenthusiastic Marxists might say. Certainly there is no one-to-one relationship. Who we are and who we want to be is complex and often contradictory, and it is something over which we do have a measure of control. Nevertheless who we are *is* constrained by our circumstances of birth and upbringing, and by the attitudes of family and peers. Even who we want to be, or want to be seen as being, is not altogether unconstrained. And when it comes to choices in the field of expressive culture, the possession of what Pierre Bourdieu calls educational capital becomes an important factor—linked once again of course to social class.

I use the term "classical music" with some diffidence. We all know the conceptual traps it sets, and yet what other term is there to qualify that socially elevated and subsidized way of musicking that all of us here like to engage in? I refuse to talk about "serious" music, since all music—or, rather, all musicking—is serious. If we think of classical music as a style of musicking, rather than as a repertory of musical works, we can understand a little more clearly what makes some love it and others resent it. Paradoxically, the modern style of musicking that we call classical, with its rituals, its customs and conventions of behavior, and even the kind of building in which it is housed, grow to a great extent out of the modern attitude of performers and listeners towards individual works that I discussed earlier, as permanent, transcendent and ahistorical. The individual work demands the total attention of the listener to the exclusion of all other stimuli, and it demands also a setting for its performance which is adequate to its splendor and its elevated social status. It was when those notions came together, over the nineteenth century, that we began to get something like the modern concept of classical music. And we should be sure that classical musicking as we know it today *is* a modern style, even if the repertory on which it is based is old. It is certainly not a style of musicking that Mozart or J. S. Bach would have recognized.

Even the purpose-built concert hall is a nineteenth-century invention, which did not reach its full development until well into the twentieth century. And audience manners have changed a lot since the delighted Parisians burst into applause at the sudden fortissimo in the last Allegro of Mozart's thirty-first symphony in 1778. Or even maybe since the disturbances that accompanied the premiere of *The Rite of Spring* in 1913.

As the style of musicking has changed, so has the meaning of performing the works. To perform and to listen to Beethoven's mighty symphonies and quartets may bring comfort and inspiration to modern listeners, but when they were first performed they were an in-your-face assertion of the values of the rising bourgeoisie of Europe and Euro-America, devoted to crisis and change as constants in human life.

The teleological power of these performances, and of those that followed through the nineteenth and early twentieth centuries, as they hurtled through time by way of crisis and climax towards a preordained resolution, resonated strongly with the preoccupations of the bourgeoisie in the same period. The headlong pace of events in the performance matches the headlong pace of events in Europe from the French Revolution to 1848 and beyond, when those who put down the proletarian rebellions were the grandsons of those who had seized power from the aristocracy in 1789. Over and over again in widely different ways these performances tell the story of the transformation of an individual soul, creating itself through conflict and overcoming and through a struggle that has a beginning and a final ending. In their internal relationships we hear the supremacy of logical and functional relationships, and above all a teleology, an impulse toward closure and finality, which is clearly audible even in the two-chord harmonic cell from which the whole great organism has developed—the succession known as the perfect cadence, in which the sounding of a triad of the dominant leads us to expect the sounding of the tonic triad. How that expectation is played with, teased, frustrated and finally always satisfied is the basis of the whole temporal succession that is a performance of a work of classical music.

The social order of the work is mirrored in the organization of the instrument that plays it. It has been frequently pointed out that the social order of the symphony orchestra is the very model of industrial order, with the conductor the boss, the section leaders the foremen and the players the proletariat, whose skills and talents are alienated from them and used in the service of someone else's purposes. The performance is the product and the anonymous audience the consumers, who have no more control over the product than they have over the cars or the breakfast cereals they buy.

The great spectacle of the symphony concert, in all its undoubted beauty and splendor, can be seen as a ceremony in which takes place the exploration, the affirmation and the celebration of certain values, certain kinds of ideal relationships. It is the ritual enactment of the power of certain members of industrial society to affirm, loudly and clearly—and how loud that is!—that This is who we are and This is how we ought to relate. It is an exhibition, not only of symbolic power but also of the splendor that only power can create, and if there is a loss of intimacy and ordinary human engagement between the participants, well, that as always is the price of power. The participants must feel the price is worth paying; otherwise they wouldn't be taking part in the ceremony. They might go off instead to a blues club, where they could feel at least the illusion of intimacy and conviviality—they might stay home and play string quartets with friends and family members, as Mozart, Haydn, Dittersdorf and Vanhal did in Mozart's lodgings in Vienna back in 1787. What conviviality must have been created there!

If we do consider a group of friends sitting down to play together in the home of one of them there is brought into existence a different kind of social order from that of the symphony concert. It may be the same Mozart quartet that the four friends played that night, one of the six he dedicated to Haydn, or it might be the latest creation of a young genius scored for harmonica, hubcaps, kazoo and harp with prerecorded sounds of car crashes. It doesn't make much difference. As a mode of performance it provides rewards for the performers that orchestral playing cannot. It is much more sociable and even intimate; it affords greater autonomy, more self-direction, to the individual performer and the opportunity for more spontaneous interaction with others. Up to a point it is, or can be, a very convivial society, even an egalitarian one, that is brought into existence for the duration of the performance.

And yet the players as they play still relate to one another, not directly but through the composer's instructions. Their responses to one another in that human encounter which is a musical performance are still mediated through the written notes, which establish and maintain a distance between them. The score provides an immutable given factor to the encounter and in this way accords it a measure of safety and mutual comprehension while preventing it from attaining total intimacy. The fact that they engage in this kind of musical performance which brings into existence such a social situation shows perhaps that that is as far as they are prepared to go in the direction of intimacy. Such distanced relationships are characteristic of certain social groups—let us be sweeping and call them, without too much attempt at precision, the bourgeoisie—and the performance as a whole can be seen as the exploration, affirmation and celebration of the values of that group.

When chamber musicking becomes professionalized, of course, and is removed from the living room—people nowadays don't have chambers, and maybe it's time to rethink the term—to the concert hall, as has been happening increasingly since Beethoven started to compose works that are outside the technical range of those who play for love rather than money, there is introduced into the encounter a further distancing. Under the day-to-day pressures of professional performance the little society can become less and less egalitarian and may fall increasingly under the command of one strong member of the group. As that happens, relationships with listeners become also more distanced, and the larger the setting the more distancing there will be, until finally, however wonderful the musical works may be that are being played, however superb the performers, the conviviality that gave birth in the first place to that mode of musicking has fled. Maybe we are prepared to pay that price, in the interest of greater refinement of playing, but we should be aware that there *is* a price. It's something we might remember when we use the word "professional" as a term of approval and "amateur" as one of abuse.

What kind of social situation is brought into existence when relationships are not mediated by written notes? Let's consider a quartet of instrumentalists who have come together to play jazz for themselves and perhaps a few friends. They will agree on a tune on which to improvise and on a tempo, and they will start to play. They are bound together, not by written notes, but by the common idiom, the common stock of material and by the melody and its harmonies. They are free to respond directly to one another's playing, to imitate or to branch off in another direction, to flatter and to criticize, to unite or to dominate the group. The striving for greater intimacy and more direct mutual response introduces an element of danger into the situation that is not there when all are playing from a score—the danger of social disintegration and musical failure that cannot take place as long as all the players follow the instructions given by a score.

But we notice that they are still bound by the requirements of the idiom. There are still ways in which they may respond to one another and ways in which they may not. There are choices they may make and choices that they may not. They are in fact caught in the ancient and creative paradox that rules all human relationships, that on the one hand, those relationships can only be established and maintained by the mutual acceptance of some common idiom, whether of speech or gesture, and on the other, that those very conventions which permit the creation of relationships also structure them and prevent the participants from attaining more than a certain degree of intimacy. We could say that it is that paradox that is at the root of all artistic activity.

With jazz, however, as well as with blues and its offshoots rock'n'roll and rock in all its varieties, there has traditionally been another factor that affects the relationships within the performing space, and that is dancing. Dancing, like musicking, is a language of gesture, and gestural language is the language in which relationships too rich and complex to be articulated in words can be articulated clearly and easily. When people are dancing as well as playing and listening the social order of the performance space is immeasurably enriched. The musicians fire the dancers and the dancers fire the musicians. The great Hollywood dancer Leon James described Dizzy Gillespie's playing in the Savoy Ballroom in Harlem in the 1930s. He said, "A lot of people had him pegged as a clown, but we loved him. Every time he played a crazy lick, we cut a crazy step to go with it. And he dug us and blew even crazier stuff to see if we could dance to it, a kind of game, with the musicians and the dancers challenging each other" (Stearns and Stearns 1968). And Lester Young used to mourn the Basie band's translation from the dance hall to the concert stage: "I wish jazz was played more often for dancing. The rhythms of the dancers comes back to you when you're playing." Both musicians and dancers, of course, were masters of their idiom and within that idiom were able to bring into existence a powerful and liberated society for the duration of the performance. There are those that hold that it was the moment when the musicians stopped playing for dancers and began playing concerts that jazz as a creative, living, *political* force died and it became just another genre of chamber music.

So, maybe we *should* start dancing to the *Heiliger Dankgesang*? Well, it's not all that inconceivable. If we were to do so it would certainly create a set of values and ideal relationships that was very different from that which I dare swear most of us bring to a performance of the piece. It might even bring into being unsuspected richnesses of relationship, which we in our reverential relation to the work and its composer have not imagined.

You can imagine, then, that I find it interesting that when we ask, "Why doesn't the whole world love chamber music?" it doesn't seem to occur to us to ask, "Why doesn't the whole world love heavy metal music?" Or "Why doesn't the whole world love hip hop?" Or "Why doesn't the whole world love rock'n'roll, or sacred harp singing, or country-and-western music?" If you don't believe heavy metal is serious and highly skilled read Robert Walser's *Running with the Devil*, in which he tells how guitarists spend their waking hours practicing virtuoso figurations derived from the concertos of Vivaldi and J. S. Bach. Or read Tricia Rose's *Black Noise* and its description of the skill and dedication of those who sample and mix tracks, and the power of the poetic idiom used by the rappers, even though what they have to say may be a fist in the face of society. Or read Maria Rosa Menocal's beautiful book *Shards of Love*, where she discusses Eric Clapton's *Layla* cycle of songs and his conscious adoption of techniques of the medieval Provencal love lyric. I'm not trying to claim respectability for these styles of musicking by linking them to respectable artistic genres. The point is that all these ways of musicking are just as serious and demanding for their devotees as chamber music is for us, and they are just as appropriate to their senses of who they are and of how the relationships of the world are and should be.

I must confess I find it hard to understand the aura of something like sacredness that surrounds chamber music, or chamber musicking. After all, it's just a very convivial way of musicking that involves a small number of performers, which is common enough the world over—gospel quartets, polka bands, coblas and highlife bands, for example. I've been unable to find out when the term first started to be used to denote a separate genre. Histories of music tend to apply it retroactively to performance as far back as the sixteenth century to madrigals and consort music, but I can find no evidence that the term itself was used at that time. There would have seemed to be no need for the term as it was the only kind of musicking there was outside of the church—all concerted music was what we would call chamber music. The term can only have started to mean something with the larger ensembles of concerto and opera, when a distinction began to be made between private and public musicking, necessitating larger performance spaces and initiating the separation of performers and audience.

I can only conclude that the sacred aura is a legacy of people like Immanuel Kant, who made what seems to me a silly distinction between sensuous pleasure and real beauty and value. Only a culture hung up on a puritan denial of the body would buy into such an idea. The idea that austerity is somehow morally or ethically better than sensuousness finds no resonance in my mind. And anyway, who said that chamber music is austere? To me, as I said, it is a very convivial way of musicking.

There's no reason in the wide world why the whole world should love any specific way of musicking. All ways of musicking, and all individual performances, are to be judged, if judged at all, on their efficacy in articulating, in exploring, affirming and celebrating their participants' sense of ideal relationships, their sense of who they are. We may not like who they are, we may perceive who they are as antipathetic or even threatening, but that has nothing to do with the matter. And conversely, when we maintain, as that Catalan brochure does, that our way of musicking is the best, that it is the one that can give most satisfaction to those who practice it and to those who listen, that it is the most educative and formative of solidarity and discipline of character, of respect for others and the satisfaction of forming part of a collective enterprise, and so on, it only serves to reveal how little we know of how musicking operates outside our own social group. I have taken a modest part in jazz groups and I know what solidarity and discipline it demands, precisely because the performers do not have the social safety net of a score. If I'm honest, it demands more, in fact, than I was able to bring to it. And I once spent an evening watching and listening to a group of four young musicians as they created a performance without the benefit of a single written note. It was nothing more elevated than an old Eagles song, but I was astonished and inspired by the solidarity and the discipline, the respect for others and the satisfaction of forming part of a collective enterprise that was brought into being there. Not to mention the sheer instrumental, harmonic and rhythmic skills they displayed, casually and without seeming to think anything of it.

Don't misunderstand me, please. I continue to play piano pieces of the classical repertory with love and as well as my modest piano technique will permit. It's my culture and in my old age I'm happily stuck with it, after a lifetime of exploration outside and beyond. And perhaps I love it even more for having explored outside. I know I've never before got such satisfaction from playing the piano as I do today.

East west, home may be best—for me—but I don't try to maintain that my home is the finest in the world, and I don't try to wish its values on to anyone else. I am aware that those values are not universal, and I know that there's no reason why they should be. But on the other hand, I don't feel any compulsion to like all ways of musicking or all musical performances. If I don't like the values that are being articulated by a musical performance I feel at liberty to say so, just as I feel free to say I don't like someone's social attitudes or their politics. As I have tried to suggest, there is a strong link between them.

That said, I have to admit that for me the sight and sound of a group of musicians getting together and playing to one another and to anyone who will listen—and maybe to dance—is one of the most inspiring experiences of this life. I don't care too much what the style or genre may be. Any organization that like CMA is helping to produce that experience is doing a beautiful job. There is for me only one experience that is more rewarding and that's when you're doing the playing and the dancing yourself, and I commend to you the task of fostering and encouraging that. It could be in the end even more worthwhile than employing professional musicians to perform, however splendidly they may do so. My friend Charles Keil, for one, could do with some help in his project of getting kids in Buffalo to play salsa and dance. In the absence of any way of getting inside the bodies and minds of others, we have to assume that all ways of musicking are equally complex, equally demanding and equally satisfying for those who take part in them. To assume anything else is to deny to others their full humanity.

BIBLIOGRAPHY

Lipsitz, George. 1994. *Dangerous Crossroads: Popular Music, Postmodernism and the Poetics of Place*. New York: Verso.

Menocal, María Rosa. 1994. *Shards of Love: Exile and the Origins of the Lyric*. Durham, NC: Duke University Press.

Rose, Tricia. 1994. *Black Noise: Rap Music and Black Culture in Contemporary America*. Hanover, NH: Wesleyan University Press, University Press of New England.

Small, Christopher. (1977) 1996. *Music, Society, Education*. Reprint, Middletown, CT: Wesleyan University Press.

———. (1987) 1998. *Music of the Common Tongue: Survival and Celebration in African American Music*. Reprint, Middletown, CT: Wesleyan University Press.

———. 1998. *Musicking: The Meanings of Performing and Listening*. Middletown, CT: Wesleyan University Press.

Stearns, Marshall, and Jean Stearns. 1968. *Jazz Dance: The Story of American Vernacular Dance*. New York: Schirmer.

Walser, Robert. 1993. *Running with the Devil: Power, Gender and Madness in Heavy Metal Music*. Hanover, NH: Wesleyan University Press, University Press of New England.

———, ed. 1999. *Keeping Time: Readings in Jazz History*. New York: Oxford University Press.

Creative Reunderstandings

(2005)

ABSTRACT

Originally titled "Creative Misunderstandings," this paper evolved during the course of writing with the realization that works of art are never *mis*understood but rather are *re*understood by those who take part in the perception and interpretation of them. I take as an example the appropriation of Pete Seeger's 1949 anthem "If I Had a Hammer"—much sung at civil rights and antiwar events—by the far right of the U.S. Republican Party at a banquet in Washington, D.C., during 2005, for the beleaguered House majority leader Tom DeLay. That such an appropriation is possible is due to the nature of the music act, or musicking. I argue that the meaning of the act of musicking, that is, of taking part in any capacity, in a musical performance, lies in the relationships that are brought into being by performers, listeners, and anyone else who may be present as the performance proceeds. A musical performance, especially a popular-music performance, is frequently a site for the contestation of meanings, whose view of relationships, or values, will prevail. These appropriations, or reunderstandings, do not occur at random but are always a sign that members of one cultural group can find something useful to them in the musical practices—which is to say, ritual practices—of another group, something with which they can empathize. The process of reunderstanding keeps the work of creation and diversification on the move in the era of global transport and communication in which we live.

On May 12, 2005, in Washington, D.C., a group of right-wing U.S. Republicans calling themselves the American Conservative Union gave a testimonial banquet, admission $250 a plate, in support of Tom DeLay, the besieged majority leader of the House of Representatives. DeLay was at the time fighting accusations of corruption, gerrymandering, influence peddling, and a whole heap of other congressional crimes, and had been described in the media as "one of the most reviled thugs to hold public office in America" and "the most corrupt and vindictive politician in Washington." He enjoyed on Capitol Hill the nickname of "The Hammer," in tribute to his successful bullying tactics.

They hired for the occasion a bluegrass band, and it is reported that among the numbers the band played and sang was the 1949 song "If I Had a Hammer" by Pete Seeger and Lee Hays. I don't know how well you know the song. It is a defiant affirmation of democratic values, sanctified by nearly sixty years of singing at antiwar and civil rights rallies. The most famous performance must have been that by Peter, Paul, and Mary at the 1963 civil rights march on Washington, where Martin Luther King gave his great "I Have a Dream" speech. The song is described in the *Encyclopedia of the American Left* as "one of the most optimistic paeans to the possibilities of constructive social change" (Taskin 1992).

It goes like this: (*sing*)

If I had a hammer,
I'd hammer in the morning,
I'd hammer in the evening
All over this land.
I'd hammer out danger,
I'd hammer out a warning,
I'd hammer out the love between my brothers and my sisters,
All over this land.

In the second stanza the singer sings "If I had a bell," the third "If I had a song," while in the last the hammer, the bell, and the song are brought together:

Well, I've got a hammer,
And I've got a bell,
And I've got a song to sing
All over this land.
It's the hammer of justice,
It's the bell of freedom

It's the song about the love between my brothers and my sisters,
All over this land.

A timely song, we might feel, to be sung in the United States today, where a warning of the danger to the Republic is in great need of being hammered out and rung out and sung out as loudly as can be. Maybe we could use a new verse, beginning, "If I had a blog."

One might wonder what a song composed by one of the great folk-hero musicians of the political left is doing in this kind of extreme right-wing company. We may ask of it, what's a nice song like you doing in a place like this? There is, of course, the coincidence of the word "hammer," and the choice of the song might even have been the musicians' own, made for that reason. But knowing the care with which events of this sort are orchestrated in American politics, this seems to me unlikely. In addition, the fact that the press thought the choice of song was worth reporting suggests that even the reporters sensed that something significant had occurred.

American conservatives, and especially the Christian right, are forever warning about the dangers presented by not only terrorism but also everything from gay marriage to the so-called liberal press, while the words "justice" and "freedom" were a frequently heard part of George W. Bush's limited vocabulary—he used the word "freedom" no less than twenty-one times in his June 27, 2005, speech to the long-suffering soldiers at Fort Bragg. And, of course, the image of the hammer is ripe for appropriation, seeing that it has long functioned as a metaphor for the crushing of disruptive people, as in the nickname "Hammer of the Scots" given to Edward I of England, or in the fifteenth-century witch-hunters' handbook "The Hammer of Evildoers"—a fact that in our libertarian innocence we—and possibly Seeger and his collaborator—overlooked. So it's not difficult to see how easily an optimistic paean to the possibilities of constructive social change can be turned into an anthem for the extreme political right wing.

The only concern might be the line about "the love between my brothers and my sisters." American conservatives don't talk much about love, being more concerned with sex, but if they thought about it at all, they might suspect the line of advocating gay marriage. After all, if the innocuous cartoon character SpongeBob could be accused of trying to turn kids gay, then Pete Seeger had better watch his back. By the way, he had turned eighty-six just a few days earlier, and I don't imagine he would have much appreciated this Republican birthday tribute.

So I don't think it was just for the coincident appearance of the word "hammer" that the song was chosen for this occasion. I think that those who chose it understood what generations of musicologists have failed to understand, that the meaning of a song, or indeed of any piece of music, is not just that of the text on the page. That's just the beginning of it. Only when a song is performed will its multiple layers of meaning reveal themselves, and in this case the satisfaction of having appropriated one of the American left's most sacred anthems must have been a major element in the enjoyment of taking part in this performance. Musical meanings are not permanent and stable, and are certainly not built into any musical text, but are labile and changeable, with each new context in which performance takes place.

This is true even with the classical repertory. The stability of scores is inclined to blind us to the lability of the meanings of performing from them. To perform and to listen to, say, Beethoven's Fifth Symphony in our own time is a very different affair from doing it in the composer's own time, so that what was then an in-your-face affirmation of the values of a rising European bourgeoisie, with the French Revolution under its belt and looking for new worlds to conquer, has today become a source of comfort and a vision of security to the middle classes, with their—perhaps I should say "our"—values and status under attack. Even my father, who was not a sentimental man, used to call it "the dear old Fifth Symphony," which I don't think would have pleased Beethoven. We understand the piece quite differently now from how they did then. That is not to say we *mis*understand the piece. We just understand it differently. A work of art "means" whatever the beholders, in whatever "here" or "now" they might find themselves, think it means. There is no final arbiter of meanings. Everybody brings their own mindset and their own history to bear on the performance, whether it be of a symphony by Beethoven or of a song by Pete Seeger. Scholars may try to reconstruct the original meaning intended by the creator, but audiences, and performers, will make up their own minds about that.

In the case of the DeLay banquet the choice of a bluegrass band is also significant. Bluegrass is a style that is associated with the conservative blue-collar working class, who may have been devastated by the Bush administration's policies but who for reasons of their own still contributed to his electoral success in 2004. The style is characterized first and foremost by a driving beat and a general high level of tension, which is enhanced by a high vocal tessitura unlike that of other country music. I can't know for sure, of course, since I wasn't invited to that particular bash, but I would surmise that the performance would have stood in great contrast to the laid-back style of the song's most celebrated performers,

Peter, Paul, and Mary, not to mention the exuberant Latin manner of Trini Lopez, who also had a big hit with it in the sixties. I would go so far as to speculate that that night's performance would have celebrated, not love or brotherhood and sisterhood, but the striving and the tensions of those who believe in their mission to make money and to rule.

In taking the song and giving new meanings to the act of performing it, those Republicans were exploring, affirming, and celebrating what they saw then as their victory in the American culture wars. That this should be possible is due to something in the nature of music that I'd like to explore here. The most important aspect of this I have already been suggesting. It's this: Music is not a thing at all, or a collection of things. It is essentially action, something that people do. It is primarily two kinds of action, namely, performing and listening. In many musical cultures, most notably on the African continent, dancing is also an essential musical activity, so that if no one is dancing then no music is happening, but generally it is performing and listening. Other musical activities are secondary, such as composing, rehearsing, organizing, and researching. The performers, of course, are the primary listeners, in both senses of the word "primary," since they are both the first listeners, in the temporal sense, and the most intense and committed listeners. There need not, in fact, be any listeners apart from the performers themselves.

There may not be any composer apart from the performers, or any fixed and stable musical text. Many highly sophisticated musical cultures get along perfectly well without them. But—and I must emphasize this—even if there is a fixed and stable text, that text is not the whole of what music is about. It is only when a text is performed that the totality of its meanings emerge.

I came to the conclusion many years ago that if music is action and not thing, then the word that designates it should be not a noun but a verb. As you will know I coined a verb, the verb "to music," with its present participle or gerund, "musicking," for this purpose. I define it quite simply: to music is to take part, in any capacity, in a musical performance.

This is not the time or the place to elaborate on the implications of this verb. If you're interested in following them up, they're in my book *Musicking* (1998). Broadly, however, using the verb emphasizes that not only is music an activity, but also it's a form of human encounter in which everyone who is present is taking part, and for whose success or failure as an event everybody who is present has some responsibility. It is not just a matter of active performers doing something for, or to, the passive listeners. Whatever it is that is being done, we are all doing it together. So that when I spoke a minute ago about the nature of music I really should have talked about the nature of the music act, or musicking.

So, what is it that is being done when people come together to music, which is to say, to take part in a musical performance? What meanings are being created? I believe the answer lies in the relationships that are created when the performance takes place. Relations not only among the sounds that are made—that's an important part but only part—but also among the participants, that is, among the performers, between the performers and the listeners, and among the listeners. These relationships, in turn, model, or act out, ideal or desired relationships as they are imagined to be by those taking part. And since who we are is how we relate, then to take part in an act of musicking is to take part in an act of self definition, an exploration, an affirmation, and a celebration of one's identity, of who one is. In an act of musicking those taking part are exploring, affirming, and celebrating their sense of who they are—or who they think they are, or who they would like to be, or even what they would like to be thought of as being.

The relationships brought into existence in a musical performance are enormously complex, too complex in fact to be articulated in words. But that does not mean they are too complex for our minds to encompass. The act of musicking, in its entirety, provides us with a language by means of which we can come to understand and articulate, precisely and clearly, those relationships and through them the relationships of our lives.

Exploring, affirming, celebrating. I use those three words a lot, so I'd better explain what I mean by them.

A musical performance brings into existence relationships that are thought desirable by those taking part, and in doing so it not only reflects those ideal relationships but also shapes them. It teaches and inculcates those ideal relationships—we might call them values—and empowers those taking part to try them on, to see how they fit, to experience them without necessarily having to commit themselves to them, at least for more than the duration of the performance. It is thus an instrument of exploration.

In articulating those values it empowers those taking part to say, to themselves, to one another, and to anyone else that may be paying attention: these are our values, our concepts of how the relationships of the world ought to be, and consequently, since how we relate is who we are, to say, this is who we are. It is thus an instrument of affirmation.

And, third, in empowering those taking part to explore and affirm their values, it leaves them with a feeling of being more completely themselves, more in tune with the world and with their fellows. After taking part in a successful performance, one is able to feel that this is how the world *really* is, and this is how I *really* relate to it. In short, it leaves the participants feeling good about themselves and about their values. It is thus an instrument of celebration.

Of course, we don't all view the world and its relationships in the same way. Tom DeLay and Pete Seeger will surely have different ideas on the relationships of their lives and on how they should be. On the other hand, to the extent that both are white men who were born and grew up in the United States, there will probably be more overlap between those ideas than one would expect, more indeed than either of them might like. They would both, for example, have absorbed from childhood similar ideas about their country's place in the world and about matters such as the uniqueness of the American style of freedom and justice. I believe that "If I Had a Hammer" could only have been written by an American, not only in its ways of articulating those ideas in words but also in its Anglo-Celtic pentatonic melody and its blues-inflected flattened seventh.

Now we cannot question the propriety of taking a song—or indeed any piece of music—that is intended for one social context and performing it in another. It happens all the time, and in fact if it were not possible concert halls and symphony orchestras would lose a great part of their repertoire.

As I suggested earlier, this is not a distortion of meanings but the creation of new meanings, new understandings. We may not like those new meanings—that's definitely so for me in the case I am discussing—but we cannot deny their existence. In the struggle for possession of the song and its meanings there is a veiled—or often not so veiled—struggle for political power and for what we might call legitimacy. Only time will tell whose meanings will prevail, and the struggle for control of meanings is never ending.

There are sites where the struggle for control of musical meanings has been settled, it seems permanently, for instance, the concert hall and the opera house. As I suggested when talking of the Fifth Symphony of Beethoven, the message of performing the so-called classics today is one of comfort. However disturbing the performance of those great works may once have been, they can no longer disturb anyone; such performances today belong to the status quo. You can perform a liberation opera like Verdi's *Masked Ball*, which was banned by the Bourbon censors in Naples in 1859, or Beethoven's *Fidelio*, or Chopin's *Revolutionary Study* in the most oppressed country in the world without provoking any anxiety in the authorities. The work of these musicians resembles those fascinating and often beautiful shapes in the cooled lava from volcanoes, giving testimony to the violence of past eruptions but no longer capable of reshaping the landscape. Even such avowedly revolutionary musicians as John Cage, Mauricio Kagel, and Frederic Rzewski found sponsorship in university music departments, which apparently did not consider them to be any challenge to the landscape of their values.

The image of the volcano may be an apt one, in that volcanoes long thought to be extinct have been known to burst into life and once more reshape the landscape. As we have been learning only too recently, the earth has many surprises in store for us yet, and it could be that that ancient volcano we have got used to calling classical music might still burst forth and change our mental landscape. But I doubt it. So many other volcanoes have erupted, especially in African America, since the great Beethovenian explosion that it is no longer easy to detect the fracture lines within the culture of European music.

We can contrast the experiences of Cage and the others with those of many so-called popular musicians, like Fela Kuti, Milton Nascimento, Sid Vicious, Jim Morrison, Charlie Parker, the Catalan *cantautor* who calls himself Raimon, who suffered under the Franco regime's censorship, and Seeger himself, whose brush with Senator Joe McCarthy's Un-American Activities Committee earned him a year in prison in 1961. All of those musicians, and countless others, lived in the mouth of the volcano, and their work is still capable of reshaping our landscape of human relationships. All suffered in various ways from brushes with the guardians of social and musical propriety—and it's amazing how often those two roles coincide. It seems that their, and their audiences', musical definitions of who they were did not accord with those of the guardians.

Musical meanings, then, are concerned with relationships, the relationships of our world as we believe they are and as we believe they ought to be. And since how we relate is who we are, we can say that in musicking we are exploring, affirming, and celebrating who we are, or at least who we think we are, in relation to fellow humans, to the world, and even perhaps the supernatural world—if the supernatural is part of our conceptual world. So it is that in the appropriation of "If I Had a Hammer" at the DeLay banquet, we hear a triumphalist affirmation and celebration of Republican Party values, at least as held by those who participated in the event.

I come back to the idea that musicking functions as a means of exploration, affirmation, and celebration, of who we are or think we are. If members of different social groups have different values, or different concepts of ideal relationships, then the kinds of performances that enact those relationships will differ from one another also. But we mustn't be too categorical about this. We have already seen that the degree of overlap between the values of Pete Seeger on the one hand and Tom DeLay on the other was enough to allow the appropriation of the former's song by the latter.

It doesn't only work that way, with members of social groups that are, or believe themselves to be, in control of things celebrating that control by appropriating the musical rituals of those they believe they have overcome. For more generations than we can count, underdog groups have been making through musicking their own exploration, affirmation, and celebration of who they think they are, often in the face of those who would say, that is who you are, or even, that is *what* you are, which is to say, less than fully human. That is what the slave masters in the American and Caribbean colonies tried to insist to the Africans who were under their control, and their descendents.

It is in fact this serial appropriation of musical meanings that has fuelled what must surely be one of the greatest outbursts of creative musical energy in human history—the African American musical culture. By that term, I mean the musicking that took place not only within the United States but also right across the two Americas and the Caribbean, throughout the cultural region that Paul Gilroy (1999) has called the black Atlantic, and eventually across the whole human race. I call it *serial* appropriation, because it didn't happen only once and for all or in one direction only but happened again and again over the nearly five centuries since the first Africans were landed on the shores of the Americas. Sidney Mintz and Richard Price (1976) date the beginning of a new African American culture to "the moment when one person in need received ritual assistance from another who belonged to a different cultural group" (10). Such ritual assistance must have included musicking and dancing. Over and over again, and back and forth between blacks and mainly poor whites, this serial appropriation could be seen in African drummers, singers, and dancers; in Christian hymn singers of the two waves of religious fervor that are called the Great Awakening; in fiddlers and singers not only white but black too—since a slave who was adept on an instrument could find his or her condition greatly alleviated on the plantations; in traveling, guitar-playing bluesmen and women; from gospel quartets and choirs to Elvis Presley; from such an unlikely source as Guy Lombardo to Louis Armstrong; and from Chuck Berry to the Beatles and Muddy Waters to the Stones—and so on and so on. Who benefitted from these crossovers in terms of fame and fortune is of course another matter.

In my book *Music of the Common Tongue* (1987), I suggested that for members of one social group to take to themselves elements from the musicking of another social group requires a certain empathy or respect between the members of the two groups, a certain recognition of a common humanity, even possibly envy, and even in the teeth of denial in the formal social processes of the dominant group (75). I doubt if the DeLay Republicans would have bothered with "If I Had a Hammer" if they hadn't valued the song in the first place. You don't appropriate to yourself things that you don't value.

Neither a song nor a style of musicking crosses unchanged from one social or cultural group to another. Every musician and every listener bring their own style of performing and listening, their own experience and understanding of how a performance should go, and their own ideas for making it better, making it new, and making it more powerful and more interesting. This is not to be called *mis*understanding. Rather, it is creating a new understanding, a *re*understanding that keeps the work of creation on the move, adapting songs and styles to our own purposes and resisting those who would impose a single mode of understanding on us.

So it is that the African American way of musicking, far from being a juggernaut that flattens out all local styles into one global grayout, in fact has accommodated itself over and over to local styles. Coming out of poverty and oppression, it makes an immediate appeal to poor and oppressed people throughout the world, giving them a medium through which they can explore, affirm, and celebrate who they are. In New Zealand a few years ago I heard a superb band called Te Vata from the Pacific Islands playing its own brand of blues and jazz. I also heard a fine Maori reggae group and a gospel choir—all with pronounced Polynesian accents. Then there is Mandarin rock, Chinese American rap, South Korean hip-hop, and Korean American pop, as well as Japanese reggae, complete with permanent-waved dreadlocks. We hear bhangra, rai, and reggae and a host of other syncretic styles whose characteristics cross and recross those arbitrarily imposed limits that we call stylistic boundaries.

These interactions do not occur at random but are always a sign that members of one cultural group can find something useful to them in the musical practices—I'd like to say ritual practices—of another group, something they can empathize with and that calls to them. It is not a question of conscious multiculturalism, which to be honest is a word I don't much like to use, but rather a question of what we might call cultural permeability. Members of one cultural group don't take on board in their entirety the musical ritual practices of another; they don't *learn* the culture, as we hear said frequently in educational circles these

Neville Braithwaite and Christopher Small on their balcony overlooking the Mediterranean in Sitges, Spain, c. 2004. Photograph by Robert Walser.

days, but rather take bits and pieces that appeal and incorporate them into the larger body of their own practices.

It is taking bits and pieces from whatever comes to hand, a process that goes under the fancy name of syncretism, not so-called authenticity or purity, that keeps the work of creation on the move. A pure musical culture, if such a thing could exist—and I can't imagine what such a monstrosity would be like—would be one that was without life. And we needn't imagine that the great European tradition that we call classical music is any exception to this. We are all hybrids, every one of us, all creoles, and we all speak our music with some accent or other. We should strongly resist those who tell us that we speak our music with an accent while they possess the pure language. There is no pure language. If I say that even the Queen of England speaks with an accent, and if I say that I find the accent a pretty unattractive one, that says as much about my social attitudes as it does about the royal voice.

As for authenticity, there is only one authenticity, and that is in fidelity to our own experience and to our pleasure in musicking. All musicking is authentic when we are doing the best we can with what we have.

We know that today musical permeation is taking place on a global scale, with everybody listening to everybody else and all musical traditions up for grabs by whoever wants to make their musicking more interesting—or more profitable. This process of musical globalization, which is part of a process that has been going on for some five hundred years, if not more, *ought* to be a cause for celebration, but we all know that the process isn't as politically innocent as that. The much warmed-over dispute about Paul Simon's *Graceland* album shows us how right we are to be suspicious of the ways in which in practice it is being carried on, and how the perfectly natural desire in Western industrial culture for what others have to offer becomes too often a cover for greed and exploitation.

The process of globalization, which is to say, the linking together of the members of the human race by increasingly rapid and sophisticated means of transport and communication, has been going on for hundreds if not thousands of years and almost certainly represents the destiny of the human race, barring accidents. What is new in the last thirty years or so has been the way in which those who would enrich themselves at our expense have hijacked the process, along with the word, and have succeeded in convincing the world that the obscene enrichment of a few and the appalling impoverishment of millions, the uprooting of entire populations, the desolation of communities, the exclusion from work and society of tens of millions, and the increasing devastation of the environment are all unavoidable and even beneficent consequences of this globalization and of the single global free market that they present to us as inseparably linked to it.

In itself, globalization does not have to mean the destruction of diversity and the graying out of the world's cultures. On the contrary, it presents ever greater and richer opportunities for us to learn from one another and enjoy one another's company on this planet. What *is* destructive of human diversity is the insidious linking of globalization with those other processes while those who oppose those processes are dismissed contemptuously as mindless enemies of progress.

It is not cultures that we respect, or deprecate, or try to preserve, or destroy; it is people. Culture is an attribute of a person or of a group of people, and the word itself is an abstraction of those attitudes and dispositions that underlie human beings' ways of perceiving, feeling, thinking, and acting. The only way we can show respect for a person's culture is to show respect for what that person is. As all people are by definition authentic in their lives, so the words "authentic" and "inauthentic" don't seem to have much meaning in this context. If enslaved Africans, and their descendants down to the present day, had given any thought to authenticity, or to preserving a culture, we wouldn't have the way of musicking today that we call African American. What they must have had in mind was personal and communal survival, and the preservation of that precious sense of who they were without which survival was not worthwhile, and for that purpose they were prepared to take whatever lay to hand from their musical environment.

When we music we have no responsibility to any culture, not even to our own. Our only responsibility is to the pleasure we and our fellow musickers derive from our musicking. Because ultimately that's what we do it for—for the pleasure it gives us and the reciprocal pleasure of others that unites us for the duration of the performance in a community of like-feeling people. The rich and complex web of relationships that we create every time we music reaches far into the past and across the whole pattern of the living world. Even the most seemingly trivial and frivolous acts of musicking can be an exploration, an affirmation, and a celebration of the way in which we relate to one another and to that pattern.

We need not be afraid of misunderstanding others' ways of musicking. As I have suggested, what some call misunderstanding is more truthfully to be called *re*understanding, and it has always been a powerful force for keeping the work of creation on the move. We need not worry too much, either, about preservation, whether it be of the treasured works from the past or even of whole musical cultures. The true treasure is the human act of musicking, in the taking part in the act of music itself. The ability to do so, indeed the *need* to do so, is part of the evolutionary inheritance of every member of the human race. To be able to say, to ourselves and to anyone else who may be listening, *This who we are*, is central to human life and dignity, and this is surely the ultimate function of musicking in all our lives.

BIBLIOGRAPHY

Gilroy, Paul. 1999. *The Black Atlantic: Modernity and Double Consciousness.* London: Verso.

Mintz, Sidney W., and Price, Richard. 1976. *An Anthropological Approach to the Caribbean Past: A Caribbean Perspective.* ISHI Occasional Papers in Social Change 2. Philadelphia: Institute for the Study of Human Issues.

Small, Christopher. 1987. *Music of the Common Tongue: Survival and Celebration in African American Music.* Middletown, CT: Wesleyan University Press.

———. 1998. *Musicking: The Meanings of Performing and Listening.* Middletown, CT: Wesleyan University Press.

Taskin, Richard. 1992. "Pete Seeger." In *Encyclopedia of the American Left*, edited by Mari Jo Buhle, Paul Buhle, and Dan Georgakas. Urbana: University of Illinois Press.

Rock Concert

(2002)

I am thinking of a large outdoor concert I attended in Barcelona, given by a major female African American singer in one of the city's big football stadiums.

The stadium had been transformed by the erection at one end of a big temporary stage and four huge steel towers carrying lights and speakers, as well as two huge TV screens, one on either side of the stage, by means of which those who were far from the stage could at least see the star's image, even though the person herself in the distance appeared about the size of their thumb. The stage was littered with electronic keyboards and drum kits, and there was a small army of technicians carrying out last-minute adjustments and sound checks.

The stadium seats appeared to be all occupied, but the majority of the thirty thousand or so present were spread out on the turf, having brought rugs, inflatable cushions, and other aids to comfort. They waited patiently for the performance to begin, until well after the appointed time. The delay did not matter too much, since the mainly young crowd was good humored and sociable, drinking beer together and passing around joints (legal in Spain, I hasten to add), and everyone was having a good time. It seemed as if the delay were an expected part of the event, a time for strangers to get acquainted and to socialize.

A hardworking warmup band played a few numbers, of which nobody took much notice, and finally, nearly an hour after the appointed time, the star's own backing band came on stage to a burst of applause. The five musicians spread out across the huge stage, each with his umbilical electrical lead tethering him to his amplifier, and they played a number that served as a kind of overture, to summon the attention of the huge audience. As they finished, a disembodied voice through the sound system invited us to applaud the arrival of the star.

She came down an enormous staircase, previously invisible in the darkness but now brilliantly lit, as if she were descending from Olympus. She was wearing the briefest and tightest of dresses. The band played a great flourish, a flight of rockets went off, and the stage lights came on at full intensity. The noise of welcome was so great and so continuous that her first two numbers were almost lost, but it did not seem to matter, for SHE was here in the flesh, or at least on the two big screens.

She sang, she danced, she played with us, she flirted with us, she blew kisses to us through the microphone, and she made gestures of undisguised sexual invitation. She was never still for a moment, neither she nor her three backing singers and attendant dancers, all women. What she sang can hardly be remembered, but her husky voice, her air of having survived all that the world could throw at her (reinforced of course by the common knowledge of her vicissitudes), and the sexy energy she gave out were memorable enough.

She called on the audience over and over again to give back the energy she was giving out, and they obliged, with cheers and shouts, the linking of arms and the waving of lighted candles above their heads. For the duration of the performance, it seemed, thirty thousand people were welded together in a community of like-feeling people, celebrating our freedom from the restraints and frustrations of our everyday lives. Strangers to one another when we arrived at the stadium, thirty-five thousand people were united in a joyful community giving our homage to this remarkable woman. For a while the pattern that connects was tangible, palpable, and audible. It was a joyous occasion.

Was it all cleverly stage-managed illusion? The answer, I think, is yes and no. The star was remote and inaccessible, and nobody was allowed to see her outside her role on the stage. The sexual invitation, of course, was playacting, and everyone there knew it; for those misguided enough to mistake it for the real thing there was a team of heavies to keep overenthusiastic punters off the stage.

Again, everyone present had paid their tribute at the box office. We were consumers of a product, and the massive publicity campaign of the previous weeks, with press, radio and TV interviews, and saturation airplay of her songs, was there to prove it. Even the candles we waved over our heads were provided by the management at about four times what one would pay for them in a supermarket. There can be no doubt that money, and a lot of it, was involved, although how much of it found its way into the star's bank account is anyone's guess; we can take it as axiomatic that when an artist, any artist, makes a lot of money from his or her art it is only after a whole lot of other people have made a lot more money first. But the intensity of her performance that night must have another, deeper source. What it must feel like to be the center of attention for such a huge crowd I cannot begin to imagine, but I cannot believe that desire for money alone, or even for attention or fame in itself, can explain it. There seems to be a need in some people to make themselves a channel for that kind of energy, to take it on themselves to cure the loneliness of others, perhaps to cure their own. In tribal societies such people become shamans, but in our fragmented society some become psychiatrists, some become priests, and some become musicians, depending on the nature of their abilities. Each represents a fragment of the shaman's healing and self-healing art.

Surrounded as she was by all the paraphernalia of a modern rock concert, isolated up there on the huge stage, she took on the burden of thirty thousand strangers and, for a brief spell, aided only by a few musicians and dancers, overcame our isolation and made herself a catalyst for the creation of a new kind of community, and for the relationships for which we were longing.

Exploring, Affirming, Celebrating—and Teaching

(2003)

I have to confess that I am very ambivalent about the presence of music as a subject, compulsory or not, in school classrooms. We are all familiar with the claims that are made for the efficacy of music in human life and, especially, education. From Plato's "music is to instil inner harmony and its purpose is to cultivate the soul of the learner" to the contemporary American music educator David Elliott's "music education improves one's health, mind and soul," a multitude of writers and musicians have assured us of music's benefits to mind, body, and soul. It is claimed also that music relaxes the muscles, raises endorphin levels, produces general improvement in other schoolwork, and even raises IQ levels. Alas, it seems that few of these claims, true or not, have made much impression on our political masters, who continue to view music as an agreeable but quite optional extra in the school curriculum, to be discarded as soon as the going gets tough, and who see such concerns as literacy and competence in languages, mathematics, and science as having higher-priority claims on what are always scarce resources of money and time.

One can see some reason for this disregard. School systems today the world over are driven by a very narrow conception of what they are doing for their students. They see themselves primarily as engaged in equipping the students to take their place in the hierarchy of the corporate state, whether as workers, soldiers, bureaucrats, scientists, political and financial leaders, members of the seemingly permanent pool of workless—or artists whose task is to entertain the rest of us and keep us happy. The current worries about literacy, for example, are fueled by concern not so much about the pupils' inability to enjoy literature, or indeed write it, as about their ability to read instructions, advertisements, and income tax forms and to write reports and advertising copy, and so become fully functioning operatives of the industrial-corporate state. Again, after World War I it was only the demands of the British army in response to the appalling physical condition of so many of the conscripts in that war that led to the introduction of physical education in British schools. And again, I read a few months ago that the British government is becoming concerned about falling standards in mathematics in British schools. The schools, they say, are neglecting the skills that are demanded by employers and universities. Note that word, *demanded*; it was the word that was used in the press report. They are even considering offering math teachers five thousand pounds a year more than their colleagues in other subjects. The report didn't say what colleagues in other subjects thought about that.

This is not to deny the efforts of so many teachers who do genuinely see their pupils' interests in a much wider view, and who attempt to put that view into their professional work, but always precedence has to be given to the requirements of the corporate state, as they are expressed by examinations and qualifications, those tools of standardization without which no course of study can claim status or a resources.

Other objectives of schooling include the inculcation of the corporate values of regularity, punctuality, obedience to authority, and the capacity to endure monotony and boredom such as they will surely encounter in the workplace. We may be sure that even among those pupils who come out of the school system without any of the knowledge they are supposed to have acquired, none come out without a full knowledge of those objectives, even those who detest them with all their hearts.

We are, all of us, these days servants of the corporate state, even artists. We have been taught to believe that artists are special people, set aside, but nevertheless they are producers of a product, in this case called works of art, to be bought and sold like any other product, while the rest of us are consumers of their art; the phrase "production and consumption of art" is commonplace today among sociologists. Further, they can produce these artworks only if they can find someone to pay them, and that person will pay them only if, as with any other product, they can make a profit from it. From this fact comes what I call Small's Law of Artistic Production, which states, "If an artist makes a lot of money from his or her work, it is only after a lot of other people have made a lot of money from it first."

So why is it that we find music in the school curriculum at all? It is certainly not with the intention of training professional musicians, even though many conservatoire-trained teachers of music in schools tend to treat the training they themselves received as a model for their work, basing their lessons on the acquisition of literacy, even for those who will never have a chance to learn an instrument, and on other technical and historical trivia of classical music. The result is that for many students the music lesson is a time of at best boredom, at worst torture; a survey taken in British schools a few years ago found that music classes were rated second to last in order of preference, beaten into last place only by religious instruction. My own belief is that it is, first, an attempt to train pupils to be consumers of music—classical music, that is, since no one needs to be trained to consume popular music—and, second, a means of socialization into the values of the school and thus of the corporate state.

I said that I was very ambivalent about the presence of music as a school subject. This may surprise those who know I have long been a strong advocate of the powers of the musical act as a means of exploring, affirming, and celebrating that precious sense of who we are without which survival is scarcely worth fighting for. I am of course a passionate advocate of the involvement of children in musical and dance performance from the very earliest age, way before school age if possible, but I am not so sure that schools, at least as they are at present constituted, are the best places to provide such involvement.

First let me explain a little my own ideas of the nature of music and its function in human life.

The first thing to be said about music is that it is not a thing or a collection of things. Surely there do exist musical objects that we call works, and we are accustomed to treasuring these works, analyzing them, and exploring their meanings, the B Minor Mass, perhaps, or the Beethoven Ninth Symphony. But what we ought to be treasuring more than these quasi-sacred objects is the music act itself, musicking, that remarkable form of human encounter in which people come together to make meanings, to explore, to affirm, and yes, celebrate for a while their common humanity and their sense of who they are and where they belong. All those treasured music objects are nothing more than concretions of the human activity, and it is as activity first and foremost that we need to understand music. The trouble is that we become so befuddled by the tendency of language to turn ideas and actions into nouns that we come to think of them as things in themselves and attribute to them a life of their own.

I believe that to a large extent it is the befuddlement induced by this reification of music that is a source of great confusion in music education today. Music education is not alone in this; the whole of Western education is befuddled by the reification of knowledge. As an antidote to the reification of music, I offer the word *musicking*, from the verb "to music." I coined it myself, and so I claim the right to define it, which I do as follows: to music is to take part in a musical performance in any capacity, that is, not just as performer but also as listener, as dancer should anyone be dancing, and even perhaps as ticket taker at the door and piano mover. Musicking is something that people do together; all those present are taking part in it, and the fact that the one verb covers everything that is going on in the space where the performance is taking place means that it makes no distinction between what the performers are doing and what the rest are doing. It is not a matter of composers, or even performers, actively doing something for the passive rest to receive. Whatever it is we are doing, we are all doing it together, and we all bear a responsibility for the success or failure of the human encounter that is the performance.

What it is we are doing, I believe, is making meanings and giving structure to our experience. Like all encounters between human beings, it takes place in both a physical and a social setting, and that setting has to be taken into account when we ask what meanings are being generated. Musical meaning is thus to be found not only in those musical objects Western tradition teaches us are its sole repository but also in the act of musicking itself. What is being performed is of course significant, but it does not wholly determine the meaning of the event as a whole. What musical meaning is concerned with is an important question that I have no space here to go into. It is dealt with at length in two of my books, *Music of the Common Tongue* (1987) and *Musicking* (1998), but briefly, I believe it has to do with relationships, relationships between person and person, person and society, and humanity and the natural and maybe even the supernatural world. Through the act of musicking we explore, we affirm, and we celebrate those relationships we believe hold our universe together; we experience them as we feel they ought to be; and since how we relate is who we are, in doing so we are exploring, affirming, and celebrating our sense of identity, our sense of who we are and of where we belong.

During a musical performance we do not just *learn about* these relationships but actually *experience* them in all their marvelous complexity, too complex to be expressed in words, through the power of the human and musical relationships that are established in the performance space. That, I believe, is the reason that when we have taken part in a good and satisfying performance we feel more fully ourselves, more fully realized, and more in tune (the metaphor is significant) with ourselves and our fellows. We feel we have been afforded a glimpse of how the world really is.

We could say that those who are musicking are saying, to themselves, to one another, and to anyone who may be listening, *This is who we are*. That applies no less to those who are taking part in symphonic and opera performances than to those enslaved Africans and their descendants throughout the Americas for whom musicking has always been more than a source of pleasure or comfort but quite literally a weapon for survival and for the affirmation of humanity and community in the face of a society that denies both. A symphony concert in this respect is in fact no different from a blues performance or a rock concert, or for that matter a performance by a West African drum ensemble, or a Balinese gamelan. Each is a ritual that for the members of a social group serves to affirm their identity and reinforce the group's solidarity, and the values that a symphony concert embodies are no more and no less universal than those of any of the others.

Musicking has long functioned as a means of self-definition, who we are or think we are socially. For if members of different social groups have different values, that is, different concepts of ideal relationships, then the kinds of musical performances that enact those relationships will differ from one another also. We must be careful not to be too categorical about this. If there is a degree of overlap between the values of different social groups—and it is rare to find no overlap at all, even in the most seemingly opposed groups—then we can expect to find a degree of overlap between their ways of musicking. We remember of course that musicking takes in not just the sounds and their relationships but all the various activities that constitute a musical performance as a whole. And if we take into account the interest and even sympathy that can exist among members of different social groups, then we see that ways of musicking are not by any means watertight, but that they constantly interpermeate and play off one another.

Everyone, every normally endowed human being, is born with the gift of music no less than the gift of speech. And when I talk about the gift of music I do not mean only the ability to understand someone else's performance. I do not even mean the ability to perform musical utterances that someone else has created. I mean the ability to create and to perform their own musical utterances. After all, we take it for granted that every normal human being is born with the potential to make his or her own spoken utterances. Everyone does it all the time. I know there are important differences between speech acts and musical acts, but in this they are alike—that everyone is born with the potential not only to understand such acts but also to make their own.

That does not mean I think everyone is a potential Beethoven or Louis Armstrong or even Andrew Lloyd Webber. We accept without difficulty the idea that some people are more gifted with words than others, and we have poets and orators and writers, but that does not deceive us into thinking only those with those kinds of gifts are to be allowed to speak. Nor do we try to confine people to speaking only what has already been written, even if what has been written is the words of Lope de Vega or of Shakespeare. Nor do we demand that everything we say be original and emotionally powerful.

Such everyday transactions are of central importance in human life. We know that speech acts, however banal and unoriginal they may be, serve to define us as social beings, and to create and to maintain our relationships to other human beings and to the other creatures with whom we share our planet, and thus to bring us to full status as socially integrated human beings.

I am convinced that taking part in acts of music is of equal importance in human life. For the act of music is part of the ancient language of gesture that enables human beings to articulate their relationships with themselves, with one another, and with the rest of the living world, in a way in which words cannot. During a musical performance, any musical performance anywhere and at any time, people are using sounds that have been brought into certain kinds of relationships with one another as the focus for a ceremony in which their values, which is to say their concepts of what constitutes right relationships, are explored, are affirmed, and are celebrated.

And further, if each performance articulates the values of the members of a social group, then every musical performance is inescapably to some extent a political act. Politics of course is about power, and an important element of power is the power to define oneself rather than be defined, to say, *This is who I am*, or *This is who we are*, as against those who would say, *That is who you are*, or even, *That is what you are*, which is to say less than fully human. Much of the historical class struggle, not to mention the struggles against racism and sexism, consists in that struggle for the power to define oneself rather than be defined by others.

What it seems to me is needed for children of all ages (as they say) is not music education but opportunities for musical performance at every level from birth onward. Every normally endowed human being is born with the potential to take an active part in musical no less than speech acts. Newborn babies immediately start performing with adults and within weeks show considerable virtuosity in gaining their attention and interacting with gestures of body, face, and above all, voice. The more a parent responds to these gestures, the more rapidly and purposefully the child will develop his or her behavior. This is the beginning of both speech and musical skills. What is needed in the early years of life is not so much formal instruction as informal interaction with adults and with peers and contemporaries. Children need mothers, and fathers too, who will sing to them and encourage them to sing back, and perhaps above all, they need bouncing and dandling in rhythm, even before they can walk. And we need a broad social context in which these activities are taught and encouraged as an important and enjoyable activity for everyone.

The big challenge to music educators today seems to me to be how to provide that kind of social context for informal as well as formal musical interaction that leads to real development and to the musicalizing of the society as a whole. Spain is an extraordinarily fortunate society in this respect, with its powerful traditions of popular music making and dancing still very much alive and providing the kind of social context of which I am talking. I remember vividly my astonishment and joy the first time I saw the sardana being danced in the Plaça de la Catedral in Barcelona, not as folklore or as something self-conscious and archaic but as a matter-of-fact part of the citizens' everyday life. I remember equally vividly my first *Festa Mayor* in Sitges, where the sights and sounds of the dances, the grallers and drums, the devils with their marvelous petard music, and the solemn but joyful *moixeganga* moved me to tears and continue to do so year by year as the ritual repeats itself, changing almost imperceptibly year by year in response to changing social ways.

One important way of musicalizing the society is to employ popular musicians and dancers of all kinds—not only practitioners of indigenous styles but also pop, rock, and jazz musicians, and perhaps above all, Africans, African Americans, African Hispanics, and African Caribbeans, in whom there is no separation between dance and music.

There is a great richness there, a richness that inspired me to write what I think is my best book, *Music of the Common Tongue*, about the encounter that occurred between African and various European ways of musicking under the conditions of slavery and its aftermath in the Americas. In that book I affirm that it is that way, or rather those ways, of musicking, and not the once-great European classical tradition, that is the major music of the West in the twentieth and probably the twenty-first century. Far from being a behemoth that is sweeping away local ways of musicking, it has become a language that disadvantaged people the world over can use to assert their own identity, their own *This is who we are*, and it has adapted itself with extraordinary courtesy to form a medium for disadvantaged people everywhere.

It is not just a musical richness but a social richness as well, and we ought to be tapping it and its musicians in the musical development of young people. For African American traditions have inherited the African assumption that everyone is capable of making his or her own musical utterances, as well as the assumption that the whole body is involved in the music act, so that music and dance are inseparable. Thus are developed not only performance skills in the narrow sense but the creative faculty as well, and the social interaction among peers that is necessary for the making of a performance in those traditions.

In those popular traditions the creative act is open to all, and although performers can and do attain amazing levels of skill and virtuosity, those whose skills are modest or even rudimentary can still do something and be admired. They can then develop those skills through continually doing the best they can with what they have, not through studies and exercises, not through scales and arpeggios, but through performing, in social contexts that everyone understands and where everyone feels comfortable.

So it is that if we wish to develop that musicality that is born in each and every one of us, and that is an important element of our coming to full maturity as social beings, we need to start early, ideally much, much earlier than the age at which children start school. We need to provide a constant supportive background of socially approved activities in which the child's whole body is involved, and we need to encourage the children to dance, not to the mechanical thud-thud-thud of disco or techno but to the subtle, flexible rhythms of Spanish, African, and African American popular musics, especially salsa. Then can come playing instruments.

I have said that I am very ambivalent about the presence of music as a subject in the school system as we know it today, and I now have to spell out my reasons for that ambivalence. One obvious problem is that the development of musicality, like the development of speech, takes place more or less from the moment of birth, and yet a crucial six years will pass before the child enters the school system. What we can do about that gap I do not know, other than an intensive program of making parents aware of the importance of this period in their children's lives. But we should be aware of the gap and try to close it by whatever means we can.

Even when the child does enter school there are problems. It is a question primarily of values. Teachers, even those relatively few who are themselves competent in popular styles, and who want to introduce those styles into the school, are confronted by a number of difficulties, of which the possible opposition of colleagues and superiors is by no means the greatest. There is the question of examinations, those touchstones of intellectual respectability and practical worth; in school, unless there is an examination and a qualification at the end, a course has no status and no perceived value. But music examinations concern themselves exclusively with the techniques and the history of Western classical music, so that the teacher has to put those who want to make a serious study of music to the study of that tradition and of that tradition only.

The Western classical tradition has any number of limitations as an instrument of musicalization. In the first place, the social base of those who compose, perform, and listen to it is extremely narrow. It makes an appeal to only a small proportion of the population, and investigation in other countries has shown that its social base has scarcely widened at all over several generations despite attempts to enlarge it through teaching it in schools.

In the second place, it demands literacy before it is possible even to begin performing, which not only places an additional barrier between children and performance but also inhibits the creative act of which, as I have said, all normally endowed human beings are at least potentially capable, and confines it to a very small number of gifted and specially trained people called composers, who tell the rest what they are to do. And in the third place, the way a performance is organized is very hierarchical; the musical impulse flows from the composer, by means of his (rarely her, which is itself significant) score, through the director to the individual performer, so that social interaction *among* the performers is extremely limited, with no space at all for the kind of social give-and-take that is possible when they are working together on making their own. And lastly, it demands a high level of skill before any performer is deemed fit to perform in public.

There is another problem as well. On the one hand, the children as they perform and listen to music of any kind are finding their way to forms of expression that will help them in the exploration, the affirmation, and the celebration of who they are. But if they opt, as most do, for forms of musical expression that lie outside the Western classical tradition, they are likely to find themselves affirming values that may be very different from those our society expresses through its schools and enforces by means of examinations. These other ways of making music do not depend on literacy, that essential tool of school and state socialization, nor do they require the formal instruction of compliant groups of pupils.

Their performance demands not stillness, isolation, and abstract contemplation but movement, communality, and involvement, all of which are out of place in the conventional school. And I cannot imagine any form of examination that would not do violence to the very nature of these ways of musicking, because of the standardization that examinations by *their* own nature impose on the teaching methods themselves. Examinations bear their share of responsibility for the death of classical music, and they will kill other musics also if they are given half a chance.

Of course, all musical performance, like all speech, has its rules and its conventions, and without those no communication, and quite probably no thinking either, can take place. Those rules have to be learnt by performers and listeners alike, but they need a context in which they are learnt, in the same way as we learn the rules of our language, by doing, and absorbed without too much conscious thought—and certainly not through examinations.

I believe that the aims of developing musicality would be better served by a network of music centers throughout the country where children of any age can learn and practice with one another, with supervisors and instructors on hand to give aid where it is needed. The current structure of schools inhibits interaction between children of different ages, thus eliminating the ability of older children to teach younger (and the learning that takes place when one teaches something), and this would be a way of using this unused educational resource. The excellent network of local municipal conservatories that already exists in this country [Spain] could well form the basis of this kind of music center, and it seems that the conservatories themselves are eager to expand their work in something like this direction.

I enunciated earlier Small's Law of Artistic Production. It is now time to state Small's Law of Quality in Musicking. It is this: the best musicking is done by those who do the best they can with what they have. According to this law, the eager beginner can make performances of finer quality than the bored routinized professional. It is not, as some people have suggested to me, a recipe for smug mediocrity. Rather, it reminds us that we are musicking from the first moment we open our mouths to sing or when we lay our hand on our first instrument, and from those first moments the act of musicking is functioning to empower us to explore, to affirm, and above all to celebrate that precious sense of who we are.

REFERENCES

Elliott, David. 1995. *Music Matters: A New Philosophy of Music Education*. New York: Oxford University Press.

Small, Christopher. (1987) 1998. *Music of the Common Tongue: Survival and Celebration in African American Music*. London: John Calder. Reprint, Middletown, CT: Wesleyan University Press.

———. 1998. *Musicking: The Meanings of Performing and Listening*. Middletown, CT: Wesleyan University Press.

Deep and Crisp and Even

(2008)

It seems that everyone, every English-speaking person at least, but myself loves Christmas carols. They remind people of childhood, of gaiety and light, and color and festivity, at the darkest time of the year. To sing or to hear the familiar songs envelops people in a golden light, and if anyone ventures to question or criticize those songs they are provoked to feelings of distress and even of outrage.

The aesthetic, if I may use so pompous a term, of performing Christmas carols is for me summed up in a picture on the cover of a book of carols that I have on my desk. It shows a little town with steepled church where the snow lies deep and crisp and even. Earth lies hard as iron, water like a stone. Windows glow with golden light, and chimney smoke ascends gracefully and nonpollutingly through bare trees toward a full moon. In the middle distance a lamplighter and his boy go cheerfully about their business. In the foreground a couple arriving in a one-horse open sleigh are being welcomed into a house by laughing friends and by four lusty singers whom I take to be waits, while through the door left wide open, though the frost is cruel, we see a happy group singing around a piano. Their costume is vaguely early Victorian in style, the period of Mr. Pickwick. It is a convivial scene.

I grew up in a country at the other end of the world, where Christmas fell at the summer, not the winter, solstice and had no strong feelings about either Christmas or carols. Like my contemporaries, I sang them dutifully but without too much enthusiasm; this festival belonged to midwinter and was not really organic to our part of the world. Our colonial education, however, gave us to understand that Christmas in the favored north was indeed something like the cover of that carol book, and our feelings for that Mother England that our parents' generation still called "home," even though most of them had never seen it, were bound up with images of that snow-covered Dickensian Christmas that we could only imagine.

But in the twenty-five years I spent in England, I did not experience a single white Christmas (I finally experienced one in Louisville, Kentucky, of all places), let alone anything resembling Dickensian-style festivities, and I realized after a few years that the Dickensian character with whom I most identified was not Mr. Pickwick but Ebenezer Scrooge—not the deflated, scared-out-of-his-life Scrooge who was bullied into buying a goose for the Cratchit family but the unregenerate, rip-roaring Scrooge, snarling "Humbug!" whenever anyone mentioned Christmas. The anxieties and irritations of Christmas cards, each one that arrived bearing its load of guilt, and Christmas shopping, not to mention the hangovers after too many compulsory boozy parties, quickly dispersed any feelings I might have harbored of Pickwickian benevolence.

And on Christmas Day nobody went visiting, and certainly not in a one-horse open sleigh, though even that vehicle might have been welcome since all forms of public transport stopped around midday. Each nuclear family shut itself up in its house or flat, overate, and watched on television images of goodwill and gaiety that did little to compensate for the stresses of being imprisoned for the day in the exclusive company of parents and siblings. If you didn't have a nuclear family you were in an even worse plight, since you spent the day either alone or in the company of other refugees, watching on TV those same scenes of goodwill and gaiety that you imagined must be going on all around you. It is no wonder there are so many suicides around Christmas.

It is all a great pity, since the north undoubtedly needs a festival of light and color to see itself through the darkest time of the year and to persuade the sun to return (nobody seems to have figured out that the south might benefit from such a festival in June). The Christian church did well to choose the old Roman Saturnalia, those five days around the winter solstice when the cosmic and the social order were suspended, for the birthday festival of its god. But this festival of conspicuous consumption and gluttony seems to me to have little real festiveness about it, and no conviviality.

I set down my feelings about the English Christmas, not to knock it but to try to understand why it is that people, even those for whom the Christian myth and its theology no longer means much, should to all appearances treasure it so much, and in particular to enjoy to sing Christmas carols and to hear them sung.

What we hear when we sing or listen to a piece of music or a song, and a Christmas carol is no exception, is a sequence of sounds arranged in a particular order. In the case of a song, there is a complex interaction of the sung pitches and rhythms with those vocal timbres whose combinations we recognize as words. The sung pitches, in fact, are inflected with the timbre patterns of speech. In our highly literate culture, we are accustomed to think of songs as being words that are "set" to music, and I have even seen discussions of the meanings of songs that confine themselves to a discussion of the verbal texts. But songs as they are sung—and we should bear in mind that it is *only* in the singing of them that musical meaning is created—are not just "words and music" or even "words-and-music," but complex patterns of sounds in which pitches and rhythms cannot be separated out from the timbre patterns of speech without doing violence to the nature of the singing.

It is important that we think of it this way around. The account I have given elsewhere of the nature of paralanguage suggests not only that it was that which came first and verbal language later but also that paralanguage conveys meanings that are even more fundamental in human life than those of speech. Thus the significance of that complex series of vocal gestures we call singing has less to do with the meaning of the verbal texts, as read on the page, than it has to do with the meaning of the vocal gesture of singing. Those British people, for example, who sing their national anthem pay little attention to the fact that its verbal text hardly even makes sense, let alone grammatical sentences:

> Send her victorious,
> Happy and glorious,
> Long to reign over us,
> God save the queen.

What that text does do is contribute to the meaning of the act of singing the national anthem, through its articulation, in the most vague and generalized terms, of sentiments (i.e., representations in consciousness of computations about relationships) that few people would care to articulate in everyday speech. The jibe that "if it's too silly to say, then sing it" is not completely without basis in reality, though we do not have to put it so negatively.

Similarly, if we examine *on the page* the verbal texts of Christmas carols we find they range from the discredited:

> The Lord at first did Adam make
> Out of the dust and clay.

to the puerile:

> Christian children all must be
> Mild, obedient, good as he.

(an injunction that is flatly contradicted by accounts in the gospels of clashes between the Christ child and his mother) to the sentimental and nostalgic:

> Deck the hall with boughs of holly, Fa la la, etc.,
> 'Tis the season to be jolly, Fa la la, etc.
> Don we now our gay apparel, Fa la la, etc.

And from the patronizing, not to say contentious:

> Rejoice, rejoice, Emmanuel
> Has come to thee, O Israel.

(the word has gained sour overtones since Margaret Thatcher's famous injunction to the British people after the glorious victory of Goose Green in the 1982 Falklands War to "go home and rejoice!") to the downright aggressive:

> This holy tide of Christmas
> All other doth deface.

None of these assertions, of course, will stand up to a moment's cool examination when studied on the page. But when sung, these accounts of the birth of the god are only a part of that larger whole that is the performance.

So what *does* it mean to perform these songs? Whatever answer we arrive at will always be concerned with the nature of the relationships that are created by the performance. Those relationships will be ideal relationships as imagined by those who are taking part. And since, as we have seen, who we are is how we relate, it follows that a musical performance can be seen as a kind of laboratory in which we try out relationships and identities, explore them and learn about them, and finally affirm and celebrate them, all without necessarily having to commit ourselves to them. If the meaning is embodied in the whole performance, then it is not enough to say that these songs in themselves mean such and such; we can only say that for certain people to be singing them at a certain time, in a certain situation, in a certain way, creates a certain set of relationships between the participants, which provide the meaning of the performance. There are of course meanings in common over all performances, but in each different situation different meanings are also being generated.

Christmas carols are associated today with the rituals of the Christian church, but their origin and the early conditions of their performance, from the Middle Ages onward, were outside the church, and their tone is more secular than liturgical. Up to the time of the Reformation, singing them was in fact a part of popular musicking, and it was often disapproved of by the church authorities as being too frivolous for the solemnity of the Christmas festival. The foursquare melodic patterns and dancelike rhythms suggest an origin distinct from that of liturgical music, at least up to the time of Martin Luther and the Reformation, and many have a distinct modal cast of folk song about them, often masked by the conventional four-part harmonization. Others, mostly post-Reformation, are derived from the practice of Protestant hymn singing. The influence of folk art and, later, of Protestant hymnody can be seen also in the verbal texts.

There were carols for other seasons also, for Easter, for May Day, and for midsummer, all of them old pagan festivals that were taken over by the church. It is well known that some Christmas carol texts incorporate quite frankly pagan elements, such as references to the druidic sacred trees, the holly and the ivy. The singing of these secular-sounding tunes and, to modern eyes and ears, "quaint" verses, would seem to represent an attempt to retain the spirit of the older festivities in a form the church would tolerate.

Singing Christmas carols in church is a modern custom. Some "traditional" carol services, like the Festival of Nine Lessons and Carols, which is televised across the British nations every Christmas Eve from King's College Chapel, Cambridge, and widely imitated in parish churches, date only from the middle years of the twentieth century and have no foundation in earlier liturgies. The acceptance by the church of these songs into its liturgy looks very much like an attempt to regain a popular base by assimilating elements of popular culture. In order to justify the assimilation an "ancient" tradition has to be invented, a not unusual tactic on the part of people in authority. On the other hand, carol singing has gained legitimacy through assimilation into the church, so that the old popular songs have become respectable among the higher orders of society. It is a process not unlike the assimilation of surviving popular music into the "classical" tradition on which I have remarked elsewhere.

The extent of this assimilation was brought home to me one Christmas Eve in London a few years ago, when a friend and I went to the midnight service in a church in Chelsea, hoping to catch a little Christmas spirit. Not a bit of it. The choir, remote and invisible in its loft, sang the carols to us, or for us, beautifully of course (but who needs such beauty?) while the congregation just stood in silence and listened. My friend and I felt unwanted and vaguely insulted, as if our singing were not deemed worthy to contribute to the occasion. We left as soon as we decently could. For us, the relationships of the event were decidedly wrong, though for others who were present it seemed that they were decidedly right.

Most carol singing, of course, still takes place not in churches but in the street, in homes, in shops and supermarkets (if we allow, as I think we must, the playing of recordings to be a type of performance), on radio and TV, in bars and pubs, and in schools and other educational institutions. Each of these situations sets up its own relationships. I have not the space to go into them all separately, but broadly, I believe the key to the meaning of all these performances is to be found on the cover of my carol book.

If I had to sum up in a word the scene it depicts, that word would be "nostalgic." It is set in a comfortable, affluent-looking village, and all the smiling people portrayed are clearly well fed and prosperous, not a beggar, or even a Bob Cratchit, and certainly not a Scrooge, in sight. The rosy-cheeked waits, members of the lower orders as can be seen from their clothes, are cheerfully singing for the pleasure of their social betters. The lamplighter and his boy go about their business without bothering anyone. More than anything else, the image is one of social stability and harmony, where everyone knows and accepts his or her place in society, which is all the more powerful for being so unselfconsciously and almost naively depicted. Above all, it is set in the past—understandably, for who would dare to depict such a harmonious scene in a present-day setting?

Now I have no desire to knock images of social stability and harmony; it is one of the businesses of artistic activity to deal in such images. But in the case of this image, we have to ask, *Whose image is it of Christmas past? What kind of social stability does it depict?* I do not imagine that those who composed the carols had in mind such images, for our past was their present and they would most likely not have found such images to be true of their own time any more than they are of ours. Some might have done so, of course, but the coincidence between the feeling conjured up for most people today by the singing of carols and those conjured up by this picture is too great to be ignored. (The village, by the way, bears a strong resemblance to certain affluent suburbs of modern North American cities, which adds another layer to the palimpsest of meanings; the book was published in the United States, but the location is certainly not Bethlehem, Pennsylvania.)

The feeling in both cases is profoundly nostalgic, a longing for past times when social and stability and harmony still existed. Those lines I have quoted from carols leave room for interpretation in this way, even if their writers did not intend it. Nostalgia for past social stability is a way not only of justifying present social relationships but also of freezing them. It is common among ruling and dominant classes, and is particularly prevalent among the English, and I suspect the American, middle and upper classes. It is in my opinion the most dangerous of social poisons.

Christmas today for most people in Anglophone societies has little to do with the birth of Christ. The Christ child is a convention, a lay figure on which to hang the eating, the drinking, the spending, and the buying and giving of presents. The response that the singing of Christmas carols arouses in most people has more to do with secular social relationships than with the birth of the god. Of course, musicking, religion, and the social order are inextricably intertwined; all religions attempt to order social life by aligning the social order with that of visible nature and with an invisible cosmic order that has to be imagined. In that sense the singing of Christmas carols is no quaint survival but is on the one hand a thoroughly contemporary activity, and on the other a religious activity in the most profound way.

Six Aphorisms and Five Commentaries

(2007)

Robert Schumann, in his writings on music, was fond of using aphorisms, short pithy sayings, to encapsulate his advice to young musicians. To the original edition of his *Album for the Young* of 1848, he attached a collection of nearly seventy of these, for the benefit of those youngsters who would be playing the pieces in the album. They are sound advice, even if some appear to today's readers a bit priggish, and as one would expect, they are confined to the practices of the European tradition. I too have been coining aphorisms over the years, and in this essay I offer half a dozen of them. Unlike Schumann I shall attach to each a commentary that enlarges on and, hopefully, clarifies those perhaps cryptic sayings that form the pillars on which my text rests.

APHORISM 1: THERE IS NO SUCH THING AS MUSIC

Music is not a thing at all. It is an activity in which humans like to engage. The essence of that activity lies not in created works but in the act of performance.

It is a pity, therefore, that Western scholars of music are generally in agreement that the essence of music lies in created works and that that idea governs their researches and their writings. Whatever meaning music may have is thought to reside in those created objects. They are thought of as floating through history, untouched by time and change, waiting for their listeners to draw that meaning out. A succinct formulation of this idea comes from the doyen of modern German musicologists, Carl Dahlhaus (1983), who tells us, flatly, that "the subject matter of music is made up, primarily, of significant works of music that have outlived the culture of their age" and that "the concept 'work' and not 'event' is the cornerstone of music history."

This concept of the nature of music comes with a few corollaries. The first is that musical performance plays no part in the creative process but is only the medium through which the work has to pass if it is to reach its listener. We read little in the literature about performance as an activity in its own right, other than in the limited sense of following the composer's notations and realizing them in sound. We learn little about performers, either, as creators of musical meaning. Their performances may clarify or obscure a work, but they have nothing to contribute to its core meanings; those have been determined by the composer before a performer ever lays eyes on it.

Second, a musical performance is thought of as a one-way communication system that runs from composer through performer to listener. This means that the listener's task is to contemplate the work, to try to understand it, and to respond but that like performers they have nothing to contribute to its meaning, which is the composer's business. The idea also implies that music is an individual matter, that composing, performing, and listening take place in a social vacuum. The way in which the act of listening takes place in a classical concert is evidence of this; each listener sits, silent and immobile in the midst of a crowd of people, not communicating with those beside him or her or with the performers for the duration of the performance.

These are of course all attitudes that belong more or less exclusively to the Western classical tradition. In other great traditions there may be no such thing as a stable and permanent musical work at all; performers enjoy inventing their own material as they perform, drawing on remembered melodies and rhythms and on their own power of invention within the strict order of tradition. Communication between performers and listeners is two way, often taking place through the medium of dance. John M. Chernoff (1979) says that when he was studying drumming among the Ewe of Ghana, "When I played poorly for dancers, they *danced* their criticism by executing their steps in a half-hearted way, or they helped me by simplifying their steps."

But even within an exclusively literate musical culture such as the Western classical tradition, this exclusive concentration on musical works and the relegation of the act of performance to subordinate status has, I believe, resulted in a misunderstanding of the nature, and an impoverishment of the experience, of music. For it is not true that performance takes place to present a musical work. That is to put things the wrong way around.

APHORISM 2: MUSICAL WORKS EXIST TO GIVE PERFORMERS SOMETHING TO PERFORM

J. S. Bach knew this and so did Mozart and their contemporaries. They composed what they composed to give performers something to perform. Their work was aimed directly at specific performers (as often as not, themselves) and at the audiences that were to hear them on a specific occasion, with little thought for the opinions of posterity. The rot, as Benjamin Britten once said, started with Beethoven, with his "What-do-I-care-for-your-silly-box-of-wires?" attitude toward performers. Perhaps it would be better, and more respectful, to say that the rot started with the unfortunate fact that the greatest European musician of his time by far was as deaf as a post and could no longer perform.

Performing and listening are activities; they are something that people do. That being so, the word for the activity of music ought to be a verb, not a noun, and I have taken the liberty of coining a new verb (or reviving an old one with a new meaning)—the verb "to music." Having coined it I claim the right to define it, as follows: *To music is to take part, in any capacity, in a musical performance.* We can include within the definition of the verb not only the activities of performing but also those of listening, of rehearsing or practicing, of preparing material for performance (what we call composing), or of dancing, should anyone be dancing (in many musical cultures, if no one is dancing then no musicking is happening).

Apart from favoring the idea that musicking is first and foremost action, the verb has other useful implications. In making no distinction between what the performers are doing and what the rest of those taking part are doing, it reminds us that musicking is an activity in which all those present are engaged, and for whose nature and quality, success or failure, everyone present bears some responsibility. It is not a matter of active performers doing something for, or to, passive listeners. Whatever is being done, we are all doing it together, and all the activities associated with the performance add up to a single event, whose nature is affected by all the ways in which these activities—composing, rehearsing, performing, listening, and so on—are carried out. We could fruitfully think of a musical performance as a human encounter that takes place through the mediation of sounds that are organized in specific ways and into specific sets of relationships.

That being so, it is not enough to ask, *What is the meaning of this piece of music?* which is the conventional question asked by scholars and musicologists, and even performers, who ought to know better. The wider, more interesting and more fruitful question is, *What does it mean when this performance takes place at this time, in this place, and with these participants?* By framing the question in that way, the meanings generated by the work of music itself, should there be one, will be part, but only part, of the answer. The second question, in fact, does not exclude the first but rather subsumes it.

What those meanings may be is too complex a question for me to examine here (they can be read in my book *Musicking* [1998, 13 et seq.]), but briefly, they are concerned with relationships. Those relationships are to be found not only among those organized sounds, which are conventionally thought of as being the stuff of music, but also among the people who are taking part, in any capacity, in the performance. They model, or stand as metaphor for, ideal human relationships as they are imagined to be by those taking part: relationships between person and person, between individual and society, between humanity and the natural, and perhaps even the supernatural, world. These are important matters, perhaps the most important in human life, and we learn them through the act of musicking, any act of musicking, no matter how trivial and frivolous it may appear to be. In the act of musicking we do not just *learn about* these relationships; we actually *experience* them in all their wonderful complexity, a complexity that is too great to be expressed in words.

APHORISM 3: EVERY NORMALLY ENDOWED HUMAN BEING IS BORN WITH THE GIFT OF MUSIC NO LESS THAN THE GIFT OF SPEECH

When I talk about the gift of music, I do not mean just the gift to understand someone else's musical utterances. I do not even mean the ability to perform musical utterances that someone else has created. I mean the ability to create and to perform one's own musical utterances. We take it for granted that every normal human being is born with the potential to make his or her own speech utterances; everyone does it all the time. I am aware that there are important differences between musical and speech utterances, but in this respect they are alike: that everyone is born with the potential not only to understand but also to create them.

That does not mean I think everybody is a potential Louis Armstrong or

Beethoven or even Andrew Lloyd Webber (well, perhaps the last of these). We accept without difficulty the idea that some people are more gifted with words than others, and we have poets and orators and writers, but that does not deceive us into thinking that only those with those kinds of gifts are to be permitted to speak. Nor do we try to confine people to speaking only what has already been written, even if it is the words of Dante, Cervantes, or Shakespeare. Nor do we demand that everything we say be original or emotionally powerful. In fact the vast bulk of what any human being says in his or her everyday speech transactions is banal, unoriginal, and repetitious.

But nevertheless these transactions are of central importance in human life. We know that these everyday speech acts are serving to define us as social beings and to create and maintain our relationships to other humans and with the creatures with which we share our planet, and thus bring us to full status as socially integrated human beings.

I am convinced that taking part in acts of music is of equal importance in human life. For the act of music is part of the ancient language of gesture, which enables us to articulate our relationships with ourselves, with other humans, and with the rest of the living world, in ways that words cannot. It is almost certain that gestural utterances appeared before spoken ones; certainly that is the case in the early development of individual human beings.

During a musical performance, any musical performance at any time and in any place, members of a human group are using sounds that have been brought into certain kinds of relationships, both simultaneous and over time, as the focus for a ceremony, a ritual if you like, in which their values, that is, their concepts of right relationships, are explored, are affirmed, and are celebrated.

I find myself using those three words a lot, so I shall explain briefly why I do so.

Exploration

By bringing into existence, for as long as the performance lasts, relationships that those taking part feel to be desirable, a musical performance not only reflects those relationships but also shapes them. It allows those taking part to experience those ideal relationships without having to try to articulate them in words. It allows us to try them on, so to speak, to see how they fit emotionally (emotions being the representation in consciousness of computations concerning relationships), without having to commit ourselves to them for more than the duration of the performance. A musical performance is thus an instrument of exploration.

Affirmation

In articulating those ideal relationships, those values, it empowers us to say, to ourselves, to one another, and to anyone else who may be paying attention, *these* are the relationships we value in this world, and consequently (since how we relate is who we are), *this* is who we are. In the case of underdog groups like enslaved Africans, and their descendants, in the Americas this may be a way of affirming their humanity and their value in the face of those who would deny both. But by the same token, taking part in a symphony concert may be a way for members of the industrial middle and upper classes to affirm who they (or we) believe themselves (or ourselves) to be. A musical performance is thus an instrument of affirmation.

Celebration

In empowering us to explore and affirm our values, taking part in an act of musicking leaves us with a feeling of being more completely ourselves, more in tune with the world and with our fellows. When we have taken part in a good and satisfying performance, we are able to feel that *this* is how the world really is and *this* is how we relate to it. In short, it leaves the participants feeling good. It is thus an instrument of celebration.

I need hardly add that the more actively we take part in the musical act, whether as performers, listeners, or dancers, or indeed as composers, who provide the material from which the performers perform, the more alert and effective will be our exploration, our affirmation, and our celebration.

APHORISM 4: ALL MUSICAL KNOWLEDGE ARISES FROM PERFORMANCE

It follows that theoretical musical knowledge (i.e., any knowledge that is transmitted by means of marks on paper) is of interest or value only insofar as it relates to musical performance.

We know that human beings do not come into the world with the ability fully formed to take part in speech acts. We have the potential to do so, but that potential has to be developed, and in all but the most deprived young children, that development takes place more or less from the moment of birth, through interaction, first with the mother and with other family members, and later with peers and elders. The child's potential for speech is developed in countless daily encounters and interactions, and that means not only the ability to manipulate words themselves and the syntax by which relations between words are governed but also the ancient language of vocal intonation and inflexion, as well as bodily posture and gesture, which is older than words themselves and which can articulate the multilayered quicksilver nature of our relationships more effectively than can words, with their linear, one-thing-at-a-time slowness. All this happens long before the child enters school or learns to read and write.

The changes in sensory ratios that occur when a person learns to read have been extensively discussed by Marshall McLuhan (1964). His conclusions, that reading, like all technologies, opens up new possibilities while closing off others, have since been confirmed by later neurological studies. These show that by a process Gerald Edelman (1992) has called "neural Darwinism" unused groups of nerve channels in the brain atrophy and become unusable. Something similar occurs when a person learns to read musical notation without prior stimulation of their movement and dance faculties and the aural stimulation of singing and placing of sounds. The faculty of spontaneous performance (whose spontaneity is of course always mediated by culture) never develops fully and a whole area of experience is closed off.

What is needed in the early years is not so much formal training as informal musical interaction, with adults and with peers and contemporaries. It needs mothers, and fathers too, who will sing to the young child and encourage him or her to sing back, and it needs, perhaps above all, dancing—not the constricted gestural repertory of classical ballet but the free movement of the whole body, perhaps initiated by dandling even before the child has learnt to walk—that takes place in the African American tradition.

The big challenge to music educators today seems to be how to provide that kind of social context for informal as well as formal musical and dancing interaction that leads to real development and to the musicalization of the society as a whole. Spain is extraordinarily fortunate in this respect, with its powerful traditions of popular music making and dance very much alive and providing something of the social context of which I am writing. I remember vividly my astonishment and joy the first time I saw the sardana being danced in the Plaça de la Catedral in Barcelona, not as folklore or something self-conscious and archaic but as a matter-of-fact part of the citizens' social and (as I am well aware) political life. I remember equally vividly my first *Festa Mayor* in the Catalan town where I live, where the sights and sounds of the dances, the grallers and drums, the devils with their marvelous petard music, and the solemn but joyful *moixeganga* moved me to tears and continue to do so year by year as the ritual repeats itself.

Something that strikes the Anglo-Saxon in Spain is how physical Spanish parents are with their children, how much touching and caressing and stroking there is, how much picking up and swinging around and bouncing up and down. That is another richness that should be tapped in the service of musicalizing the society. (I sometimes think that if this behavior were seen in the United States, where a teacher can be fired for laying a hand on a pupil, or indeed in Britain, someone would be calling the cops.)

APHORISM 5: MUSICIANS ARE GENERALLY AS LITERATE AS THEY FEEL THE NEED TO BE

This does not require much comment, except to point out that it is not difficult to acquire the skills of reading and writing musical notation—once one has acquired elementary skills on an instrument or with the voice. My own memory is that my reading skills developed naturally, in tandem with those of performance. Certainly trying to teach children to read in a vocal or instrumental vacuum is a cruel waste of everybody's time (see aphorism 3). Many popular musicians of my acquaintance have told me that notation for them is often a nuisance when it comes to improvisation, that great and noble art. Such a superbly cultured musician as John Coltrane once said of the way another superbly cultivated musician, Thelonious Monk, taught him his tunes, "He would rather a guy would learn it without reading because you feel it better and quicker that way" (Carr 1982). Notation is a good servant but a bad master, and those who are wholly dependent on musical scores for their performance are to be pitied as being deprived of an important dimension of musical experience.

Mozart, J. S. Bach, and Beethoven and the host of their contemporaries and successors through the nineteenth century were certainly not dependent on notation for their performances. In fact, the accounts of Mozart's improvised performances suggest that these were even more daring, exciting, and moving than those of his written-down works that have come down to us.

I do not believe that those teachers and musicians in Spain who lament that their country has the lowest musical literacy rate in the European Union need worry. A vibrant musical culture does not depend on literacy. I very much doubt that the singer of *saeta* who made my blood run cold during Semana Santa in the Plaza Nueva of Granada, or the flamenco guitarists of Sacromonte, or the Andean musicians of the Barrio Gótico in Barcelona, or the musicians and dancers of the Danza Guerrera of Castellón (to cite just some of my own experiences), or the musicians who perform in dozens of other indigenous traditions owe much of their beautiful and sophisticated art to notation.

APHORISM 6: THE LACK OF AFRICAN AMERICAN MUSICKING IN SCHOOL CURRICULUMS IS SCANDALOUS

Since it is through musicking in the African American tradition that most people in the Western world find their most satisfying musical expression, the fact that musicking in that tradition is virtually absent in institutions that are supposed to be developing the musicality of young people is nothing short of scandalous.

By "African American" I mean that way of musicking that was born out of the encounter in the Americas between African and European traditions during and after the times of slavery, a way of musicking that, like all offspring, partakes of both its parents but is not the same as either. It is an immensely rich tradition. Its richness inspired me to write the book of which I am most proud: *Music of the Common Tongue*, in which I maintain that it is that tradition, and not the once-great European classical tradition, that is the major musicking of the twentieth century, and probably of the twenty-first as well.

It is not only a purely musical richness but a social richness as well. For the African American tradition has inherited the African assumption that everyone is capable of making his or her own musical utterances, as well as the assumption that the whole body is involved in the music act, so that musicking and dancing are inseparable. Thus are treasured not only performance skills in the narrow sense but the creative faculty as well, and the nonhierarchical social interaction between peers that is necessary for the making of such performances.

And, always, dance. We tend to forget today that jazz, until its recent beatification as a respectable concert music, was essentially a dance music. One of the dancers who used to frequent the Savoy Ballroom in Harlem in the 1930s said of Dizzy Gillespie "A lot of people had him pegged as a clown, but we loved him. Every time he played a crazy lick, we cut a crazy step to go with it. And he dug us and blew even crazier stuff to see if we could dance to it, a kind of game, with the musicians and the dancers challenging each other." Marshall and Jean Stearns comment, "Great musicians inspire great dancers—and vice versa—until the combination pyramids into the greatest performances of both" (Stearns and Stearns 1968).

Jazz, unfortunately, is no longer a dance music, but the richness of the wider African American tradition encompasses plenty of the most flexible and subtle dance music to be heard today. This is especially true of those dance forms that originated in the melding of Iberian and African ways of musicking in Latin America—salsa and tango and rhumba and samba, to name but a few. In these ways of musicking the creative act is open to all, and although performers can and do attain to amazing levels of skill and virtuosity, those whose skills are modest or even rudimentary can still do something and be listened to and admired. They can develop those skills by continually doing the best they can with what they have, not through studies and exercises, not through scales and arpeggios, and certainly not through being subjected to examinations (those lethal weapons of standardization), but through performing, in social contexts that everyone understands and in which everyone feels secure.

That brings me to my last aphorism, which I leave without commentary.

APHORISM 7: THE BEST MUSICKING IS DONE BY THOSE WHO ARE DOING THE BEST THEY CAN WITH WHAT THEY HAVE

BIBLIOGRAPHY

Carr, Ian. 1982. *Miles Davis: A Critical Biography*. London: Quartet Books.

Chernoff, John Miller. 1979. *African Rhythm and African Sensibility: Aesthetics and Social Action in African Musical Rhythms*. Chicago: University of Chicago Press.

Dahlhaus, Carl. 1983. *Foundations of Music History*. Translated by J. B. Robinson. Cambridge: Cambridge University Press.

Edelman, Gerald. 1992. *Bright Air, Brilliant Fire: On the Matter of the Mind*. London: Allan Lane, Penguin.

McLuhan, Marshall. 1964. *Understanding Media: The Extensions of Man*. London: Sphere Books.

Small, Christopher. (1987) 1998. *Music of the Common Tongue: Survival and Celebration in African American Music*. London: John Calder. Reprint, Middletown, CT: Wesleyan University Press.

———. 1998. *Musicking: The Meanings of Performing and Listening*. Middletown, CT: Wesleyan University Press.

Stearns, Marshall, and Jean Stearns. 1968. *Jazz Dance: The Story of American Vernacular Dance*. New York: Schirmer.

Afterword

On Music Education

(2009)

ABSTRACT

This article takes issue with the reification of the music act into the thing called music, whose essence is the music object, or work. It affirms that the essence of music lies not in works but in performance, for which a fixed and stable musical work is not necessary. It is not that performance takes place in order to present a musical work, as is commonly assumed, but rather that musical works exist to give performers something to perform, should they not be capable of inventing their own material. It affirms also that all normally endowed human beings are born with the gift of creating their own musical acts, no less than their own speech acts, and investigates the implications of this idea for music education. Important among these is the idea that musical literacy is not essential for performance, that musicians generally become as literate as they feel the need to be. And finally it advocates the presence of African American ways of musicking—and dancing—in those institutions that are devoted to the development of musicality among young people.

I have said many times (see Small 1987 and 1998) that the act of musicking is a way in which we explore, affirm and celebrate our concepts of ideal relationships. We do not just *learn about* those relationships—in fact, we do not need anyone to teach them to us—but actually *experience* them in all their complexity and variety in ways that talking or reading about them can never allow us to do.

Two comments are in order. First, it does not mean that the relationships are presented to us ready-made; on the contrary, they have to be constructed by all the participants in the performance, listeners and dancers, should there be any, no less than performers, and anyone else who may be present. Some performances never bring about the experience; we think of them as poor performances, for one reason or another, and the failure to achieve it is not by any means always the fault of the performers. In addition, the space in which the performance takes place imposes its own parameters, and limitations, on the relationships that can be constructed by the performance (Small 1998, chap. 1).

Second, there is not necessarily unanimity among those present about the nature of those ideal relationships. This may mean that while some are turned on by the performance, others may be turned off. And of course some professional performers may be doing it just for the money, while their real values, their real concepts of ideal relationships, are elsewhere.

Sociology is concerned with human relationships, both actual and ideal. We might call it the science of human relationships, although the infinite complexity of those relationships makes them highly recalcitrant to scientific investigation, or even, as I have just noted, to verbal discussion at all. Nonetheless, the sociological discourse can provide us with useful insights into human social processes, and in this essay I want to consider one of these, the process of socialization of the young.

It is a commonplace these days that the process of musicking functions as an instrument of socialization. Socialization is a word with several meanings; my dictionary gives four, of which two are of concern to us here. The first is "to give someone the skills required to enable someone to function successfully in society." This definition is centered on the individual and his or her development within a social setting. We have evidence from the fieldwork of ethnomusicologists that this exists widely across the world's cultures, from the Aborigines of Australia: "music is used to teach him about his culture, about his place in it and his place in the world of nature and supernature" (Malm 1967) to the Venda of South Africa: musicking "may involve people in a powerful shared experience and thereby make them more aware of themselves and of their responsibilities towards one another" (Blacking 1976).

The second definition that concerns us is "to convert or adapt someone to the needs of society." There seems to me to be a dissonance between this and the previous definition, in that it implies that the needs of society take precedence over those of the individuals that comprise it. I do not think the two definitions are necessarily mutually contradictory; they simply emphasize different aspects of the same process. Those different emphases, however, can have deep consequences for the person on the receiving end of the socialization. Both are aspects of that enterprise in which we teachers are engaged, which we call education.

We like to think about our work primarily as the giving of skills required for our pupils to function successfully in society. We are certainly not unaware of the second definition—how could we be when confronted with it on a daily basis through the deadening demands of curricula and examinations?—but we try daily to keep the two definitions in some kind of balance. In chapter 3 of this volume (Ruth Wright, ed., *Sociology and Music Education* [Farnham, UK: Ashgate, 2010]), Ruth Wright and Brian Davies give an account of the tensions on a national scale in Britain between the demands of the system—what the authors call official recontextualizing fields (ORF)—and those which those in the teaching profession think beneficial—pedagogical recontextualizing fields (PRF)—that have shaped music education in Britain for the last thirty years. To me, the chapter would be an excellent piece of deadpan humor if the story it tells were not so disastrous.

We should be under no illusion why it is that governments give so much attention and money to setting up and maintaining school systems and to determining what it is that the students should be learning. We all remember that when Tony Blair found himself in the office of Prime Minister in 1997 and was asked what were his first priorities in government he replied "Education, education and education." The changes since wrought in British schools do not incline one to the view that he was thinking of education as the development of the human potential of each individual student, but rather as thinking of the adapting of pupils to the needs of the British industrial (such of it as still exists) and service-industry state, in which those pupils will become political and social leaders, academics, bureaucrats, technicians, tradesmen, laborers—and members of the seemingly permanent pool of workless. And, further, the process of socialization in the second sense inculcates in the pupils an acceptance of the social category into which they are placed as inevitable and correct.

Despite whatever efforts we may make, as individual teachers, to further the individual development of our pupils, it is the demands of the state, as expressed through national curricula and above all through examinations, that finally determine not only what we teach but also how we teach it, that in the long run take precedence.

We might use the two words "education" and "schooling" to characterize the two definitions I have been discussing above. I first came across the distinction in

Christopher Small at Santes Creus monastery in Aiguamúrcia, Spain, 2008.
Photograph by Robert Walser.

Ivan Illich's *Deschooling Society* (Illich 1971). (I recently learned that Mark Twain got there first, as he often did, with his remark: "I never allowed my schooling to interfere with my education.") As Illich points out, you do not have to go to school to get an education, while going to school does not necessarily give you an education, as many frustrated pupils and ex-pupils can testify. However, no matter how well or badly they have learnt what the school expects them to learn, every one of them does learn well what it expects of them—those industrial virtues of punctuality, obedience, toleration of boredom and standardization that are necessary to fit into and work in the (post-) industrial state. We know that many pupils will have utterly rejected those values, but we may be sure that they will have thoroughly learnt what they are—what has been called the Hidden Curriculum. I suppose that is education of a kind.

The practice of socializing children, of incorporating them into the fabric of knowledge, belief and custom of the society into which they were born is of course universal across the human race. What is quite recent is the idea of universal, state-sponsored institutions as a tool for doing this. In England, for example, the enactment of the idea into law happened as recently as the Education Act of 1870. There is an interesting piece of history attached to that act, which I learned from a remarkable but little-known book, *The Lost Elementary Schools of Victorian England* (Gardner 1984). He tells us that before the 1870 act and for some time after there was a vigorous network of elementary schools in working-class areas of English cities whose nature was completely different from that of the schools that were set up under the act. They taught the basics of literacy and numeracy, and little more, and were generally organized around the day-to-day needs of the local community, in which they were deeply embedded. What these schools did not set out to do was inculcate those so-called industrial values without which the industrial state would not be able to function.

When I was in teachers' college, the lectures I received on the history of education referred to these schools, with something of a curl of the lip, as "dame schools," with a clear implication that they were run by a crew of at best incompetent and semi-literate old women who had no idea what they were doing. But according to Gardner, as many were run by men as by women, many of whom had lost their factory occupation as a result of an industrial accident or war-inflicted wounds. The teachers, or schoolkeepers as they were called, were members of the community who had acquired a degree of literacy and numeracy. They generally enjoyed respect in the community and also frequently acted as scribes and as advisers in dealing with the law and authority. They would charge each pupil a few pence weekly, amounts that in those days could be a substantial portion of the family's budget. For this reason, if for no other, the parents expected to see concrete results from the instruction. As Gardner says, "To the extent that the working-class users of private schools sought particular—if limited—educational results, the teachers had to be able to offer particular instrumental skills and the ability to communicate them . . . the illiterate simply could not operate as school-keepers. Working-class educational demand was too sensitive to allow this" (118).

There was no age-grading, no formal examinations or standardized curriculum. Gardner says, "The working-class private school was a product of a broader working-class culture and as such it was attuned, in personnel and in atmosphere and organization, to the demands of that culture. It was *an education that was fully under the control of its users*; it was an education truly 'of' the working class and not 'for' it . . . the classrooms of the working-class private school were the true focuses of an alternative educational culture, physically and financially constrained, but effectively unregulated by middle-class morality. They were places where the basic skills of literacy and numeracy could be quickly and effectively picked up at times and *in ways that suited the user and not the provider*" (173, my italics).

We can see why these schools were popular in their communities, so much so that when the 1870 act came into force the state-school managers had a hard time attracting working-class children into their schools and in convincing parents that they could do better for their children. It was not just that the new state schools were run by middle-class people whose aim was to inculcate the middle-class industrial values, but also that the children found themselves lifted physically out of the community setting and placed in the charge of strangers whose experience and values were completely alien to their own. And then there were examinations, which turned the schooling process into a series of hoops the children had to jump through, and replaced the culture of mutual aid with one of competitiveness, which remains today the dominant ethos of schooling. (Successive English governments have carried the culture of competitiveness into new levels of refinement. Not only are pupils pitted against one another but also schools are being pitted against one another by the device known as league table—a metaphor that we recognize as being taken from that most competitive of human activities, sports.)

Generally speaking, for the new state schools working-class culture was the enemy, not the environment, of education, and in these schools every effort was made to eradicate the signs of that culture, and replace it with those of the middle class—"good" manners, "good" speech, punctuality, obedience and so on. The new schools were organized in ways that suited the provider, not the user. In so far as the values that middle-class children had absorbed from birth coincided with those of the teachers, they tended to do well in the new schools, while working-class children found that many things were stacked against them.

So it was that the newly appointed school inspectors had to find a way to coerce those children into the state schools, and to coerce not only the children but their parents as well. They did not dare risk the outcry that simply outlawing the popular "dame" schools would produce, so they developed an ingenious backdoor way of killing them that touched the working-class families where it would hurt: their shallow pockets. With the passing of a second act of Parliament in 1876, no child under the age of thirteen was allowed to take employment without a certificate of proficiency, and that certificate could be obtained only by at least two years' attendance at one of the public elementary schools. Working-class parents were thus faced with a cruel dilemma: either they sent their children to the public schools or the family suffered from the loss of the three years' wages that could be earned by a child between the ages of ten, below which no child could be employed, and thirteen. Gardner again: "For most, the only realistic alternative was to accept the regime of the public school, trading the losses in preference, convenience and cultural consonance against the right to early employment" (206).

The ruse worked, and the working-class schools slowly faded away, though some lasted into the early twentieth century. Today they are scarcely a memory, and today's schools are governed, not by user need, or even by users' own perceptions of their needs, but by assumptions about what the state needs, enforced by a system of examinations and qualifications. But the old working-class schools, however limited they must have been, however cramped and lacking in resources, show that other concepts of education are possible, ways that do not require the pupils to swallow the whole package of industrial values if they are to get the skills that enable them to function successfully in society. I believe it is those industrial values that are alienating pupils from today's schools.

Whatever else examinations might be, they are above all instruments of standardization. In so far as they enforce uniformity across a whole age group they deal severe blows to creativity and individuality. Where musicking is concerned, I am convinced that they played a considerable part in the slowing-down of creation in the classical tradition, even perhaps its death. (I am reminded of the story of the forty-year-old Erik Satie showing to friends his certificate in counterpoint from the Paris Schola Cantorum and declaring that he now had a license to engage in the practice of composition.)

If musicking is a means of exploring, affirming and celebrating one's sense of who one is, or who one thinks one is, the way of musicking that explores, affirms and celebrates middle-class identity, and that of those who aspire to the middle classes, is what is called classical music. It was natural, then, that when music was introduced as a subject into the school curriculum it was classical musicking that was primarily held up to the pupils as the norm and ideal of all musical experience, augmented by carefully selected songs from the dead or dying rural tradition, probably published in collections edited and provided with genteel piano accompaniments by classically trained musicians happy to earn a few extra pounds. Urban workers' songs, with their often-inflammatory social content, were excluded, as were items from the lively urban vernacular of the music hall. That tendency was reinforced by the practice of hiring music teachers from the ranks of music school or university graduates. It is therefore not surprising that music did best in schools whose roll was drawn from the middle classes. One might say that, to put it crudely, to take part in a classical-music performance is to explore, affirm and celebrate, whether one is aware of it or not, the valued relationships of the middle classes in the modern industrial state—the same values that modern schools seek to inculcate.

Recent attempts to introduce various styles of vernacular music, the music of the common tongue, into schools have not had more than partial success. This seems to be due, first, to that consonance of values between the aims and pedagogical methods of schools with that of classical-music performances; second, to the lack of congruence between the values embodied in vernacular musicking, especially African American, and those embodied in the school classroom; third, that music teachers themselves have generally little skill or experience, and in many cases little interest, in vernacular styles; and finally to the fact that without examinations and tangible qualification, those touchstones of practical worth and intellectual respectability, no school activity is going to attain the status and the resources it needs. But if examinations have played their part in the decline of classical musicking, what would they do to the dazzling array of individual styles that vernacular musicking presents to us? How could one possibly, for example, give comparative marks to such widely different piano players as Jerry Lee Lewis, Elton John, Count Basie and Thelonious Monk, each of them brilliant in their own individual ways? If each had had to pass an examination, what would be left of their joyous individuality?

School pupils as they perform and listen to music outside the school setting will be finding their way, as people will if left to themselves, to ways of musicking that will help them in their formulation and articulation of values. Those, probably the majority, who opt for African American ways of musicking are affirming and celebrating values that may be very different from the official values of our society as expressed through the schools.

The value conflict here confronts us head on, in that forms of musical expression that are natural and important to the sense of identity of a majority of people are excluded from full participation in the institution that is ostensibly there to serve the people. It is a conflict that we all know has been disastrous for the work that teachers of music are trying to do, and we all know in our hearts that all our efforts, however carefully thought out and applied, to advance the musical experience of our pupils are reaching only a small proportion of them.

If the conflict is to be resolved, something has to change, either in the way schools are ordered or in the ways in which musical education takes place. Schools are not going to change, unless the official values of our society change, and I do not see that happening in the foreseeable future. If anything, societal demands are gaining an ever-tighter hold on the schools; the needs of industry and commerce are increasingly coming to dominate the practices of schooling.

I can see no alternative to taking the teaching of music out of schools. It is a solution that we have heard put forward many times, though always qualified by the question, Without music in the classroom during school time, how will children obtain that musical experience that is so valuable for their socialization?—in whichever of its two meanings that word may be used. It is a very valid, not to say disturbing, question, but finally I think that removing music from the schools' curriculum would do more good than harm to the pupils' experience. Classrooms are not good places for the gaining of significant musical experience. I am not saying that it never happens, but the odds are cruelly stacked against it.

Nor am I suggesting that music education should be abolished. Rather, I envisage a network of music centers throughout the country, where people of all ages can engage in musicking and dancing as and when it suits them ("user-directed"), where older can help younger, and perhaps vice versa, and where instruction is offered as the need is felt for it.

I have seen this kind of operation in several places. For me the most impressive was that in Hartford, CT, founded by the great saxophonist Jackie McLean. The City of Hartford had lent a disused primary school, and when I was there the place was bursting at the seams and exploding with energy, in dancing as well as musicking. In London, Community Music, co-founded by a great English musician and teacher, John Stevens, started its life on an industrial estate among the machinery and the delivery vans, and has since exploded into East Anglia with Community Music East. In Spain where I now live, there has long been a network of small conservatories of music in small- and medium-sized towns, which have in the past been content to deal exclusively with the conventional materials and methods of conservatories but are now looking to expand their operations as centers of musicking for everybody in the town who wants it. Their organization and their methods bear a striking resemblance to the working-class schools discussed by Phil Gardner. It will be interesting to see how they develop.

These expanded music centers can be wonderful places for children and adults alike. They can be places where formal instruction goes hand-in-hand with informal musical interaction, where older students can instruct younger, and perhaps vice versa, where dancing as well as musicking can go on from a very early age, where the western classical tradition coexists happily with other modes of musicking, possibly to create any number of hybrids, where all kinds of ensemble, from string quartets to rock bands to African-style dance-and-drum ensembles to salsa bands, and of course choral groups of many kinds, are at work, and dancing is fostered. Most important perhaps of all, rehearsal and recording space is available for young musicians, ideally twenty-four hours a day as in the wonderful Midlands Arts Centre in Birmingham.

Music education, as we have understood the term, gives way to getting together and playing, and music educators, as we have understood the term, become leaders and pacemakers in the communal work of musicking. If music teachers can come to think of themselves in that way then I believe they can find a new and enormously expanded and infinitely more satisfying role, not within the narrow and frustrating confines of school and classroom but in the wider setting of the community as a whole.

BIBLIOGRAPHY

Blacking, John. 1976. *How Musical Is Man?* London: Faber and Faber.

Gardner, Philip W. 1984. *The Lost Elementary Schools of Victorian England: A People's Education*. Beckenham, UK: Croom Helm.

Illich, Ivan. 1971. *Deschooling Society*. New York: Harper and Row.

Malm, William P. 1967. *Music Cultures of the Pacific, Near East and Asia*. Englewood Cliffs, NJ: Prentice-Hall.

Small, Christopher. (1977) 1996. *Music, Society, Education*. London: John Calder. Reprint, Middletown, CT: Wesleyan University Press.

———. 1987. *Music of the Common Tongue: Survival and Celebration in African American Music*. Middletown, CT: Wesleyan University Press.

———. 1998. *Musicking: The Meanings of Performing and Listening*. Middletown, CT: Wesleyan University Press.

Pelicans

(2009)

It is some years ago now that I spent the months of winter into spring in Texas. A friend who was professor at the University of North Texas had dragged me out of retirement and got me to teach a semester there. We had the great good luck to be able to live on an estate of some five hundred acres outside the town of Denton, with a two-mile wooded shoreline on Lake Dallas. There we were able to watch cottonmouths and armadillos and feed crumbs of bread to the fire ants. The god of the ignorant must have protected me, for I never got bitten or stung by those fearsome creatures. Then there was the evolution of the spring, the coming into leaf of the oaks and hickories and other trees whose names I never learned, and the appearance of the famous Texas wildflowers, whole fields of Texas bluebonnets and the dazzling red flowers they call Indian paintbrushes.

But the most memorable and life-illuminating experience happened for me on a mild, still day in early April, when I was enjoying the sunshine on the stoop of the house where we were living. A flock of big white birds, fifty or more, came in from the south at just above rooftop height, lazily flapping their wings. They had long, orange beaks and straight wings with black undersides, with a wingspan of about a meter, and although I had never seen such birds before, I knew that I was having the great good fortune to see part of the annual northward migration of the pelicans, one of the great natural sights of that region of the United States.

As I watched they started to circle slowly, practically over my head, with their wings stretched out unmoving. Then I saw that they were gaining height, riding a thermal air current that they had somehow located. Up and up they went, never moving their wings, circling around and around in the invisible current of rising air. I could see no features on the ground that should cause such a rising current, but the birds had found it anyway. As they rose higher and higher another flock of about the same number came in and joined the thermal at the bottom, and both flocks rose effortlessly until after about a quarter of an hour they were only tiny crosses weaving around against the blue of the sky. Then the two flocks, first one and then the other, turned and headed northward, still gliding. I watched them until I could see them no more. I suppose they were going to keep gliding northward using god knows what navigation equipment, slowly losing height until they found another thermal, going on and on with minimum expenditure of energy until they got to the Canadian lakes or the Pacific Northwest where I have learned that they spend the summer eating and breeding.

I don't think I have ever seen a more beautiful sight than those big birds riding up in that invisible stream of air that was surging so powerfully upward under the sun's heat. It was not just the birds themselves, elegant as they were, but what they were doing, their joyous use of the earth's resources of energy. I cannot believe that nature, which has endowed us humans with such rich and varied sources of pleasure, should not have granted some kind of avian pleasure to those great birds as they discovered and rode those currents, feeling the warm air beneath their wings as they soared ever higher.

They probably didn't even notice the fat, elderly human that was staring up at them with his mouth open, but I felt a very strong sense of kinship with those pelicans and an admiration for the intelligence that I didn't share.

As I savored the experience over the next days, there came to my mind a remark of Gregory Bateson's that had puzzled me. He had said that the question "How do I relate to this creature?" is fundamentally an aesthetic one. I could understand that there was a link between my aesthetic perception, that is, my perception of beauty such I had found in this passing glimpse of the life of those great birds, and the way I felt I was related to them. But, I thought, what about my relationship, say, with the pilot who drops a bomb on me? What of beauty is there in that? Maybe Count Ciano, who celebrated from his plane the flower-like patterns of flame created by bombs exploding on Abyssinian villages during Mussolini's invasion, or Karlheinz Stockhausen, who envied the Twin Towers attackers for having created what he called "the greatest work of art imaginable for the whole cosmos," could have something to tell us about aesthetics, but I think their concepts of desirable human relationships would not stand up to much examination.

I think that Bateson, as usual, opened up a great area of enquiry with this one throwaway remark, but I have to venture to suggest that he came up with the wrong answer, or rather had the answer the wrong way around. It is not that questions concerning relationships are aesthetic in their nature but rather that any investigations into aesthetic concepts, that is, concepts of beauty such as that which I found in Texas that April afternoon in 1995, are most fruitfully approached by thinking about our concepts of relationships, especially those relationships we believe we ought to have, with the creatures and the objects with which we share our world. Concepts of beauty, in other words, follow from, rather than govern, our concepts of how we ought to relate. Then again, few of those who witnessed the destruction of those giant buildings can have failed to feel in some way a sensation of Yeats's "terrible beauty." And yet again, if, as Bateson suggests, emotions are the representation in consciousness of relationships, then perhaps the sensation of beauty is the representation in consciousness of right, or ideal relationships as imagined by the perceiver. That would certainly jibe with what we know about Ciano (who was Mussolini's son-in-law) and about Stockhausen. One corollary of this idea could be that the sensation of ugliness is the representation in consciousness of wrong relationships. We are all too familiar with the lack of agreement between people about what is beautiful and what is ugly; this might help to explain it. A factory operating in a countryside may satisfy its owner's idea of right relationships, whereas to a conservationist it is an affront to right relationships, that is, relationships not only among humans but also between humans and the natural world. Even the supernatural world could be involved if, for instance, the factory were built in what had been a sacred spot to the inhabitants of the place. The treatment of the ruins of Babylon by American troops is a clear demonstration of this gulf in values.

Bateson went on to say that if his observation were true then the whole basis of aesthetics would have to be revised. This is what I believe I am doing. Artistic creation is concerned not with the creation of beauty or of beautiful objects—that can only lead to trivial forms like Fabergé eggs—but with the articulation of ideal, or perhaps desired, relationships. The sensation of beauty arises from the appreciation of those relationships. Charles Ives said that art has nothing to do with beauty, and from this point of view he was right.

Afterword by Susan McClary

Remembering Neville Braithwaite

Chris used to love to tell this story. He arrived at a gathering in London only to find everyone whispering excitedly: "Just wait until Braithwaite shows up. That's when the party will *really* start." Quite put out at being reduced to the status of a spectator, Chris muttered to himself, "Bloody hell! Who is this fucking Braithwaite?" Then the door opened and Neville stepped in, his beaming smile and infectious exuberance quickly eclipsing everything around him.

Indeed, that's when Chris's party started. He took Neville home with him that night in 1973, and the party lasted for thirty-three years. When Neville died in 2006, the lights went out in Chris's life, and he soon followed.

Although I already knew Chris's first two books, I first met him and Neville together in 1994. Chris had invited Rob to stop by to see "us" if we ever found ourselves in Spain. That summer, we happened to be in the neighborhood and took him up on his offer. As we approached his door, Rob wondered out loud what Mrs. Small would be like; I asked why he thought that "us" included a woman. Again, a door opened, and here was not only Chris but also the ever-luminous Neville. I fairly worshiped Chris for his work, but I could not take my eyes off his partner. When Neville beamed, everyone around him beamed. Not even the most dour of us could resist that charisma. Like Chris and so many before me, I fell in love at first sight.

Neville's physical beauty had something to do with it. A professional model in his youth and a teacher of dance for most of his career, he had a sculpted, powerful body; even in his eighties he attracted admiring stares at his beloved "naked beach" in Sitges. But it was his brilliant smile and contagious laugh that drew you in and held you. He simply exuded joy. Some of Chris's snottier English friends used to accuse him of hooking up with Neville for superficial reasons. Yet however much Chris appreciated Neville's pulchritude and unflagging high spirits (which he most certainly did), he benefited even more deeply from his partner's mind. For Neville brought with him an entirely different cluster of cultural experiences.

Before he met Neville, Chris was pursuing the intellectual path of a European-trained musicologist. To be sure, he had already started to chafe at what he perceived as the elitism and inhumaneness of the ideologies surrounding the Western canon. He had already bailed from the world of avant-garde composition for which he had left his native New Zealand in order to study with Luigi Nono in London. He preferred teaching in colleges, in which context he began to piece together the critical narratives about Western classical music that burst on the scene in his *Music, Society, Education*.

But the radical swerve that resulted in *Music of the Common Tongue* cannot be explained without Neville's powerful influence. Neville had arrived in London from Jamaica to study law. Although he had a lovely tenor voice and sang German Lieder and Handel arias throughout his life, his principal medium was dance, particularly idioms of the African diaspora. In London, he founded a number of youth centers in ethnically troubled neighborhoods, making use of dance to instill mutual respect among young people; in 1976, the Queen Mother herself bestowed an award on Neville for this important work. He received a Winston Churchill Memorial Fellowship in 1977 (one of only three in the UK that year) for a project titled *Dance and Movement in the Promotion of Racial Harmony*—a project that allowed him residencies with such groups as the Alvin Ailey American Dance Theater and supported his own dance workshops in San Francisco and St. Louis. Neville was always a social activist, and he anticipated in his particular concept of dancing what Chris would come to call, in his own medium, musicking.

Like most musicologists, Chris had tended to ignore the function of the body in art, and he had had little contact with musics of other societies. Neville removed those blinders and encouraged Chris to rethink everything from the ground up. As Chris delved into practices he had previously ignored, he acquired a very different set of aesthetic criteria. And this experience not only opened up a new world of embodied sound and movement but also led him to reconsider the core assumptions of the European repertories to which he had previously devoted his energies. Becoming bi-musical with Neville meant refusing any longer to privilege the classical tradition. We all stand as beneficiaries of their love child, Chris's second book.

Anyone who spent any time with Neville quickly recognized his deep personal wisdom. Like Chris, Neville kept notebooks into which he copied passages from books that mattered to him. He read widely on dance, of course, but also on African and Caribbean cultures, on the slave trade, on problems of racism in the UK, and on sociology and anthropology. It is clear that the two of them worked closely together, sharing their insights and experiences with both Western classical and African-based practices, each giving the other the moral support he needed to keep going in the face of academic indifference.

I want to close with an account of an astonishing event in 2005. Chris, Neville, Rob, and I had gone to Trondheim, Norway, to give talks at an international conference. Neville had been diagnosed as having Parkinson's and was having tremendous difficulty getting round; we even wondered if we ought to have brought him along, given his condition. At a certain point in the conference, a group of young musicians arrived to play some African-based music. Suddenly, Neville—who could not walk without support on both sides—levitated and raced down to the stage. There he proceeded to dance vigorously for a very long time. The spirit had seized him and bypassed the parts of his illness that had prohibited standing or walking. It was his last hurrah.

Neville could barely move after that miraculous moment. He died the following year of a brain tumor so large that his doctors did not know how he had continued to function at all. But six months before he passed, he and Chris got to experience something they never could have imagined at that legendary party three decades before in London: Spain passed laws to allow same-sex marriage, and Chris and Neville were wed in a joyous ceremony in Sitges in 2006. They scarcely needed the law, however, to legitimize what they and we had long since recognized. Theirs had always been the marriage of true minds.

In his dedication to *Music of the Common Tongue*, Chris wrote, "To Neville Braithwaite, who taught me what it was all about." And Chris, in turn, taught us what it was all about.

NOTES

1. Robert Farris Thompson, "An Aesthetic of the Cool: West African Dance," *African Forum* 2, no. 2 (Fall 1966): 85.
2. Henry Pleasants, *The Agony of Modern Music* (New York: Simon and Schuster, 1955); *Death of a Music?* (London: Victor Gollancz, 1961); *Serious Music—And All That Jazz* (London: Victor Gollancz, 1969).

ACKNOWLEDGMENTS

Many thanks to Chris's dear friend Patrick Satge, who helped me rescue Chris's notebooks and other unpublished writings after his passing.

The interview with Robert Christgau is reprinted courtesy of Robert Christgau.

"Afterword" is reprinted by permission of the publishers from "Afterword," in *Sociology and Music Education*, edited by Ruth Wright, 283–89 (Farnham, UK: Ashgate, 2010). Copyright © 2010.

The excerpts from Christopher Small's books are reprinted courtesy of Wesleyan University Press.

"Why Doesn't the Whole World Love Chamber Music?," from *American Music*, vol. 19, no. 3. Copyright 2001 by the Board of Trustees of the University of Illinois. Used with permission of the University of Illinois Press.

Editing of the individual pieces in this volume has been limited to the correction of obvious typos or other errors.

INDEX

MUSIC / CULTURE

A series from Wesleyan University Press
Edited by Deborah Wong, Sherrie Tucker, and Jeremy Wallach
Originating editors: George Lipsitz, Susan McClary, and Robert Walser

Frances Aparicio
Listening to Salsa: Gender, Latin Popular Music, and Puerto Rican Cultures

Paul Austerlitz
Jazz Consciousness: Music, Race, and Humanity

Harris M. Berger
Metal, Rock, and Jazz: Perception and the Phenomenology of Musical Experience

Harris M. Berger
Stance: Ideas about Emotion, Style, and Meaning for the Study of Expressive Culture

Harris M. Berger and Giovanna P. Del Negro
Identity and Everyday Life: Essays in the Study of Folklore, Music, and Popular Culture

Franya J. Berkman
Monument Eternal: The Music of Alice Coltrane

Dick Blau, Angeliki Vellou Keil and Charles Keil
Bright Balkan Morning: Romani Lives and the Power of Music in Greek Macedonia

Susan Boynton and Roe-Min Kok, editors
Musical Childhoods and the Cultures of Youth

James Buhler, Caryl Flinn and David Neumeyer, editors
Music and Cinema

Thomas Burkhalter, Kay Dickinson, and Benjamin J. Harbert, editors
The Arab Avant-Garde: Music, Politics, Modernity

Patrick Burkart
Music and Cyberliberties

Julia Byl
Antiphonal Histories: Resonant Pasts in the Toba Batak Musical Present

Daniel Cavicchi
Listening and Longing: Music Lovers in the Age of Barnum

Susan D. Crafts, Daniel Cavicchi, Charles Keil, and the Music in Daily Life Project
My Music: Explorations of Music in Daily Life

Jim Cullen
Born in the USA: Bruce Springsteen and the American Tradition

Anne Danielsen
Presence and Pleasure: The Funk Grooves of James Brown and Parliament

Peter Doyle
Echo and Reverb: Fabricating Space in Popular Music Recording, 1900–1960

Ron Emoff
Recollecting from the Past: Musical Practice and Spirit Possession on the East Coast of Madagascar

Yayoi Uno Everett and Frederick Lau, editors
Locating East Asia in Western Art Music

Susan Fast and Kip Pegley, editors
Music, Politics, and Violence

Heidi Feldman
Black Rhythms of Peru: Reviving African Musical Heritage in the Black Pacific

Kai Fikentscher
"You Better Work!" Underground Dance Music in New York City

Ruth Finnegan
The Hidden Musicians: Music-Making in an English Town

Daniel Fischlin and Ajay Heble, editors
The Other Side of Nowhere: Jazz, Improvisation, and Communities in Dialogue

Wendy Fonarow
Empire of Dirt: The Aesthetics and Rituals of British "Indie" Music

Murray Forman
The 'Hood Comes First: Race, Space, and Place in Rap and Hip-Hop

Lisa Gilman
My Music, My War: The Listening Habits of U.S. Troops in Iraq and Afghanistan

Paul D. Greene and Thomas Porcello, editors
Wired for Sound: Engineering and Technologies in Sonic Cultures

Tomie Hahn
Sensational Knowledge: Embodying Culture Through Japanese Dance

Edward Herbst
Voices in Bali: Energies and Perceptions in Vocal Music and Dance Theater

Deborah Kapchan
Traveling Spirit Masters: Moroccan Gnawa Trance and Music in the Global Marketplace

Raymond Knapp
Symphonic Metamorphoses: Subjectivity and Alienation in Mahler's Re-Cycled Songs

Laura Lohman
Umm Kulthūm: Artistic Agency and the Shaping of an Arab Legend, 1967–2007

Preston Love
A Thousand Honey Creeks Later: My Life in Music from Basie to Motown—and Beyond

René T.A. Lysloff and
Leslie C. Gay Jr., editors
Music and Technoculture

Allan Marett
Songs, Dreamings, and Ghosts: The Wangga of North Australia

Ian Maxwell
Phat Beats, Dope Rhymes: Hip Hop Down Under Comin' Upper

Kristin A. McGee
Some Liked It Hot: Jazz Women in Film and Television, 1928–1959

Rebecca S. Miller
Carriacou String Band Serenade: Performing Identity in the Eastern Caribbean

Tony Mitchell, editor
Global Noise: Rap and Hip-Hop Outside the USA

Keith Negus
Popular Music in Theory: An Introduction

Johnny Otis
Upside Your Head!: Rhythm and Blues on Central Avenue

Kip Pegley
Coming to You Wherever You Are: MuchMusic, MTV, and Youth Identities

Jonathan Pieslak
Radicalism and Music: An Introduction to the Music Cultures of al-Qa'ida, Racist Skinheads, Christian-Affiliated Radicals, and Eco-Animal Rights Militants

Matthew Rahaim
Musicking Bodies: Gesture and Voice in Hindustani Music

John Richardson
Singing Archaeology: Philip Glass's Akhnaten

Tricia Rose
Black Noise: Rap Music and Black Culture in Contemporary America

David Rothenberg
and Marta Ulvaeus, editors
The Book of Music and Nature: An Anthology of Sounds, Words, Thoughts

Marta Elena Savigliano
Angora Matta: Fatal Acts of North-South Translation

Joseph G. Schloss
Making Beats: The Art of Sample-Based Hip-Hop

Barry Shank
Dissonant Identities: The Rock 'n' Roll Scene in Austin, Texas

Jonathan Holt Shannon
Among the Jasmine Trees: Music and Modernity in Contemporary Syria

Daniel B. Sharp
Between Nostalgia and Apocalypse: Popular Music and the Staging of Brazil

Helena Simonett
Banda: Mexican Musical Life across Borders

Mark Slobin
Subcultural Sounds: Micromusics of the West

Mark Slobin, editor
Global Soundtracks: Worlds of Film Music

Christopher Small
The Christopher Small Reader

Christopher Small
Music of the Common Tongue: Survival and Celebration in African American Music

Christopher Small
Music, Society, Education

Christopher Small
Musicking: The Meanings of Performing and Listening

Regina M. Sweeney
Singing Our Way to Victory: French Cultural Politics and Music During the Great War

Colin Symes
Setting the Record Straight: A Material History of Classical Recording

Steven Taylor
False Prophet: Fieldnotes from the Punk Underground

Paul Théberge
Any Sound You Can Imagine: Making Music/Consuming Technology

Sarah Thornton
Club Cultures: Music, Media and Sub-cultural Capital

Michael E. Veal
Dub: Songscape and Shattered Songs in Jamaican Reggae

Robert Walser
Running with the Devil: Power, Gender, and Madness in Heavy Metal Music

Dennis Waring
Manufacturing the Muse: Estey Organs and Consumer Culture in Victorian America

Lise A. Waxer
The City of Musical Memory: Salsa, Record Grooves, and Popular Culture in Cali, Colombia

Mina Yang
Planet Beethoven: Classical Music at the Turn of the Millennium

CHRISTOPHER SMALL (1927–2011) is the author of *Music, Society, Education*, *Music of the Common Tongue*, and *Musicking*, all published by Wesleyan University Press. He was a senior lecturer at Ealing College of Higher Education in London until 1986, and he lived in Sitges, Spain.

ROBERT WALSER is professor and chairman of musicology at UCLA. He is the editor of *Keeping Time: Readings in Jazz History* and of the journal *American Music* and author of *Running with the Devil*.

SUSAN MCCLARY is a professor at Case Western Reserve University and teaches courses in music history, music theory, and historical performance practices. Her published works include *Feminine Endings: Music, Gender, and Sexuality*, *Georges Bizet: Carmen*, *Conventional Wisdom: The Content of Musical Form*, *Modal Subjectives: Renaissance Self-Fashioning in the Italian Madrigal*, and *Desire and Pleasure in Seventeenth-Century Music*. She is also coeditor of *Music and Society: The Politics of Composition, Performance, and Reception*.